Foreword to introduction:

Every movie has a rating before starting the story to warn the viewers of the content about to be seen. This book could be a movie one day. No doubt about it. I would say it is PG 13 because of the stories mentioned in England, Cambodia, Australia or University of Vermont. There are many places God has sent me that were full of darkness and abominations. I felt like Noah pleading with people to get into the Ark of Safety because of a rain storm coming that will flood the entire earth. These assignments were not easy, but His grace was there for me. Not every street preacher that I have worked with in this 5-year journey is someone that I would endorse as a mouth piece for God. Being brave doesn't mean that God has anointed that person to speak for Him. However, I am thankful for every one that has been a part of my life. Iron sharpens iron. By the way readers, I will be quoting from my journals in this book. I did not allow anyone to professionally edit my book in the final stages of the book. Mainly, because I am not a professional Evangelist and want my book to be raw. I want the book to sound like me and not too polished or churchy sounding. Therefore, I have fixed up some of the quotes for proper grammar. Yet, there will still be possible typos. When they are found, no worries I will fix them for next printing. This is just how I roll. Keeping it real, Angela Cummings

May the Lamb of God be glorified with this book because without Him I am nothing.

John 15:5 "I am the vine, ye are the branches: He that abideth in me, and I in him, the same bringeth forth much fruit: for without me ye can do nothing." Jesus Messiah, Lamb of God

Chapters Index:

Introduction

Inspired by the Great Commission

by Angela Cummings

INTRODUCTION

A small crowd was gathered around me at Reno University campus in the free speech area across from the third largest knowledge center when an Atheist gave me, Angela Cummings, a 3-question challenge. I stood my ground; firm, unshaken by his three requests for me to explain in detail "How I live in my car," "How I travel the world," and "Do not use God in your details."

"The fool has said in his heart, there is no God..." (Psalm 53:1)

Knowing that a University student in front of me God calls a fool. I had to handle his challenge carefully because God wanted to bring this seeker into the Light and Truth of God's Word. I remember when I used to be lost in my sins and couldn't stand religious talk with no substance of power. My response to him was fun, colorful and calming with stories of amazing adventures of the open road.

As I began to paint him a picture with my words, of the "Motel Honda" journey, slowly I brought God back into the spotlight by the help of the Holy Spirit. This student became relaxed, hanging out with me and honestly found my stories as good, free entertainment.

Words of Jesus

"Ye are the salt of the earth..." (Matthew 5:13)

"Ye are the light of the world..." (Matthew 5:14)

"Ye shall be witnesses..." (Acts 1:8)

Regardless of the challenge that he presented to me in front of the small, listening crowd, my goal in this conversation was not to make a friend for life, but to give him and the crowd a clear explanation of the Kingdom of God. God's Word is my authority, not his demand or any of the books in the large Knowledge Center on campus. King Jesus' words tell me, *"Angela, be salt, light and a witness."*

Salt: to cause him to thirst for more of God. **Light** to shine into his unbelieving lost soul with the story of the Glory of the Lamb, crucified and risen again on the third day from the precious Holy Word of

God. ***Witness***: that Jesus is not dead in the grave. Let me tell you something; I am a witness that Jesus Christ is alive, well and ready to take his repentance call.

"Call to me, and I will answer you, and show you great and mighty things, which you do not know." (Jeremiah 33:3)

My challenger at Reno University allowed me to share the entire gospel with him. He then told me he had a Chinese pug. Away I went with more stories because pugs are my favorite dogs. God brings me pugs all over the world as a token of His great unfailing love for me. My photo on the back of the book was of me holding a Pug in Oslo, Norway. God loves me like a Father and sees me as His cute, little, warrior princess, resting under the stars in the Honda Fit before our next big, bad battle. This university student without any hesitation blurted out with a radiant smile, "You have more stories than anyone that I ever met before. You should write a book!" Several other friends and professional writers have told me the same. "Write the book, Angela." God has used the words and face of this atheist, pug-loving campus student to be the fuel on my fire to give birth to "Motel Honda" that has now grown into a bigger story called "Inspired by the Great Commission" because of God sending me around the world several times without getting in debt.

Motel Honda helped put my ministry on the map. My favorite scripture in the Word of God is: *"And the Lord said to the servant, 'Go out into the highways and hedges, and compel them to come in, that my house may be filled.'"* (Luke 14:23)

John Wesley said "I look upon the whole world as my parish."

CHAPTER 1

Motel Honda

Why would a grown woman that knows how to run a successful business choose to move into her car? Because I can. Yes, this is my answer. I can live in my car and give up status quo living for adventures in Motel Honda. This book would not be written, if I had of stayed in an apartment in same city with same church and same friends. Motel Honda gave me FREEDOM!!!!

Do you think Warriors are made in comfortable church buildings? Warriors are made in the heat of the battlefield. I believe the local church can disciple people to walk in the righteousness, holiness and with conviction of God's Word. However, if you want to be a warrior for Christ, then you must go get involved in a few battles. Someone rolling their eyes at you is not spiritual warfare.

Motel Honda has had a few different types of beds over the years. Dog beds with extra comforters laid across the back of my Honda Fit/Honda Jazz is what is inside my car now for me to sleep on top of with turquoise sheets and tan comforter. My toilet is a simple garbage can with handle. After I use it for only getting me through the night, I pour it outside car or on grass. Then, clean it out with supplies and wash my hands. I took baths in sinks for over a year in this journey. After a while I learned to have hair washing days and sink bathing separate. That way I was not taking too long in a locked public bathroom. Someone begin to pay for me a gym membership the 2nd year into my car living lifestyle. What a blessing this was to have real hot showers to look forward instead of sticking my leg on a toilet to shave my legs, while people in the coffee shop were having lattes. Simple gift of a gym membership made a big difference in my car living adventures. Surprisingly, my 2 videos on YouTube about living in my car get lots of views. I am not a dumb educated loser for moving into my car. Motel Honda was one of the greatest decisions of my life. My wisest choice in life has been to follow Jesus.

Just a brief testimony about who I am before you read the gospel adventures to 45 countries by 45 years old. I am a former crack addict/alcoholic that got radically forgiven, saved and transformed by the power of God. Jesus Christ is my Hero. I am NOT ashamed of the gospel. From 1995 to 2011 I ran my own cleaning business called "Compulsive Cleaning." I operated Compulsive Cleaning in Chattanooga, TN, Pensacola, FL and DFW Texas regions. This was one state at a time, though while living there. My business made the nighttime and daytime news, front page of Chamber of Commerce and often had such large contracts that I hired employees in every state. This was part of my preparation for Full Time traveling evangelistic ministry. I was a hard worker and still have a passion for business. My heart desired to be about God's business more than anything. God enlisted me at 29 years old into the Brownsville Revival School of Ministry from 2000 to 2004. The day I graduated from BRSM in Pensacola, Florida my 13-year-old son, Nicholas, was in front of the whole church standing with red roses at the bottom of the steps of the pulpit as I stepped down in my cap and gown with my diploma. Nicholas was 20 when I took a leap of faith to move into my car in DFW area of Texas. He was in Chattanooga, TN with family and enjoying growing in a relationship with a beautiful girl. I have never been married by the way. People need to relax and enjoy this book. Don't be screaming how my Adult son needs me or my family. My son is 26 at the time of first publishing. Christians should be happy when someone leaves everything to share the gospel all over the world. My family encourages my journey with adventures with God. They have never made me feel bad for living in my car. Mom said "It's your life. You can do what you want to do."

Matthew 9: 37 "Then He said to His disciples, 'The Harvest truly is plentiful, but the laborers are few."

The final episode for me to let go of my cleaning business came from cleaning a Christian family's home in Texas. They had so much stuff and lived in a 9,000-sq. foot mansion. I made up to $600 a month cleaning their home. This client was paying $400 to $600 a month for a maid. I was so grieved working there, even if it was good money. I have seen stuff, stuff and more stuff because of cleaning homes for 16 years. I got sick of people's stuff, including my own stuff. I have friends that have big houses because they have large families. Nothing wrong with that and no one must live by personal convictions, anyway. I am just telling you what caused me to hit bottom in my life to move into my car and close my business soon afterwards to move to California for a new start.

Matthew 6:19 "Do NOT lay up for yourselves treasures on earth, where moth and rust destroy and where thieves do not break in and steal;"

FREEDOM! That is what I wanted, so I could preach the gospel full time. I used to weep crying over their bath tubs saying to God "God, is this what I went to bible school for 4 years for to clean for Rich Christians?" I didn't mind cleaning the homes of non-believers because I always shared the gospel. God used my business as a lighthouse for 16 years. Yet, I was feeling an ending coming soon. God was breaking my heart to give birth to the new season. Yahweh knew putting me in this home would drive me into prayer for liberation. My tears were like a woman in travail about to give birth. My dream of full time ministry was the baby. This required me to PUSH. (Pray until something happens=PUSH)

Motel Honda was my deliverance and answer to 100% freedom. You will understand more about these early decisions, as you travel with me through the USA and then around the world. Apostle Paul has scriptures about him being a tent maker and scriptures about living by faith. I choose to live by faith and see what God would do with my living sacrifice.

1 Corinthians 9:14 "Even so the Lord has commanded that those who preach the gospel should live from the gospel."

CHAPTER 2

California Dreamer

After I moved into my car on March 17, 2011, God began to take me on special, small road trips to increase my faith. Chips was my favorite TV show as a kid and Los Angeles highways and bright lights of Hollywood sounded like a great place for a street preacher to live. 40 years was long enough for me living in the "Bible Belt." I cried out to God to get me out of the heavily churched areas of the USA for a place without a church on every corner. I wanted to reach people that may have never heard the gospel. The Bible Belt is full of drinking Christians listening to their rock and roll having sex outside marriage and attending church on Sunday to praise the Lord. I wanted a new mission field with sinners that didn't go to church. My faith had to be built first, though.

Three stories impacted me most to trust God and to leave everything for my childhood, California dreams. Those are the stories I would like to share with you next.

First, my campus revival teacher, Dr. Sandy Kirk, watched a video of me in her home on one of my visits to Pensacola from TX. I showed her how crowds listened to me preach when I was at University of Georgia campus recently. Glowing with pride and joy, Dr. Sandy said, "I think you have found your calling? Go make a promo video. God is about to launch you into something."

At the time, I didn't really want to yield to the calling of being a campus preacher. It is harder, in my opinion, than being a street preacher because all the crowds have questions. Small crowds have always gathered, but on campuses I've had over 200 people for over an hour interacting with me.

My second story starts when a HSM student was at his home in Arkansas. I contacted him to ask if he would make a new promo video, as Dr. Sandy suggested. Arkansas road trip and sleeping in Motel Honda. The next day, while he worked on the video, I snuck in the church bathroom, bolted the door for my sink bath. No big deal! The water in the sink was there to be used for God's people. Twelve hours later the new video was birthed and we watched it on the big screen of his church, believing God was about to explode my ministry. God did, but not with the traditional church formula for launching Evangelists to the Nations. Thank God for the Holy Ghost that allows forerunners to bulldoze new grounds.

Whoops! Out of gas and not back in Dallas yet! A client was waiting on me to clean her home. There I was on the freeway almost empty and had to think quickly. Unconventional thinking was now my emergency mindset. I parked the car and went into the gas station, asked for a piece of cardboard that was ripped off an old box, then borrowed a marker. I made a bold sign like homeless people make:

HELP – NEED GAS TO DALLAS

If someone helped me, praise the Lord, because there was nothing else to do but wait on the provision. I marched with glee to the freeway and stood for the first time with my cardboard sign. Within ten minutes a man and his wife pulled up. He told me to meet him at the gas pump. Motel Honda got her belly full of gas. Yeah God! Bless you sir for help.

San Antonio, TX was having a huge street festival with thousands on the streets. I was walking alone in the city with my backpack full of gospel tracts, Bible, and water bottle. I purposely came a day early and chose to go preach somewhere. Fear gripped me as I walked, not because of people, but because I had no gas money to get home. I started looking on the ground for money, as I walked. Maybe an angel left some for me somehow. Hey, this faith walk was new to me. The Holy Ghost of God spoke to my heart "You look for souls. When you are done, I will make sure you get home. Don't look for money." What a mighty God I serve. John 10 talks about the sheep hearing the voice of the shepherd. There are Christians that have never had a dream, vision, heard God or felt His spirit before. I must say that I am thankful for all the encounters with God that I have had over the years. My heart craves the Living God. Thank you, Holy Spirit, for your guidance, conviction and comfort. It's good to be a Child of God.

After I got to the park, a nineteen-year-old girl told me that she had never heard about Jesus in her whole life. God used me that day and the next day as well. God put me on a team of strangers for the huge parade. Police shut down their bullhorn, so my voice was loudest on team. I did most of the preaching that day. My voice is loud enough without needing a bullhorn. To God be the glory for my mega voice.

When I got done preaching I walked inside a fancy hotel to sit down to rest and charge my cell phone. Then I prayed to the Father, "God, I did what you asked me to, now I need gas money to get home." Within a few minutes a man walked up. He asked me "Why are you sitting on the ground?" My response with confidence was "charging my cell phone and waiting on my angel from God to bring me some gas money to get home. Are you my angel?" Well, the man began to chitchat about his weird beliefs, so I had to share the truth with him that he was wrong. I sternly told this man that Hell is real. He gave me $20.I asked if he would give me food money as well? He gave me $10.00 more. Thank you, sir. I celebrated with a coffee and food and of course smiled at Heaven gratefully thanking God Almighty. This must really upset some people that I asked strangers for money. Its ok if you are, but are you willing to live in your car for the gospel? There is a word for what I was doing and it's called a "mendicant." A mendicant begs for money for religious purposes. It is humbling, of course. Sometimes I would have rather found money on the ground than looked a stranger in the eye to ask for help. There is a scripture about God's people not having to beg, however there is also a scripture about "You have not, because you ask not." Again, argument can be made both ways. However, God has asked me to humble myself many times to ask for help. Begging and asking are 2 different things. Its ok if you get mad and call me a "beggar." At least, I am trying to change the world with the gospel.

Proverbs 15:33 KJV

"The Fear of the Lord is the instruction of wisdom; and before honor is humility."

I returned to DFW, Texas area living in Motel Honda. Here came my big announcement to move West. Attention: church friends and bible school students: I am moving to California! It's time to go to the Promised Land. Texas heat will be too hot living in my Motel Honda in the summer. They were shocked by my announcement. My Pastor was my favorite preacher for the past 14 years. Pastor Steve was the Evangelist in Pensacola that pointed at me through a crowd at the revival for me to come receive prayer from him. I was called to preach the day he laid hands on me 2/27/1999. Now, he was a pastor and did less traveling as an Evangelist. Cancer was killing him and it had been a year since he even came to church. I needed to go on with my destiny. Waiting was no longer an option. The Lord is my Shephard. There will be seasons as a Christian that you will serve another man's vision. Christians should serve their local church and be a disciple in the house of God. It was time for me to fly my own wings now. My mother asked me on phone "Why did you stay in Texas so long?" I think it was because my pastor was sick and wanted to help his bible school students to become world changers. I cared about those students. They called me "Mama Fuego." Leaving made me feel like a jerk, but staying made me miserable. I left the night of their graduation in May 2011. One of the mothers of the graduates thanked me with a card with $40.00. That was nice. Good bye, Texas!

Psalm 37:4 KJV "Delight yourself also in the Lord; And He will give you the desires of your heart."

Anticipation was flooding my soul with California dreams as I drove 3 days across the famous Route 66. Someone suggested I contact this street preacher named, Ruben Israel. So, I did and it was awesome getting my first California phone call. There was a huge beautiful rainbow and God was promising me of a happy new life.

When I checked my voice mail on the phone, Ruben had called. He said "Welcome to California, sister. Our outreach will be this weekend at Long Beach gay pride march." After we chatted on the phone for the first time, I knew God was linking me up with a real General in the Faith for a season. Scary excitement! Oh, my goodness, I am in California! My heart was full of HOPE.

Ruben suggested that I go to Hollywood to preach at the Chinese Theater on the famous walk of stars on Hollywood Boulevard. Way before I moved to California, I told the Lord that I wanted to preach on top of Motley Crue's star. I forgot that I prayed that prayer until the voice of God said to my heart, "Look down." "No way, Father God! Really? Right here, right now?" It was Motley Crue's Hollywood star. The first tattoo I ever got in my drunken Hell Bound sinner years before Jesus was Motley Crue tattooed on my right ankle. It is now covered with a horrible looking Christian fish. I regret both tattoos now.

This weekend was special because it was 10 years to the day of my first open air preaching sermon in Pensacola, Florida. Now, 10 years later I am standing on top of the band's star that influenced me the most to rebel against God in my teen years. Shout, shout, shout at the devil!

That was the name of one of their songs "Shout at the devil!" I decided it was a GREAT IDEA to shout at the devil in the name of Jesus!!! Woooo hoooooo! Oh yeah, the devil's ears were hurting from my loud voice that day. Even a man across the street came over to video tape me preaching the gospel. Thank you, God, for this moment to be reminded of just how far Jesus has brought me since I surrendered all at the foot of the Cross in Rome, Georgia in 1996. Jesus set me free from drugs in 1994 and will share about this in later chapter. Praise God!

I went to Bible Believers Fellowship church that night in Ruben's home. His wife baked me a cake for my ten-year anniversary of preaching. Only a street preacher would understand the milestone of ten years because if street preaching were easy then more people would be doing it. I have seen a few preachers preach on the streets like it is a stepping stone to the church pulpits. There is a lot of rejection from even Christians for being a street preacher. If you are called to this frontline ministry than ask God to make your heart strong. You will be misunderstood. Just obey God and don't let the critics kill your spirit. John the Baptist was Jesus favorite preacher. However, John was beheaded within a year of his ministry. Prosperity preachers don't seem to mention having favor with God may get your head chopped off.

Bible Believers Home Fellowship meetings felt like I was at a "John the Baptist Support Group." I felt like I finally was normal being in this group and this helped me grow in confidence. Ruben said "We are the armpits in the Body of Christ." I agree street preachers can annoy people. Especially if they are not anointed by God.

Apostle Paul was a Street Preacher.

Acts 24:5 KJV "For we have found this man a PESTILENT fellow…"

Dictionary.com

Definition of Pestilent:

1. Producing or tending to produce infectious or contagious, often epidemic, disease.
2. Destructive to life; deadly; poisonous
3. Injurious to peace, morals, etc.
4. Troublesome, annoying, or mischievous

After coming to this Fellowship, I learned that preaching outside of churches was approved of by the Holy Bible. I never thought about it before, but away I went to start preaching at a few unholy churches. God sure let me know where to go, too. A guy locally and I rebuked a church starting the Chrislam movement. The lesbian pastor came out to ask me "What issue are you here today for?" I said, "All your issues." I showed her my Bible opened to I Corinthians 6:9-11 and she pushed my Holy Bible away from her eyes. I regret not having my YouTube channel back in 2011.

Then, one day Ruben posted something on Facebook about homosexual churches. I was driving through Santa Monica thinking about that post and spotted a church with a rainbow decoration hanging on church. The Holy Ghost told me, "Preach there right now." Apostle Paul was the one that wrote the most about homosexuality being sinful and worthy of death. This church was using Martin Luther's name and Apostle Paul's name dragging them through the mud. This church was celebrating "reformation day and 80 years established." My mouth opened and God filled it. Neighbors could hear me in their homes and came out to tell me to "shut up!" A man dressed in a long dress and high heels (Transgender) came out of church across the street to push me in attempts to silence me. I kept prophesying the words God was giving me to shout as a Trumpet to awaken hearts. I finished the message and a cop drove to scene. I smiled and walked off to the car, satisfied that I obeyed the Lord. Police did nothing, because I broke NO law. USA! USA! USA! We have great free speech laws.

Our church fellowship went to a few Muslim events while I lived there in Motel Honda. An Angry Muslim asked at Orange County Arab event if I was with that group holding signs. I said "yes." Muslim said, "If the police were not here, then I would kill you." My first death threat as a preacher had finally come after 10 years of labor. I lost count now how many people have threatened to kill me, break my knee caps and stone me.

We went to concerts, car races, gay pride marches, MTV awards, Grammys, Emmys, Academy Awards, SAG Awards, sports events, Catholic conventions, the Christmas parade, Israel March, Hispanic parade, porn conventions, marijuana conventions and really, whatever else was happening.

A funny story happened at the LA Convention Center one day because a porn convention and marijuana convention were both going on inside in separate conference rooms. Which sin was worse? Ruben stayed outside to preach with banner and like a seasoned leader told me to go inside to talk to people. Thank God, Ruben told me to go in building because I stood at the bottom of the escalator of the porn convention. All the porn ticket holders and porn stars going upstairs had to pass by me with my "Trust Jesus" tee shirt. I didn't shake hands with anyone for sanitary reasons. I rebuked over ten Porn stars and told them to "Repent!" I also shared my testimony and told them "Jesus Christ will set you free." A Hispanic man asked me, "How can I stop having these thoughts?" He wanted to be free from his bondage to Lust. He was another good reason to be a risk taker. There stood a lost soul at bottom of stairs talking to the preacher, instead of going up the stairs on the highway to Hell. I felt like I was standing at the gates of Hell with my bible that day trying to pull people from the flames. That day God gave me a new courage in evangelism. We should always be growing in faith. Never get comfortable or think you don't need the Holy Spirit of God.

Mark 16:20 KJV

"And they went forth, and preached everywhere, the Lord WORKING WITH THEM, and confirming the word with signs following. Amen."

California is also where I finally got to meet Brother Jed Smock for the first time. His book, "Who will Rise Up?", inspired me over ten years prior. I admire his dedication in reaching college campuses for over 45 years. When he came to town I went to the campus to join him. Interestingly, he mentored his wife to preach and raised five daughters. He encouraged me to take a turn preaching on the campus. To be honest, I didn't want to be a campus preacher. The campus preachers at UGA prayed for me to "take the burden of the Lord for USA college campuses" the week I moved into Motel Honda spring 2011. I had already preached on several college campuses over the years, just preferred street preaching. College students are the future leaders of America, so this is one reason I embraced this Cross when Brother Jed arrived to launch me into a new ministry.

Oh yeah, I get to deal with this now, instead of cleaning toilets and bathtubs. I closed my cleaning business to be available for God full time. Campus ministry is a lot like soap scum on a bathtub. Sometimes a hard stain on a bathtub will take extra supplies to cut through the tough grime, germs and bacteria build up. After I begin as a cleaning agent to apply pressure to the areas that need cleaning, this begins the process. It brings it back to its original state of being squeaky clean and smelling lemony fresh. I see many of them as soap scum stains. They will only get clean again by the blood of Jesus Christ. I know my heart was like a huge soap scum stain when Jesus washed, sanctified and justified me by the Spirit of God. I am ONLY righteous because of Jesus, not because of my good works. My message is about the cleansing power of the Blood of Jesus through the finished work on the Cross. Wooo Hooo! Good news to the future leaders of America: You don't have to be a Scum Bucket. Jesus will make you clean! Glory to God!

To respect Brother Jed's request, I got up to preach and a large crowd gathered to listen to me. Over one hundred people gathered at California State Fullerton Campus free speech area. Something happened in my heart that week. I decided it wasn't so bad after all to preach to college students. God had a huge USA College adventure ahead of me. All I wanted at this point in my life was just to live in California. I didn't want to lose my car/home for being behind on payments. God was guiding and providing. People have said to me over the years "Where God guides, He provides." I think some people are shocked that God would pick me, though. Why Angela Cummings? Why did God pick her?

1 Corinthians 1:27 KJV

"But God hath CHOSEN the foolish things of the world to shame the wise, and God has CHOOSEN the weak things of the world to confound the things which are mighty:"

CHAPTER 3

Scary Moments

About a year after living in my car, an older street preacher got overly concerned for me. My lifestyle bothered him to the breaking point of needing to hear my parents say on the phone that they were at peace. My parents said that I am grown and could live in a car if I want to. The old street preacher without any children of his own, said to me one day on the phone, while I was washing clothes at a Laundromat, "What if someone opens your car while you are sleeping, pulls you out and rapes you, cuts your throat and leaves you for dead?"

There are always the "What ifs?" in life. My response is "What if God and His holy angels continue to protect me, hide me and anoint me for service and one day I leave a legacy and Jesus gives me a huge, soul winners crown. What if I am supposed to trust Jesus like my T-shirt says?

Growing up my parents took my older brother and I camping. We didn't have the flashy RV or travel trailer with a shower. No, we had a basic pop-up camper. My parents slept on one side of the popup camper. Kerry and I slept on the other side of the camper. Pop-up campers have only fabric to protect us from wind, rain, sun and crazy serial killers with big knives. Someone could have taken a chain saw with a hockey mask and cut open our Pop Up camper. A simple pair of scissors could have cut open the camper. My training for outdoor living came as a child. Now, I live in a black car, tinted windows and you cannot use scissors to cut fabric. My car is so small that most people would never even consider that a person could be inside snoozing. Vans are the most obvious vehicle of a homeless person. I meet a street preacher living in a van once way before I moved into my car. His lifestyle seemed so free and meeting him planted a seed in my mind. When I slept in my car my windows had to always be cracked for air to breathe. This is a risk, because a hand can try to crawl in like a snake.

I was sleeping one night over in Van Nuys, California on a side street in a neighborhood. I drove over there to sell my plasma (blood) for some quick cash. My iron was too low, so I had to get orange juice in me and try the next day to donate. All four windows were cracked open in my car. Snoozing away, I awoke at 4 am to a man by Motel Honda's back window on the driver's side. His fingers began to crawl inside like a spider. Without thinking, I shot straight up out of bed to "Roar!! Roar!" I roared like a lion, for real. My voice was like a Hollywood action clip because two Hispanics, not just one, took off running away from my car. Did I cry or even move the car? No, because it was such a supernatural voice that roared that I sat up in awe of God. I asked God how He did that with my voice. God has given me a Gift of Faith. Like a child, I just closed my eyes to go back to sleep. Thanked God for His protection and told the precious Holy Ghost, good night.

One night I was parked at the Wal-Mart in Santa Fe Springs, California, talking to a friend on the phone before going to sleep. He was talking about demons and the spirit world, which is not always something I enjoy talking about before sleeping. However, that night when I fell asleep, a homeless man began to walk in front of my car, back and forth on the sidewalk. Motel Honda was parked far away from the front entrance and closer to the back-parking spots near other buildings. I saw him and prayed with my covers pulled up around my face. "God don't let him see me." He must have felt the presence of God around my car and those demons in him began to manifest. The crazy guy began saying "I am wind. I am fire." As he paced back and forth, his facial expressions were even changing. I would peek up under covers to look some at him. It was witchcraft and demons overtaking him. Then after thirty minutes, possibly shorter than that, he left to the other side of the parking lot. After praying for peace, soon I feel asleep again in same parking spot.

When you have a hotel, campsite or a home, then you are forced to drive to your destination, just so you can brush your teeth there, put on sleeping clothes and lie down in that bed. Motel Honda parks anywhere. I can wake up next to a coffee shop right outside my door. Oh yeah! Many times, I have slept by a coffee shop, so I could wake up there for a cup of coffee, brushing my teeth for the day, sink bath for refreshment and charging phone for the day's adventure. Thank you, local coffee shops for being my living room of Motel Honda.

There is a church parking lot in Norwalk, California that has a nice place to hide a car with no bright lights around for a peaceful rest. A few times I have parked there and even taken a sink bath on a Sunday morning in the church bathroom (with dead-bolted door) before going to preach the gospel. Late one night, as I was resting with sleeping clothes on in my bed, a flashlight shined in the backseat. An angry homeless man was screaming at me from outside the window that I was in his parking spot. Apparently, he moved into the church parking lot. Homeless people do get territorial over their spots. Many homeless people have mental disorders and schizophrenia. Watch out for their mood swings! He wanted me to leave ASAP! The problem was that I couldn't because too much stuff was put in my driver's seat. This was scary, but I was praying. I grabbed stuff from the front, pulling it into the back of the car. Early in my journey of Motel Honda I didn't have a storage unit in California, only in Texas. My back was hurting from moving all that stuff so quickly to calm down the homeless Mad Man. After it was all in the back of the car, I hopped into the front seat to drive off. He was still shining his light in my eyes. I rolled the window down to say, "shut up devil in the name of Jesus." I never slept there again and learned that night to always have my front seat clear to leave somewhere quickly.

My aunt once asked me to speak to her senior adults Sunday school class about my journey of Motel Honda. The questions seemed more about handling my fears along the way than about why I choose to live this way. Women have a need for security and comfort. Danger is attractive to me. Status quo normal life bores me, but it is nice watching others live normal. I love to see family photos with dogs, homes and dinners. Normal people seem to enjoy reading my journey of being single and traveling the world for the gospel. God has given me grace for this pioneer journey. There would be no world tours to write about if I had of got tired of Motel Honda and went back to my normal life of work, paying rent and going to the same church every single week.

Before I became a Christian, my crack cocaine addiction and alcoholism had me in dangerous situations because my body screamed for another high. This physical need drove me to go to the crack dealers alone at 3 am in my car. I was risking my life at 23 years old to get a drug that could stop my heart after I inhaled it. Thank God for Jesus, rescuing me out of that living nightmare. I am not living in darkness anymore. Now I am a born-again Child of God. God has His angels watching over me. When is the last time you tried something risky for the Kingdom of God?

Psalm 91:11 KJV

"For He shall give His angels charge over thee, to keep thee in all thy ways."

The scariest night of my life happened because of my thrill of the unknown and it happened soon after I moved to California. Pioneer Angela wanted to go check out Azusa, California and see the Los Angeles Mountains. Let me set the scene a moment before taking you up the mountain with me.

I was low on gas, had no money in the bank and a phone plan that didn't get good reception. I looked at that mountain as my friend, because I was raised at the bottom of Signal Mountain in TN. I had already discovered Malibu having a road to go to Calabasas and a freeway waiting on the top of that mountain to get to Hwy 101, assuming this mountain had the same set up. I traveled up the quiet road. The sun went down and the sky turned darker. No one else was around except one car camping on the side of the road. Soon my phone went out of range and then my "get some gas" yellow light came on. I paused in the moment. My fun music that had been playing was turned off to hear the silence and my own heart beating. The road was taking me deeper into the woods. Should I keep going or turn around, put in neutral to coast down all the way? Quick prayers went up and a few small tears of "help me God!" were really on my cold face, frozen with fear. California has bears! The state flag has a Bear for the logo. I didn't tell anyone what I was about to do. It was spontaneous.

My quick prayers and thoughts were "press forward and see what else is up there." Within a few miles a road pointed to the right to a day park with a camp store. This sign gave me hope. Upon arrival, it was dark everywhere. A house had lights on, with smoke going up from the chimney. It was so quiet, like nowhere on earth I had ever traveled.

My car horn honk was my cry for help. "Lord, please let them hear my car horn." Sure, I could have gone to sleep there without honking and froze or been attacked by bears. Wisdom told me to honk! Wisdom has also taught to me that night; never ever do that again!

Within a few minutes, Adam came out to the cries of my horn from Motel Honda. We chatted. He contacted the police. I sat in my car an hour. When the police arrived, I heard them discussing my drama and how I was believing for a miracle. Overhearing them saying that made me laugh and pray at the same time. ABBA GOD HELP…

16

The 2 police then came to my car window and I slowly rolled it down for their answer. The officer said, "Adam said you can sleep in one of his cabins until the morning. It will be too cold to sleep in the car. Park it right over there and then in the morning maybe someone will come up the mountain with gas to get you back down again."

Relieved, I went into my free cabin on the mountains of Azusa, thinking about the Azusa Street revival. Another thought struck me, as I carried my night time bag inside the cabin. I prayed for a real shower. My cabin was cold, but I got my free shower. When I got in the nice cozy bed after my warm shower, I burst out with laughter. I felt like a little girl being tucked into bed by her Daddy. Thanks Abba God for the cabin party.

The next morning was beautiful and I even made coffee in my cabin. I went to the campground store (now open) to thank Adam. He decided to just give me the gas he had saved up in his red gas can. Whoa!! That means he had gas last night. I could have gotten the gas and went back down. Nope, God gave me favor to stay in a cabin that normally runs close to $100 per night. I got to stay there for free. Adam filled up my tank then went back inside. Several times after this drama I have gone to revisit Azusa Mountains. My purpose is to thank Adam again and spent money in his camp store.

Before I left to go back down the mountain that day, I chatted with a few people. They told me that this road to camp was closed for the past nine years. The road I got lost on was just recently reopened. Oh, my goodness, God knew that I was going to get stuck up there and had to hurry opening the road just for me. Call me dumb if you want. I have been called way worse. Pioneer is a great word for who I am in Christ. I love and depend on the favor of the Lord.

Shield of favor, *"for you, Lord, will bless the righteous; with favor, will you compass him as with a shield."* (Psalm 5:12)

CHAPTER 4

PIONEER CHAPTER

Pioneer by Honey tree

Pioneer Pioneer
Keep pressing onward
Beyond your fear
Only the Father
Goes before you
To your own frontier
You're a Pioneer
Uncharted wilderness
Stretches before you
And you thrive on going
Where no one has gone
Still it gets lonely
When darkness deepens
So, sing by the fire
Until the dawn
You travel on
You travel alone
And when you arrive
Nobody knows
But your Father in Heaven
He is glad you could go
For those who come after you
Will need the road
Pioneer...

My first Thanksgiving outside the Bible Belt in California was spent at a Catholic Church. I was poor and hungry. This was my only invite. I had a sink bath at a grocery store in Santa Monica before walking there dressed up in black cowgirl boots, black jeans and peach button down with blonde highlights in my hair. Homeless people were there by the hundreds to get some free food and clothes. My best friend in Malibu was a homeless Jew named David with thick glasses from Maryland. He lived in Beverly Hills and Malibu in woods. I always preached the gospel to David. He always picked on me about being a Christian too. However, he invited me to come. So, I went. He saw me preach once at Sag awards and became nicer to me after that. We saw each other a lot in Malibu, because I wanted to preach to the famous people. David wanted to meet the famous people for a conversation.

I got myself a number for my free dinner seat and got in line with everyone else. Daniel was there with his dog "Chewie the Chihuahua." He was a homeless man living in a van. I met him on his bike in Hollywood a long time ago. I shared the gospel with him. He talked me into getting a storage unit months later, when I ran into him again. His advice was the best advice I ever got for car living.

Someone in line mentioned that I didn't look homeless. My reaction was "well, yes I am one of you all, but I sleep in my car." My joke of the month after this day was perhaps I can win "Best Looking Homeless" award. What an unforgettable night for me! Suddenly, as I was waiting in line, I saw this good looking Catholic priest, with blonde hair and blue eyes, walking slowly down the sidewalk, welcoming people to the church dinner. My heart was hurting because of a personal pain from the past throbbing in my heart earlier that day. God knows I have loved a blonde-blue-eyed package since I was five years old. Why was I attracted to a Catholic priest though? This attractive priest was checking me out too. Oh yeah, he was because when he warmly shook my hand and wouldn't let go he gazed into my brown eyes. This Blonde Priest said to me "I think you might be my wife." Quick on my feet I flirted back to the eye-catching priest, "I was thinking the same thing about you." We had chemistry, people. Even the older couple sitting on the steps watching the fireworks going off, suggested for me to stay in touch with him. What is going on with me? "Angela, you can't marry a Catholic priest. Snap out of it," I told myself. It took me going to see him do a Mass service to get him off my thoughts. Yes, I seriously went to see this good-looking priest do his Mass. I can't stand the Catholic Church. That is why it was not good having these feelings. The feelings died when I saw him raise the Word of God with his robe before the crowd. It is different from the way I raise the Word. When I raise the Word of God, it's like a battle cry for war.

When I went to the door to leave Mass I decided to not make eye contact and shake his hand. My Thanksgiving Day crush finally ended. I will not recant, Blondie! Love live the Reformation!!! Thank God, I was back to being my normal anti Catholic self. No one will ever convince me Catholics are Christians with all their idol worship, praying to dead saints and changing the 10 commandments.

A month later, I had a horrible cold for ten days and the weather was in the 40's. Winter was hard because of colder temps and darker nights with loneliness at holidays. Coughing, cold, tossing back and forth, trying to find a way to fall asleep I slept outside the massive Baptist Church in Santa Monica, because I missed my Baptist parents. They never knew I slept outside Baptist Churches on my journey because, I was homesick for family. God had me on His path, His journey and His adventure. God knew I would leave it all behind to say yes to this journey. I didn't know how hard it would be at times. He gave me grace. He filled me with His love that I needed He also, continued to show me visions of the future. God is the God of all hope.

19

Romans 15:13 KJV

"May the God of hope fill you with all joy and peace as you trust in Him, so that you may overflow with hope by the power of the Holy Spirit."

Summer was hard at times in car too. I got sick once with a headache and slight fever. My body was weak, but decided to get out of small car to at least sit inside of the coffee shop to be near the bathroom. A Jewish lady named Gabby between 35 to 40 years old saw me in my bedtime clothes inside the coffee shop. She came up to me stoned on either her pills or medical marijuana. She asked if I was sick and needed anything. Then, I explained that I was sick. Immediately in her forceful way, she asked me to follow her to a grocery store. There she bought me cold medicine, and then we came back to where she found me. She ordered me an expensive sandwich and the tallest hot tea in the place. Quietly, I slowly ate my food God had provided through this Jewish stoner. We stayed in touch for a few weeks. I took her to her psychiatrist a few times in Beverly Hills. I tried to give her the gospel several times in my car, as I drove her. She had no car or license.

 She had serious issues and think she maybe the stripper on the ad of a billboard in town. She mentioned she stripped in conversation. I watched her leave my car at a gas pump. Walk straight up to an old man and begin to make out with him. She got in his car and bossed me around demanding I follow her. She gave me the gas money, so I did not know what she was going to do next. I didn't want to leave her stranded. She took the old man to Beverly Hills to get her a new dress. Our fellowships ended quickly after that day because she brought her medical marijuana in my car. Gabby didn't tell me why we stopped at a local pharmacy. She opened the bag. There was a marijuana sucker, brownie and weed. Danger! Get away from this Jezebel.

Wisdom is HUGE for a disciple of Christ. Light and darkness are in opposition. I gave her the gospel and she even started to tear up listening to worship music. Now, it was time to let go because she was putting me in danger. She was mad at me for not helping her after this day. I had to change my phone number to keep her from stalking me. My goal was not friendship, but to point her to Jewish King. Jesus wanted to set her free. She was living with a Persian man in an expensive home on Pacific Coast Highway. She even screamed on the phone at him that she would burn the place down. Gabby was the most dangerous woman I ever met in my life. God will allow danger in a Christian's life to reach a soul. Don't ignore the heart of God for your own personal safety. If God leads you to a dark place, then He will be your Light and Salvation. Remember Apostle Peter walked on water with Jesus, while the other disciples watched. I am not surprised Peter was the first street preacher after the Fire of heaven came down in the Upper Room of Jerusalem. Peter was a Risk Taker. Are you ready to take some risks?

Lonely days can be overcome a lot quicker than lonely, rainy, cold days. That combo is deadly for the human heart. Rain during the day, when there is no schedule is very hard. You find yourself trying to figure out where to go and wait out the time till bedtime. Never spend the whole day in your car, unless you are driving somewhere. It messes with your head. I got free counseling a few times at my lowest periods of life in Motel Honda. There were even a few times I considered suicide. My friends walked me through it, I kept going to Ruben's church and preaching the gospel. It was my dark night of the soul. No one could rescue me. I was like a worm in the cocoon about to come out as a Butterfly. Before the butterfly comes out it struggles and fights inside. No one is supposed to try to help the butterfly out in the struggle because it will mess up the wings. When someone is going through the dark night of the soul, they need to work through this to be stronger for the beautiful flight.

"First the attack and then the blessing." Pastor John Kilpatrick

I was willing to be homeless. Seriously, I counted the cost and was willing to allow the Honda Repo company to come get my car. 4 years I diligently made payments on that black Honda Fit. A stranger that I never met already paid off my credit debt after I obeyed God to move to California. Praise God! I only had one more debt to be cancelled. Then, I could be debt free. God would not let me rescue myself by getting a job. All I could do was pray, because I was behind 3 payments. My amazing parents didn't want me to be homeless, so they called Honda. They paid off a HUGE debt, that I couldn't pay for myself. Wow, I was in shock when Honda called me. I was just waking up in my car on the West Coast in the Azusa Walmart parking lot. The Honda employee was so happy to inform me on the phone that I don't have to worry about losing my car anymore. My debt had been paid in Full! Glory to God! Thank you, mom, and dad for helping me keep my car. I called to thank them and then went to the Azusa mountains to worship God in Thanksgiving and Praise.

Later, I had to stand on a street corner and beg for food. God was teaching me humility and how to receive help from others. It was not easy to ask someone for help. Can you imagine getting your car paid off and then having to beg for lunch? My parents did not need to make sure I got lunch that day. They wanted to make sure I didn't lose that car. Motel Honda was my only home and transportation. I can remember wearing a Navy Sweatshirt with HSM on it. HSM was the bible school that I helped for free for over 2 years encouraging those students to become World Changers. This was so humiliating standing there with a sign that I was hungry. Watching a man eat pizza in his car at the stop light about to burst into tears from my stomach growling at me. Suddenly, a middle-aged man drove up to my street corner with a bag of hamburger and fries with a fountain coke. I bowed my head and humbly said "Thank you." Deep sigh and thanks to God. I then walked to the grass behind a business to sit out of the view of everyone. I sat with my food crying and thanking God for His gracious provision of my daily bread.

Genesis 6:8 KJV "But Noah found grace in the eyes of the Lord."

CHAPTER 5

3.3 Million Dollar Parking Spot

Why keep sleeping in the Wal-Mart parking lots looking at ugly, big bulky 18-wheelers every night? Instead I can wake up to glorious mountain views of Malibu on a million-dollar piece of real estate and drink my coffee alongside the rich and famous? When you live in your car you choose your own zip code. More joy was added to my journey of homelessness in Motel Honda when I decided to upgrade my nightly parking spot. I found paradise in Malibu on top of a hill blending in with other cars. Right outside my Honda home were beautiful flowers, sunrise views fit for a princess and the Pacific Ocean breezes blowing up the hill, not too far from my parking spot. Thank You, Jesus!

On October 11, 2011 Buzzle.com author Rutuja Jathar wrote an article "The Top Ten Most Expensive Places to Live in California." Beverly Hills, not surprisingly, was voted number one. Malibu was number seven. The article said about Malibu, "The warm and sandy beaches and breathtaking scenic beauty of Malibu has made it a popular tourist destination. Malibu is also the second home to many popular personalities including the entertainment industry. Median income for a household in Malibu is around USD $100,000. An average house in Malibu, sizing 2,200 sq. ft. may cost you somewhere near USD $3,300,000.00."

Someone told me on my journey that many celebrities were spotted shopping at Malibu Mart. Being raised up in Tennessee, watching television like most folks in America, that sounded like a whole new adventure to evangelism. Ruben even encouraged me to be bold when I met them, because they need the gospel and are just people. Ruben has personally preached to celebrities at many events in LA over the years, but the fact that he reached Elton John fired me up. My prayers became like arrows with love letters on the end to God to please allow me to reach Hollywood stars for Jesus.

One morning I went to a local bathroom at Malibu Mart when the workers opened it. I was first customer. Quickly I dead-bolted the door for my morning sink bath. I changed into my jeans, "Trust Jesus" t-shirt with camo jacket over it and no makeup. I walked around Malibu Country Mart for fun just to people watch and get coffee. Extreme Fish Alert! My first celebrity sighting was Jerry Seinfeld having some breakfast outside on the porch of the country restaurant closest to the gas station. I walked in the back by my car to pray with my heart beating wildly. "God give me courage!" This man is worth over $800 million and is Jewish. Clapping happy, I began to walk back. However, with my thumbnail I tried to get an annoying booger out of my nose, before talking Jerry. Too late! As I rounded the corner with thumb nail wiping my nose, there came Jerry to his car. Great! A professional comedian just saw a Jesus lady picking her nose with thumb nail. Well, whatever. I walked up to him, not to shake his hand but show him my "Trust Jesus" t-shirt. He gave me a half-smile and did look at the shirt. I asked him if he "knew Jesus Christ." He was not clearly not interested, but still got a message. Trust Jesus Jerry! He is your King.

David, the homeless Jew, loved looking for celebrities too. That is how we became friends. Another good friend in Malibu that I would talk to when lonely was Joseph, who was from Egypt. He didn't leave Malibu often and would wear the same clothes for weeks. One day while I was shopping with my only monthly donation of $50 from a couple in Ohio, God spoke to me to buy him a new outfit.

The night that I did my very first acting role, the only friend around to tell my story to was Joseph. I worked as an actress on a Judge show called "We the people" for $50.00. Most judge shows are real. "We the People" is actors off craigslist and other casting companies. This was only acting job I ever had while there, but I worked background jobs a lot more.

Joseph never complained about being homeless, hungry, tired or broke. He was a quiet man that was just surviving in paradise. Occasionally, he would tell me about a celebrity he saw. He saw Mel Gibson and I never did. Joseph loved his sweatpants with pockets and even wore my Uncle Dallas t-shirts. A few months later he still had it on. I needed to buy him another outfit because he was dirty. I adopted him as my homeless buddy and clothing extension of ministry. One day, I was in a Goodwill store shopping and told a lady I lived in Malibu and was a minister. She got angry! Yeah, I didn't think long enough on that. Some preachers have overindulged in the ministry causing other ministers to be judged wrongly. I didn't have a chance to tell her that I lived in my car in Malibu. She was too mad to talk to me anymore.

Paparazzi are in your face with cameras and personal space when you are famous; therefore, many people despise their careers as celebrities. Someone's got to take the photos because lovers of this world crave gossip with juicy photos.

My first encounter with a large group of Brazilian paparazzi was one late afternoon, after meeting Jerry Seinfeld that morning. When I saw a group of over seven men standing on the grassy hill by a name brand clothing store, gazing at the playground no one had to tell me that something BIG was going down. Aaron Spelling's daughter, Tori was there with her husband, Dean and the kids. Jack, his teenage son, from Dean's first marriage was there too. I walked straight up to the paparazzi and asked what they were waiting on. The leader said, "Tori is pregnant. We want to wait till she gets up for a pregnant shot." Her dad was the dude that made the TV show "Love Boat" that I used to watch as a kid. Whoa! Let the action begin people. My former evangelism pastor in Texas told me once, "You need a hobby." Well, now I found one. Chasing famous people with the gospel became my new hobby. When the famous family got up to leave, I followed the paparazzi to watch them in action. Since I was a missionary I was free to do my own thing in this situation. As they began to get into their dark tinted Cadillac Escalade, I asked a simple question, "Do you know Jesus Christ as your personal Lord and Savior?" Tori didn't answer. She just got into the front seat and pulled her visor down to see how she looked. Her husband, Dean, responded, "No, not personally." I then told the teenage boy that "Jesus loved him." Normally, I don't say that to people because people take "Jesus loves you" as a license to sin at times.

The following day I was on the playground at Malibu on the swing set. Jack, the stepson of Tori Spelling, came to sit by me and swing. He probably appreciated someone caring for his soul. I had no idea the drama behind this family and that they had a reality TV show. I wanted his father to know my intention, so I went across the playground to speak to him. "Dean, yesterday I talked to you all about Jesus and I just want you to know I am a missionary. I just care about your souls is all." He was so nice, that his simple words have helped me approach all of Hollywood afterwards. Dean said, "I know," smiling. Then the little children began to tell me about the hotels in Malibu. God was allowing me to feel the moment and relax. Yes, I can do this. I can talk to the rich and famous, just as easily as the homeless down and outers. After that first day, I knew God was going to bring more in my path because God cares for their souls. Imagine some of the big Hollywood influencers getting born again and following Jesus with their whole life.

"For I am not ashamed of the gospel of Christ: for it is the power of God to salvation to everyone that believes; to the Jew first, and also to the Greek." (Romans 1:16)

The word of God says to the "Jew first." When I was in Bible school, I took a Jewish Roots class and made a D. That is horrible grade, yet God has brought me so many Jews to preach to in the past few years. Malibu is nicknamed by some locals as "Mali-Jew". Some famous Jews that I met, besides Jerry Seinfeld and Tori Spelling are Adam Sandler, Jillian Michaels, Rob Reiner, Robert Downey Jr, Ben Stein, Jeremy Pivens, Pink, Gloria Allred, and Kenny G.

Malibu used to have a popular restaurant located inside Malibu Country Mart called, "Nobu." After I went to Texas for a season it closed and relocated to California Hwy 1. Most of the divine appointments were right there. When I returned after being gone six months my homeless Jewish friend said, "We hardly get any celebrity sightings any more since you left." God brought them out so they could get the gospel, not so David could get an autograph.

Oh yeah, God brought not just the rich and famous, but the homeless, paparazzi, autograph-seekers and random others in my path. We were like a small community; the autograph seekers, photo-takers, camera TMZ reporters and the professional paparazzi. Hours I spent with each of them over the season of my Malibu assignment. One group of paparazzi asked me once, "Who is the worst sinner in Hollywood?" Wow, what a question! The paparazzi said they thought Lindsey Lohan was the biggest sinner and they wanted me to preach to her. Man, they gave me a burden for her and they weren't even born again Christians yet. When I moved back to Malibu to wait for my trip to Europe in 2013, I found out that Lindsey Lohan was in a rehab in Malibu. I found out where it was and drove there. There was a private road with a policeman on the hill to guard the expensive place. I was hoping to stand with a banner to get her outside to hear my story.

Adam Sandler heard my testimony as he sat quietly listening on the playground of Malibu Mart. He said, "I hope nothing but good for your future." His words were like a Jewish blessing to me because after that I got a part time job working in Hollywood as an extra. I didn't work much, but enough to survive. Adam means "first man." Not only did I begin to work in Hollywood after meeting him, this was the day I got a burden for Israel. Whenever I meet Jews now, it's different. God just downloaded something in my heart talking to this Jewish comedian that day. I hope Adam will take his family to Israel someday for a visit and get in touch with his roots. Most of all I hope he surrenders his life to Yeshua as His Messiah. That was my whole purpose for walking up to him that day. I told him first thing in conversation that I didn't want a photo. I was there to tell him what Jesus has done for me. Glory to the Lamb of God!

Being a Hollywood extra, I did not have a set schedule and sometimes no work was there for weeks. God provided and as Christians we can understand about the mysteries of God more than the unbeliever. This subject really bugs the atheist because they refuse to see God in my provisions and miracles. Only God can open your eyes, like He did mine. I used to curse God, but now I am a preacher filled with His love and compassion for others.

The paparazzi gave me tips sometimes for phone calls, if they got the shot or the story for TMZ. Once I got $40 for pointing out an actress from Desperate Housewives. The only reason I knew her was because of another paparazzi getting bad treatment from her another day. Paparazzi talked to me often about who people were and let me know who they wanted to snap photos of the most. TMZ guy was too scared to interview Robert Downey JR because he was his favorite actor. I had just told him 24 hours before that I wanted to share Jesus with him. When he walked by I got to speak to Iron Man freely because the paid TMZ professional lost his courage. He was star struck.

I was star struck the most with Rick Springfield because he was on my bedroom wall as a teenager. I repented to God for not preaching to him and asked God to bring him again. God brought Rick Springfield 3 more times after that sincere prayer. I shared gospel and 4th time got his photo. He was Atheist. He said he didn't believe in a God in the sky with white hair ready to pounce on people. One time I told him that I was praying for him still and he thanked me. He got a DUI that year in Malibu.

Dean Cain was Atheist too. I saw him 3 times and he thanked me for our talk about God. Superman waited at his car for me to walk to him since he was too busy on phone the first time. Dean ended up playing in a great Christian movie about a year or 2 after that divine appointment at Malibu Mart. He stared in the movie playing an atheist in "God's Not Dead." When I saw that movie, it warmed my heart how God used me in this actor's life. Others I reached with gospel are Martin Sheen, Pierce Bronson, Melissa Etheridge, Courtney Cox, Sean Penn, Cheech Martin and Cindy Crawford. There are many stories I could share because it was such an interesting season of my life. The paparazzi have even asked me for prayer. David even went to church with me once. That was a miracle. I love Malibu!

Malibu is still my favorite city in America. I have seen famous people that I have preached to on billboards, posters, make up and TV as I traveled around the world. The Holy Spirit would spot light them for me. I would smile and thank Him for using me to share the gospel with that person. However, when I think about Malibu I think of my poor stinky homeless buddies too. One time David told me a Mexican lived in the back yard of Cher. She did not even know it. I love that story, because many famous people unapproachable and prideful. Jesus walked and talked to all people groups.

Proverbs 22:2 KJV "The rich and poor meet together: The Lord is maker of them all."

CHAPTER 6

Oktoberfest to Red Light District

Early one morning at Starbucks in Freemont, California, I began daydreaming of preaching at Oktoberfest in Munich, Germany, as I looked at photos of the previous year on my phone. In walked a man wearing a military jacket with a German flag patch on it. Call it a small sign from God, but to me I took it as a nod from God. Right away I began declaring that I would be going to Germany. As I was leaving the small group of street preachers there, Kevin blessed me with a five-foot banner with poles that would fit in a carryon bag. The banner said "Fear God" and on the other side "Trust Jesus." It was black with yellow letters. He gave me a beautiful royal blue t-shirt with "Jesus saves from Hell" on it. Kevin showed me a picture of him preaching in Amsterdam. He believed in me. At the time, all I could think of was just getting by week to week in California and now I want to go to Germany. Jensen Franklin, preached a message at Brownsville called "How?" Then he would say "The Holy Ghost." That was what I would hear in my heart as I got nervous about the money "How? The Holy Ghost."

Since it was summer time in California I chose the long scenic way home, along California Highway 1. It was so beautiful and nothing to hurry to get to. I was just enjoying life with God. One night I slept in the parking lot of Calvary Church along the way. The next morning I enjoyed the small town I found myself in. God asked me to write my testimony in a tract to give people on my journey. I noticed my phone was not getting any service in that city and realized that was a good thing. Social media can be a distraction when you are trying to accomplish something, like a writing assignment. I got a cute room upstairs with a desk and balcony at a bed and breakfast, with some extra money I had been given by a street preacher on Kevin's Cry to God ministry team.

The Word of the Lord came to me there in that writer's room. Not only was the tract written or at least started, but faith came in full from Heaven to trust God for the Munich, Germany trip. The Holy Spirit spoke to me not to get a job, but that He (Holy Ghost) could get the money quicker than I could. "Ask one hundred people on Facebook for $30." What a plan and who is crazy enough to be the first giver to a woman preacher living in her car? I rarely ever got a donation back then. My faith was real, because I know God's voice. Something big was about to happen. Praise the Lord!

People believed in me and began to help. Only a few people didn't come up with their promised donation, but it was ok because God provided through some giving $100 or more. All I knew was that after seven days of no food and lots of prayer, God moved in a powerful way.

The home that I used to live in for free in Texas reopened to me for a season. Grampa needed a ride to the airport and back. Unbelievable, yes! I drove from California to Texas just so I could housesit and make sure he got to the airport. What a blessing that was to stay in a home again to prepare my Europe trip on his computer.

No more libraries waiting for my turn to use the computer for an hour. July and August were spent in a huge room in the back of his house. That is where I lived a long time before as a live-in maid in exchange for rent. Right before I went to Europe in Fall 2012, someone blessed me with a camera, laptop, four new tires, alignment, bag and clothes for the trip. Please, understand this was my first camera and laptop of my whole Christian walk. I prayed for 5 years for a laptop. Thank you, Jesus!

While still in Malibu, before my move back to Texas, I got travel books of Italy, Switzerland and Germany and videos from the library. Because Italy was so close to Germany I wanted to watch those videos first. After exploring Italy through books and videos, God told me "no". Then, God told me "no" to Switzerland too. One day I was in the lobby of the YMCA waiting for a girl to get off work to go eat. There was a travel book about Amsterdam, a sinful city in Europe. When I started to read how wicked the city was, my heart was stirred to go preach there. I showed the book to the girl working there and she said, "Someone just dropped that book off today. You can have it." That is the day God called me to preach in Amsterdam.

I purposely planned my trip to leave on Rosh Hashanah, the Jewish New Year. I heard somewhere that it is very important what you do during those high holy days because it represents what you will do all year. I believed that, because the year before I had my first acting job on "We the People" TV shows that day. The next year I preached to so many celebrities and worked in Hollywood.

September 17, 2012 to October 23, 2012

Germany, Austria and the Netherlands

Several people asked me if I was going to Berlin while in Europe. I kept saying no because I had been there before. God dealt with me about going to Berlin. When I told God "yes" at 4 am, His presence flooded the room and I knew He had something special ahead for me.

What then shall we say to these things? If God is for us, who can be against us? (Romans 8:31)

All alone I arrived in Munich, Germany and immediately took a picture of my stuffed lamb, Behold, with a "Munich loves you" billboard in the airport. Behold, the lamb has always been a great travel buddy for me. My stuffed lamb reminds me why I do what I do. I stayed in a home close by the airport for several days to overcome jetlag. I walked the streets in awe of every car, house, plant, flower and store in the German community. No longer was I in my car, wondering where I would get my next meal. God promoted me to the foreign mission field. A huge five-week mission trip was in front of me. What a glorious prayer walk I was having, thanking God for sending me to the nations! Simple desire birthed a bigger dream. I had a chocolate covered banana one day at a café shop. I was not lonely at all, because I knew God was with me. This is a dream come true.

I was off on the train to Garmisch-Partenkirchen, Germany which became my favorite German city. I loved the scenery; mountains, flowers, churches and small village atmosphere. My hostel had over-booked and upgraded me free to my own room. Yeah God! I stayed there and traveled to Munich by train to preach at Oktoberfest. I had to take trains and buses to get to my destination.

What a great feeling to know I was going to preach at the most famous drunken party in the world and Jesus set me free from alcoholism! Glory to God! Repent, drunkards! Jesus has new wine and a better way. My first day, I went all the way inside Oktoberfest preaching the gospel with my raised banner. Crowds of people walked by, wave after wave, seeing Jesus on my sign. People came to me with questions. One guy could not believe I came alone all the way from America just to preach there. He said "What is it you want to tell us?" "Glad you asked," and away I went with my biblical message.

The next day I stood by a huge Oktoberfest sign that everyone was getting photos under. Only a few that knew no English talked to me in German. Most of the people walking by spoke English and stopped to chitchat. I met people from all over the world. This is a great place to take missions teams.

Soon I moved to Salzburg, Austria to stay a few days. My train rides were the same price because of the Bavarian ticket I bought daily to go back and forth to Munich. The weather began to get colder and I used my winter coat some. I caught a cold and had to push myself to go anyway. Ruben encouraged me to go preach with a cold anyway. The outreach went very well and I wore a warm coat.

My question is, "Where was the church of Germany?" Every year Germany knows millions are coming to get drunk in their own backyard. Why not show up and serve these millions of people with gospel tracts and share the love of God? Christians all read the same Holy Bible. Jesus gave every disciple the great commission. So why was I standing alone for five days for hours reaching out to so many, with no local churches helping? Only once did I run into Bible school students there for a few hours and then they left. Maybe there were Christians there and we didn't run into each other. It was a two-week event and I only preached there five days. God was sending me to Frankfurt, Berlin and Amsterdam after Oktoberfest. I hope Germans are covering this event with the gospel.

For two days at Oktoberfest, I stood across the street from the large entrance sign and saw lots of people walking by. This was my most fruitful place because it was more of a relaxed, laid back spot to talk. One vendor selling food and drinks refused to sell me a peach tea. She cursed me out in German. Another vendor was mad at me too. My preaching was loud and was reaching the crowds going in to the beer fest. The worst foul mouth I met was there from Dallas, Texas. She did not appreciate me being there at all because she was trying to enjoy her debauchery. People were passed out during the middle of the day on the sidewalks and a few even puked.

Two young people were napping from the beers, so I quietly left a gospel tract next to them. The young guy woke up and began reading the tract while lying down. I tried to talk with him. He was from Hungary, which caused me to want to preach in Hungary. Several people wanted photos with the banner and one guy flipped a bird at Jesus name on the banner with his friends, all dressed in Bavarian clothes. Imagine how God viewed his bride. God gave this young man breath and life, but he chose to curse his maker by saying "F--- you, Jesus!" Heartbreaking how many people will end up in eternal flames of Hell for ignoring this great gift that God offers through His Son, Jesus Christ.

My final night, I decided to go ahead and stay in Munich so I could catch the train to Frankfurt easier the next day. Oktoberfest was packed and people were drinking beers in tents all over the large property. I went in without my banner and just decided to preach short messages all over the walking areas where crowds were going by. One guy tried to steal my Bible, one girl put her hand on my mouth, two men pinched my butt, and the day before, one German slapped my butt. When he slapped my butt, he said, "Don't forget, it's all about grace." Well, I never forgot that, but not butt-slapping grace. Grace is not a license to sin.

My final night was also filled with guys from Norway picking on me, UK guys asking for prayers and Scottish men complaining about how much money they had spent on beers without getting drunk. The men were shocked that I had overcome my alcohol problem and wanted to share with others about Jesus there. These people caused me to want to preach in Norway, UK and Scotland. Thousands of souls were reached with the gospel during my visit to Munich. Praise God!

The nations need the gospel of Jesus Christ. Missions should not be something we do once a year. Missions should be a lifestyle and the heartbeat of the church.

A very nice break in my schedule was Christian fellowship in the home of BRSM grads in Germany. I brought their son a cookie necklace from Oktoberfest as a gift. It was great timing for my visit because October 3rd was German day and they were off from work. We had a great day sightseeing and visiting a castle. We laughed a lot and Christa made wonderful food. Praise God! Always, nice to see friends and relax from frontline ministry a few days.

Next, off again after two nights, to Berlin for a few days, October fourth to October eighth. Normally, I don't like four hour historical tours of a city. I really felt like God wanted me to do the Berlin walking tour though. Most of my mission trips over the years have been to Germany. Berlin is where Hitler held his rallies on the grounds. Wearing my winter coat, I walked in the rain with a tour guide. Very interesting and crazy how some bombs from former wars are still being discovered as they work on the cities upgrade. I got the coolest photo of my left foot in West Germany and my right foot in East Germany with a sign under my feet, "Berlin Wall." You can walk on top of where the Berlin Wall used to be 25 years ago, and still see pieces of the wall standing. I heard amazing stories about people escaping. It made me so thankful to have all my freedoms in America. Hitler was not a Christian. He was a Catholic. He was nothing like Jesus Christ. A Christian is Christ like.

The Next day there was an ice hockey game going on in the O2 Center. The arena was about two blocks from my hostel. I did get in trouble from security both days for trespassing, so I had to be careful how close I got to the entrance. The second day I had to run with my banner because security wanted to take me to the police. They grabbed my arm. I pulled away and began to run with my banner against the wind. My boots were hurting my feet and I had no belt to hold my new trousers up. They begin to slip as I ran. I pulled them up and continued to run. They followed me several blocks. I was not going to jail. The next day I had to go to Amsterdam.

My day was interesting because it poured down rain as I carried my banner around the city. My goal after the ice hockey short outreach was to get to the steps of the mayor of Berlin. I heard he was a homosexual. I wanted to preach on his steps and declare holiness over the area. Right before I got there a rainbow came out over the city. It was so beautiful. God was with me on my day adventure in Berlin for sure. I walked one more block to the mayor's steps and preached.

Soon a Christian guy on a bicycle came by with his huge banner with scriptures on it. He even had an Israeli flag on his banner. What a great encounter to have with a brother in Christ. The cops didn't want either of us getting our banners out any more or even hanging out there. His banner was in German. I know it was probably from Matthew 28, possibly verse 19.

"Go therefore and teach all nations, baptizing them in the name of the Father, and the Son and of the Holy Spirit."

Later that night a guy from UK stopped me. He felt God called him to Berlin for missions. He was waiting on God for laborers. There I was a five-foot two-inch woman alone standing working Berlin without an evangelism partner. Surely, my life was a loud wakeup call not to wait on a partner. I just start preaching the gospel and left the partner issue to God. I will stand before God alone, not with some partner at the Judgment Seat; just me. Hello God! Wow, what a scary day when we will face God. I do not take that day lightly. Jesus is not my homeboy. Jesus is my Master.

On a prayer walk in Berlin one of the days there, I was carrying my banner with my music jamming in my ears. Right before I crossed the street, someone tapped me on my shoulder. Wow! I turned around to two girls, college age, standing there. One girl poured out her heart to me. She was a Muslim and a lesbian that had a powerful encounter with Jesus while in Jerusalem. He came to her and tried to convert her. She knew Jesus was real and all she wanted to know from me was can she still come to Him? That was the moment I knew why God had asked me to please go to Berlin. Berlin was about this precious, lost soul. She asked many questions about Hell, her lifestyle and asked if Jesus would still God!

"What man of you, having a hundred sheep, if he loses one of them, does not leave the ninety-nine in the wilderness, and go after the one which is lost until he finds it? ⁵ And when he has found it, he lays it on his shoulders, rejoicing. ⁶ And when he comes home, he calls together his friends and neighbors, saying to them, 'Rejoice with me, for I have found my sheep which was lost!' ⁷ I say to you that likewise there will be more joy in heaven over one sinner who repents than over ninety-nine just persons who need no repentance." (Luke 15:4-7)

Long train ride from Berlin to Amsterdam and cannot believe I am living this missions dream. Amsterdam rocked! I met a lot of cool people there working the streets for Jesus. My hostel was in the Red-Light District where all the sin is celebrated. Lots of sin means lots of sinners. My calling is to help sinners meet the savior of the world. Woot! Woot! I love Jesus.

"Christ said, I came into this world for one reason – to reach and save lost souls! Yet this was not only Jesus' mission, but He made it our mission as well; and he said unto them, go ye into all the world and preach the gospel to every creature." (Mark 16:15) David Wilkerson.

Amsterdam is, in my opinion worse than Las Vegas. It is hard enough walking around Las Vegas looking at everything going on without either crying or puking from the demonic spirits taking over the area. Amsterdam was even more disturbing, because of sexual photos more in your face. Hookers in windows for sale legally too. I was not prepared for just how bad it was going to be, even from the book.

When I first walked through the Red-Light District to find lunch one day, my eyes felt raped for the wicked pictures on the businesses on this walk. One photo was so filthy that I began to weep. I leaned up against a business wall corner, out of the way of people walking by. The photo made my stomach sick. As I stood crying like a child that lost her parents, a police officer walked up to me.

"Why are you crying?" he asked. My response was, "Because there is so much sin in this city." He said, "Sh?" I said, "No. Sin." Twice he thought I said the curse word that is like the word "crap." He asked "Where is your home?" I pointed the way to my hostel. The officer than suggested I go home and take a nap. All the years of my open air preaching ministry, never has a cop told me to go take a nap. Let me tell you something, I did go home, grabbed my banner and went back to confront those demons from Hell. Then this preacher woman went to the hostel and cried herself to sleep. I took my nap. Then, went later back to the streets and began open air preaching crusades.

First, I started in the train station areas. Then I went to Dam Square and then did a few outreaches in the Red-Light District. Hell's Angels bikers walked by me once as I preached and didn't throw me into the canal. YWAM is in Amsterdam, but I never ran into anyone on the streets doing evangelism. There are two Christian hostels there and they are doing a good job of inviting people to nightly Bible studies. I went to one and got to share with a guy there asking questions. One desire I have for those starting in ministry is that they would try just a little harder to share the whole gospel. Sometimes people that are new at sharing their faith are too concerned with making friends and not hurting anyone's feelings. The gospel has a bloody cross and there is no way around the bloody cruel-cross. Christianity is all about a Lamb sacrificed. We need to be concerned with the fact that God sets up these divine appointments and expects us to tell people the truth of God's Word. Otherwise, what kind of an ambassador are we if we start changing the message to make the lost sinner happy. *No blood = No forgiveness of sin.* Pray for boldness, if you struggle. Just don't be a faker and a coward because Heaven is counting on you to speak the truth with conviction.

One day I was preaching and several young people stopped to ask me about God. "If He had a Son, where is He now?" One young teenager showed me a Bible that he had just received in the mail that day and then gave me a walking tour of Amsterdam. He gave me so much hope for the next generation. He was happy about reading God's word and growing in fellowship with God. He wasn't cursing, drinking beer and picking on the prostitutes in the Red-Light District. *This young man had just gotten born again and found his pearl. Jesus is the pearl.*

God gave me some fun times in Amsterdam. A girl from Korea invited me to go visit another town in Holland to see windmills with her. We had a blast and walked past a building where they were making chocolate. Irresistible smells came from the chocolate factory. What a great neighbor that would be! We saw wooden shoes made and ate cheese samples together. My day was filled with great joy and memories. I bought an Amsterdam jacket that day and when I wear it, I remember how much fun my roommate from my hostel and I had. I believe in preaching the gospel and enjoying the places God sends me. I won't deny myself a great photo, a piece of cheese, laughter with new friends or looking at some wooden shoes being built, just because I am on a mission trip.

Another guy I met at my hostel was about 35 years old and from China. He was a believer in Christ and was very interested in street evangelism after I shared my stories with him. We arranged for him to come with me. We walked with my banner during the day, slowly through the Red-Light District.

We stood outside of a busy bar where we could see people drinking beer. A window about 50 feet away had a hooker inside ready to work. She was in her underwear and not very attractive at all. Close by was a tattoo parlor and a pot smoking bar. We began talking to one table of beer drinkers together. A man asked us "Why should I fear God?" As soon as he asked about fearing God, an explosion went off in the area. It was so powerful that we felt the ground shake under our feet. My Chinese partner said the mafia may be involved. We went immediately to see what happened and waited for the police. What a serious Amsterdam moment on the streets! The explosion happened close to the tattoo parlor. We never did find out if anyone was hurt.

We walked onto Dam Square and ran into other Christian women preachers that I had already been enjoying fellowship with on the streets. There are awesome hearted people there that love Jesus and care about lost souls. They look pretty rough and remind me of David's army in the Bible. Beauty is in the eye of the beholder and these people for sure are beautiful because of their big hearts to serve Amsterdam with the Word of God.

My last day in Amsterdam was my birthday. I went to a castle in another city and took my stuffed lamb with me for cool photos. I met a couple of Muslims on my journey and got to pull my lamb out of my backpack to explain the gospel. Islam has no blood atonement for sin. Only the blood of the Lamb of God can remove the stain of sin. The great news is that Jesus wants to save. One Muslim was really listening to me. We parted ways. I had walked a long way to visit that castle. My shoes were not good walking shoes at all. I decided, after exhaustion to pray for a car to give me a ride back to the train station. My first thumb out to hitchhike worked.

A very nice man picked me up and at first went the wrong way. Then I explained it was the other way, and he had no problem turning around to get me to the train station. He saved me at least a two mile walk. My feet hurt so badly. Thank You Jesus for the lift!

The next morning I was up very early, walking my two huge bags to the Amsterdam Central train station at 6 am to get myself to the airport to go back to America. Walking alone and quietly, I was in deep thought about my past five weeks of preaching the gospel adventures with God. The Holy Ghost of God whispered to me "Now, I am going to use you in America." That was great timing, because all I could say was, "OK." What God wants, God will get. Jesus is my Master.

October 23, 2012 I returned to Texas, rested in a huge mansion of a former employee for a few days and then went to a hotel for three days locally before my next mission started. The rest of the year was traveling to many college campuses, concerts, youth groups, and churches and then ending up in Miami, Florida to wrap up the year of 2012. God was using me with college students and I began to see God readjusting my calling from street ministry to college campuses of America. Motel Honda was still my home. No camper with a bow given after my return to the states. I was in content living in my car because I made it across the line to Full Time Ministry now. While on this mission's trip I started a YouTube channel to film my work overseas and after coming back I continued filming the gospel journey.

CHAPTER 7

West Coast Tour

Awe, sweet Miami for the Christmas holidays! I parked in a high rise parking garage and could feel an ocean breeze. An electric outlet by the elevator made cooking a steak on my grill possible. Parking was $15 a day and for the few days I was there, Starbuck's provided my sink baths again. I met a homeless street preacher that directed me to a street by a park with free parking. There I lived resting and getting settled into Miami life. If you are going to be homeless, then the best way to do it is in a beautiful city. Why look at trash on streets, when you can look at beautiful beaches. I have slept in some ugly places before and it takes away from the adventure. Why? Because waking up with palm trees outside my window is better than waking up looking at a spray painted wall in a dangerous part of town. Miami, Florida has excellent weather year around, unless there is a hurricane.

When Brother Jed posted his schedule for spring 2013, my interest in having a nice, peaceful, chilled out, stay-put winter went away. The Holy Ghost gave me marching orders to arrive at Florida State University to help him preach in Jan. 2013. I can even remember doing a MapQuest of Florida to California to Washington with his schedule. The schedule was for me to see all the miles that I might possibly put on my car/home that semester. Miami was my comfort zone at the moment. I was tired from traveling in 2012. My heart was on the road and those college campuses. *God gave me a ministry called "Highways and Hedges Ministries" and the highways of America were inviting me to come and ride.*

Road trip fever! From Florida to California I traveled again. That was a long journey. A friend of mine gave me four free nights in a hotel with his reward points. What a blessing that I didn't have to sleep in my car all the way there! Within a month, Brother Jed Smock of Campus Ministry USA was on his way with Sister Pat and his wife, Sister Cindy. Both these women are hardworking warriors for Christ. I joined their tour and preached with them on several California campuses. A friend bought me a gym membership for my hot showers. I would even sleep outside gym there at times. Another friend helped me rent a 5 x 5 storage unit. Having a storage unit and gym membership helps a homeless preacher greatly. Thank you so much.

The Catholic Convention was in Anaheim for four days. My heart was broken for the Catholic Church after preaching hours at this event. Ruben used to be Catholic and got them all fired up by smashing a Mary statue with his hammer. I kept the Mary head as a souvenir of the outreach. Once I even drug the statue of her head on the ground tie to a small rope, because God hates idol worship. Catholics are one of the largest cults in the world. If you defend them, then you defend Mother Terresa embracing all religions, Paul John Paul kissing the Koran and Pope Francis saying atheists go to heaven without having a relationship with Jesus.

Facebook friends kept inviting me to Italy for the summer to "Storm the Vatican" tour. Yet, I didn't think God would send me. I didn't even pray about it. Yet, Feb. 27, 2013 2 Ex Catholics dropped $2000 in my account to go do this mission. It was the 14th anniversary of my calling to ministry. The tickets were then bought and trip was being planned. This shocked me that God wanted me to go to Europe. Praise God! I was so happy to finally get to Italy, because God told me no in 2012. Now, Italy was a big green light with a team of brothers. It was scheduled after my West Coast Tour in July 2013.

The adventure alone begins. This is something I felt compelled to do before rejoining Bro Jed in Washington. I started campus preaching alone at Berkley Campus. This 6 weeks' season is where God grew my faith. West Coast Tour was my Faith Boot Camp. Bible School couldn't teach me this. God taught me this Himself. God sent me to preach at Chico, Humboldt State, Reno, Nevada for eight days; Sacramento and the Washington too. I saw on Facebook my favorite singer, Chris Tomlin, was in Seattle, Washington so I drove over 500 miles to go to his concert. I had to be there soon anyway to join Campus Ministry USA. I decided to go early. My seats were awesome too. A friend of mine gave me gas money that day, not knowing I had none. God truly provides and even cares about me enjoying a good concert. Blessings come when you work for God, but not without crosses to bear.

When I preached at Chico, a Muslim blew smoke in my face and pushed me, the day of the Boston bombing. Humboldt State wrote about me being on a campus. Called it "Bombs for Jesus" because of a comment I made about my Holy Bible being the Bomb in my Bag. I was new at shock and awe preaching. I didn't have a real bomb. I was commenting about the power of the Word of God. The cops trusted me. The police made sure I was safe from their students, as I left for Washington. The LGBT community came out as an organized army to protest me. Not one Christian there opposed me. As a matter of fact; they prayed for me and walked me to my car both days. The crowds got very big and I truly enjoyed my time there, despite the loud LGBT band, who even stopped their music to listen to me off and on.

That week in Humboldt male strippers were in town. So, a skinny student wanted to pretend he was a stripper. While I sat in my chair facing a crowd sitting down, he stripped to underwear. Then, crawled towards me with shorts in his mouth and attacked like an animal. I just begin to teach on demons and then back to the gospel. College students are excited to be free away from parents. I never knew what they will do. The Holy Ghost draws these crowds so I can cry out "JESUS!" The name above all name, praise GOD.

Brother Jed asked me to get the Washington schools warmed up for his visit. University of Washington is huge! Personally, I enjoyed Western Washington more because of the free speech area being smaller. A girl at WWU told me "I learned more about the Bible today then I have in my whole life." What a compliment! Praise the Lord! Preachers should use the Word of God to shine the light of truth.

Western Washington wrote a short article about my preaching visit there as well. One thing I have learned in 2013 is the press do not always tell the whole truth and the press doesn't care too much if a mistake is even made. They are in a hurry to get the story out and amplify it as much as possible. The West Coast Tour prepared me for many new battles that were ahead.

The Reno campus was one of my favorites on this tour because the cops appreciated me being there and several Christians got really inspired. One lady my age, was only on campus to get free counseling. She decided to stay and listen. She invited me over to stay one night in her mom's spacious home. After seeing she had a pug, I knew God had placed me there for a good night's rest. Reno had cold weather while I was there for an eight day crusade. Crazy as this may sound, I looked at my pen and it is from a hotel in Reno where a friend paid for two nights for me to be warm. God has allowed me to suffer many nights in my cold car. A cold car makes a hot fiery preacher! I am not suffering for nothing. No way! I have chosen this life so I can be in full time ministry, regardless of the cost.

After warming up the campuses in Washington, I got a strong desire to go to Portland, Oregon to preach. Portland State University must be one of the hardest campuses in America. There is lots of witchcraft there. A little Muslim boy even gave me the sign of two swords with his hands. My response to him and his mother was not to let him grow up to be a suicide bomber. Repent! Put your faith in Jesus Christ!

While I was on the computer looking at Portland News, I noticed the one and only Dali Lama was in town and that the next day he would be at a huge convention of 11,000 people 100 miles away. The Holy Ghost assigned me to go preach there. I was the only preacher there as 11,000 Buddha seekers came out. That day was a major religious showdown. God does not tolerate idols or other religions. There is only one way to God the Father and it is through Jesus Christ, Son of God. "Jesus said unto him, *'I am the way, and the truth, and the life: no one cometh unto the Father, but by me.'"* (John 14:6) Some Amish showed up at end with signs to preach, but missed most of the crowds coming out.

Those six weeks before Brother Jed showed up in Washington were life changing. I did not know anyone for forty days. Another thing I have learned is you can meet someone and connect quickly. People assume I will fall apart without a church home or constant fellowship. No, I will be miserable if I don't preach the gospel.

"For though I preach the gospel I have nothing to glory of: for necessity is laid upon me; yea, woe is unto me, if I preach not the gospel." (1 Corinthians 9:16)

I had great joy when I got to serve Campus Ministry USA as a backup preacher. Brother Jed had his schedule set up and I would just show up at the campus to help. Some days it rained hard and we had to wait it out inside with the students. One weekend some friends in Idaho invited me to come to a couple of outreaches. Normally I wouldn't drive that far for a psychic fair and to rebuke a false prophet, however this "minister" that was coming to Spokane, Washington pretends to smoke Baby Jesus like a doobie. He has a huge following and people that follow him hate words like "Repent, sin, hell and wrath." They want to be drunk in the spirit all the time and "resting in the Lord." How ridiculous, knowing Jesus could come back any day now. All those flaky Christians want to do is lay on the floor pretending to huff the Holy Ghost like a doobie. There are videos on the internet of his followers pretending to get high huffing a wooden cross. God allowed me to preach there on Pentecost Sunday. What a reminder, that the fire of the Holy Ghost was to empower the disciples to go preach the gospel!

But ye shall receive power, after that the Holy Ghost is come upon you: and ye shall be witnesses unto me both in Jerusalem, and in all Judaea, and in Samaria, and unto the uttermost part of the earth. (Acts 1:8) (KJV)

And when the day of Pentecost was fully come, they were all with one accord in one place. 2 And suddenly there came a sound from heaven as of a rushing mighty wind, and it filled all the house where they were sitting. 3 And there appeared unto them cloven tongues like as of fire, and it sat upon each of them. 4 And they were all filled with the Holy Ghost, and began to speak with other tongues, as the Spirit gave them utterance. (Acts 2:1-4) KJV

At the University of Oregon, a homosexual came out dressed as a vagina with a bullhorn and was unashamed. He got the LGBT community fired up and a lesbian grabbed my camera. She squeezed it till it broke. Campus Police told me they would look for her and if I wanted a new camera I would have to take her to Judge Judy. That night I went to Best Buy to look for a new camera, just didn't have money for one.

The next day I looked at a young, local street preacher that joined the team and said "I would be taking photos right now if that lesbian hadn't broken my camera yesterday." He smiled and opened his backpack. He handed me a brand new blue Canon camera, the very one I told God I wanted the night before. Thank You, God! Thank you man of God. I had no idea that was his first campus preaching day. He now has become a full time street/campus street preacher known as "Russian Street Preacher".

A friend of mine in California and I talked on the phone about him possibly going to East Coast to preach at all the Ivy League schools in the Fall. When he mentioned Harvard Law School, I said, "Oh man I want to go too." We decided to meet up for a day on a campus in California, so we could see how well we worked together before Fall came around. This meant I needed to leave one week early from helping Brother Jed. As we parted ways, he said, "See you again on the gospel road." I really grew a lot in drama skills and public speaking. It was good to be around a seasoned campus preacher, but to also try to do it myself alone to grow in confidence.

First, I decided to preach on the way in San Luis Obispo, California because it was voted one of the friendliest cities in America. As I arrived in San Luis Obispo I found a great spot close to the campus to park under the palm trees for free. I can remember being so broke that I wouldn't be able to eat anything before preaching except my can of tuna. My tripod was messed up, so I didn't bother filming with my new camera that day. Preachers need to always film for safety.

My fault for not being prepared, but I couldn't afford a new tripod. I was waiting for Italy missions trip money to clear in my account.

San Luis Obispo, California was a coastal town voted as one of the nicest cities in USA on Oprah show. I had preached for three hours on their University and a small clip was filmed by the students on purpose to try to make me appear outsmarted by the sodomites. They uploaded the video and next day it had gotten 400,000 hits. A lady from my high school in Tennessee saw it on social media going viral and warned me. Next ten days I got hate mail. Hey, I worked three hours that day. However, they put a two-minute clip on YouTube to mock me. 2 sodomites kissed next to me. I turned my head to read Romans 1. Students cheered. They uploaded it to make it look like their unnatural kiss stopped me from preaching. I kept preaching after that and continued with a nice size crowd. They are mocking God and His Word. They are not just mocking me. I got an email from the city asking for an interview. I attempted to contact them and they didn't answer my call. They put in paper I didn't contact them. However, the KCOY TV station took my call and it showed both sides of the story. This ended up in Huffington Post news and that is when I really got attacked by emails. I almost had my last name changed over all the press just to protect my family in future. West Coast Tour taught me that I was a "Controversial Evangelist." I already knew that, but the news made it a reality. I was going to change my name to Angela Holland, because I love the country Holland.

Blessed are they which are persecuted for righteousness' sake: for theirs is the kingdom of heaven. [11] Blessed are ye, when men shall revile you, and persecute you, and shall say all manner of evil against you falsely, for my sake. [12] Rejoice, and be exceeding glad: for great is your reward in heaven: for so persecuted they the prophets which were before you. (Matthew 5:10 - 12)

The West Coast Tour ended at University of Santa Barbara with Doug from Bible Believers Fellowship. My faith had really increased on this journey and confidence that I could handle large crowds by myself. Now, it was time to go to my favorite mission field: Europe. Praise God!

CHAPTER 8

Footsteps of Apostle Paul (July 5 to 25, 2013)

Bible Believers Fellowship watched an HBO special about the Catholic priests and seeing those grown men talk about what the perverted priests did to them as young boys caused me to wipe some tears from my eyes. The documentary about Father Murphy even showed that after he molested all the boys, the Catholic Church still buried this wolf in priest's clergy outfit in Catholic cemetery with Catholic funding. I watched this after the Catholic convention in Spring 2013. God was preparing me to rebuke the Vatican. My friends in Pensacola are ex Catholics and were sponsoring the whole trip to Italy and Greece. Can you imagine how much God hates child molesters touching children and pretending to be Holy Men of God?

Some people can go through life ignoring crimes, but this isn't just any crime. These are Priests abusing children. The Catholic Church covers it up. Maybe that is why the Pope quit. The reason I write this is to light a fire under some of the younger preachers to follow our lead. Go over there and rebuke the Vatican. Find churches in your area that have abominations going on in the so-called "House of God" and go rebuke them in Jesus name.

For the time is come that judgment must begin at the house of God: and if it first begin at us, what shall the end be of them that obey not the gospel of God? (I Peter 4:17)

I found a cheap parking spot by the airport with a camera pointed at the car. I prepaid them for three weeks and they shuttled me to LAX (Los Angeles, California International airport).

Athens, Greece looked so close to Rome, Italy on the European map. This was the place I really felt led to go before going to Rome to meet the team. I wanted to walk where Apostle Paul walked alone with God to hear God's thoughts. Mars Hills Acts 17 was a huge bucket list. A bucket list is all the things you want to do before you die or in slang terms "kick the bucket."

After overcoming my jetlag and readjusting to new schedules, I began to venture out into the city of Athens. I found locals eating outside of little delis and even a police protest forming close to my hotel. This large group of people were about to march down the streets with a banner. The words were Greek to me. All joking aside, I asked a man that spoke English what was about to happen. He said thousands of police lost their jobs yesterday and they are about to do a public demonstration in protest. Quickly, I went back to my hotel, grabbed my "Fear God" "Trust Jesus" banner. I came back to the start of the protest alone to reach these people with my banner. I wasn't sure how many of them knew English, yet what else could I do? There were two choices here; try to reach even one person with the public preaching or ignore thousands of people to go sightseeing. Trying was the honorable thing to do because Jesus' name was lifted up that day.

After the outreach was over I was pouring sweat. I went back to my hotel, got a shower and changed into "Trust Jesus" T-shirt and went to Mars Hill. On the way, the tour bus had several stops to make. A porn shop had its door open so I rebuked the from top of bus. Turn off the porn and get reborn.

We made it, finally! The Acropolis was the main attraction on this stop. However, I wanted to walk all the way up the long road to Mars Hill. When I got to the top it was breathtaking. All I could do was shout. "Wow! This is awesome!" Someone else was joyfully shouting too. The view was just magnificent, people. I set up my camera and made about five different videos speaking from Acts 17. The more I read from the book of Acts, the more I got fired up. Apostle Paul stood right here and said these very words. Now, I am here saying his words. Why would I want to only take a picture? I had to preach and the people taking photos began to listen to me talk about how powerful Mars Hill was. Excitement is contagious. Thank You, God, for allowing me this moment, even if I didn't preach to thousands of people.

When I was buying lunch one day, the owner of the restaurant spoke no English. All I wanted was lamb or beef gyros. Those are addictive. I was trying to read the menu and both of us were having a hard time connecting to make the sale. Then I noticed a picture of Jesus. I pointed and smiled. He lifted up a cheer, raised his arm in the air and shouted, "Bravo!" From now on when I think of Greece, I think of "Bravo Jesus!"

Well, it was finally time to go meet the dudes and storm the Vatican with the real Gospel of Jesus Christ! I was traveling without a cell phone, so all of my communications with team Jesus or anybody had to be through email or Facebook. Technology has come a long way from the days Apostle Paul was a missionary, John Bunyan was alive, or even when John Wesley was circuit riding across America. They would say "What's a cell phone, e-mail or Facebook?" As a world traveler, I say it's a huge blessing to be able to give instant missions reports to friends with photos and videos. What a great day to be alive and working in the harvest field!

Go Team Jesus! My concern was if we could all get along. Tracy and Pavel showed up at my hotel to personally escort me to their hotel for fellowship in their kitchen with the other two brothers in Christ named Luong and Dean. I wanted to make a video of our first meeting and have us sharing our meal and Bible study about how the Catholics miss several key points in the Bible. Like, Peter is not the first pope and not the Rock of the church. After our fellowship, we all wanted to go preach that night, instead of waiting until the morning. We went out, attempting to go "somewhere" and ended up "nowhere." Then I realized that this wasn't about us preaching that night. It was a revealed to each of us on the team who we were to each other and our strengths and weaknesses. The Bible says to know those you labor among. You can't truly get to know someone over a meal, as much as you learn about someone in the heat of a battle. God had His plans for us and it helped us bond fairly quickly. We walked a lot that night around Rome, and then we decided to make sure that I got safely home first because I was the "weaker vessel," the girl on the team.

Saying good-bye that night was an unforgettable moment. I was on an escalator going down towards my train. Four brothers in Christ were about twenty feet away on another escalator, all looking at me with this holy, pure brotherly love. That night I learned something about Christian holy men. They are protectors. Their eyes communicated their concern for me that I would make it home alone safely without them in this big, Italian city of Rome.

The next day the four soldiers of Christ were at the Trevi Foundation preaching the gospel and I arrived not knowing where they were for sure. I then unrolled my five foot banner "Trust Jesus" and "Fear God" to hold in the air. As soon as it was raised they found me and so did the Roman cops. I tried to reason with the police as long as possible to allow me to carry my banner. Finally, I had to just take it down and roll it up. We just preached around area without banners.

We went to the Roman Coliseum to preach, next. Christians were eaten by lions in the Coliseum at one point in Roman history. It was considered a sport and people cheered as believers were eaten alive by lions. Going inside may have been an interesting sight, however we didn't want to spend the money. Preaching about it was way more exciting and I got to preach there by Roman Coliseum for two days.

My favorite spot to preach the gospel was at the Spanish steps of Rome, with Pavel and Dean. I knew from photos that I would want to preach there for sure. Pavel started a sermon at the bottom of Spanish steps and hundreds were sitting down there. I enjoyed taking photos of him with this beautiful backdrop of name brand clothes behind him. He was preaching about how to get to heaven, while people were trying to buy the best of the best and enjoy worldly pleasures that will perish. There came the police again. After they told him to stop, we went up the Spanish steps one level, so I could preach to smaller crowds sitting down.

When I began preaching I started with a simple introduction about who I was and that I had something to share and would be brief. This is why I love Europe so much, because people will allow you five minutes without heckling. When I got done with my testimony and gospel presentation, I asked the crowd who would like a copy of my testimony tract of how Jesus changed my personal life? Several people raised their hands and as I began to hand them out, a Jewish guy asked for one. When he said he was Jewish I got excited. I told him how much I loved the Jewish people and how the gospel is for them first. His response was that the guy with him was Jewish too. Next thing I knew he brought me over to all his Jewish friends. I got a photo with about fifteen of them. Happy missionary! It was so nice seeing him in the picture holding my story, because I had to force myself to write it in California. Writing is great, but takes lots of focused discipline.

Next we talked to a girl from New Jersey drinking with a guy from Texas. She got really mad at me and after meeting her I knew I needed to go preach in New Jersey. She was so lost in her bottle and Rome vacation. The gospel has a way of sobering people up. We stayed about twenty minutes with them and moved to the last set of steps at this beautiful historic site. I gave another message and this time went a lot longer. "New Jersey" came up there and called me a really bad word. Leave it to an American to heckle me in a Roman gospel crusade. Go sit down Yankee! God was dealing with her.

Some time that week, Dean and Luong went with signs to the Vatican to preach inside St. Peters Square. Pavel was there filming and I was glad he was because they got arrested fairly quickly. Never tell your friend to meet you at the Vatican, ok? That is like saying meet me in Atlanta. The Vatican is huge and has many places to enter and meet. Therefore, I was in a bad mood that morning going to the Vatican to meet Team Jesus. I walked all over the area without a cell phone looking for them and complaining to God about it while in the hot July sun. About to give up, I looked across the street to see Pavel. What a relief! He quickly informed me that Dean and Luong were in a Roman jail. Tracy was at their hotel, so we chose to go to my place to get on Facebook to let Tracy know what happened. Unable to reach him, God brought Tracy to my place and Team Jesus was together thinking what to do. The Warriors were allowed out of jail that same day. What a crazy story. My hotel was less than half a mile from the Vatican. They stayed closer to the Roman Coliseum. We all were amazed at how people can find each other with the help of God's angels guiding us somehow.

I know without a doubt that God used angels on this trip. One night I was lost and clueless how to get home. A light turned green and a girl would not cross the street. She just stood there. Then I asked her if she could help me get home. Immediately, she showed me where I was on the map and how to get home. "Thank You, God."

"Be not forgetful to entertain strangers; for thereby some have entertained angels unawares." (Hebrews 13:2)

Team Jesus declared that we would be preaching the gospel by the Vatican the next day. That night I walked over to pray over the area with my music playing. Colton from American Idol was singing "Everything" on my mp3 player from "Life house" and my spirit caught fire as I walked St. Peters Square singing with him. My heart was bursting over the words, "Jesus is my everything. How can I stand next to you and not be moved by you?" Yet, I begin to think about how people view the Pope as a real man of God. Our team doesn't view The Pope as a real man of God, but as a false teacher. I personally think all the Popes carry the anti-Christ spirit the Bible warns about. The Vatican has lots of followers, but how many of them know "Jesus Is Lord and Everything?" Most Catholics seem to prefer talking to Jesus dead mama, more than God the Father in Jesus name. Catholics need to get Born Again like Jesus explained in John 3:3 and get about from the abominations of the church.

Storm the Vatican outreach report:

July 2013 Rome, Italy
Last night the Holy Ghost led me to go pray awhile alone at the Vatican/St. Peters square. I felt His hand on me strongly and knew He was going to use me powerfully today. I went home and read Rev. 17 over and over again. I believe the" Great Whore" is the Vatican sitting on" seven hills" of Rome, although I am not a prophet or doctor of the Word of God. Luong said in my inbox that **today** we would preach at "Great Whore." Him using that wording, confirmed for me

to confront this wicked religion full of child molesters and idolaters.... Tracy came and got me about noon. We walked together to meet team that was already there. It started pouring rain. Tracy bought cheap umbrellas for the whole team. The Vatican was packed with so many people under walk way. Fire was in my bones and I really wanted to preach. We discussed if the sidewalk across the street close by was Vatican City or Rome, Italy? I did not want to purposely preach inside Vatican City, because I knew that would mean jail. Dean filmed and I went over there. I lifted up my voice and said everything on my heart. God allowed me about twenty to thirty minutes there without any police issues. People were listening. One born-again girl was from Iran. She later thanked us for preaching. She was about to cry that someone would do this. I just hugged her, because Jesus saved her soul. Iran, wow! Seven years she had been a believer, she said. In one part of the message I said "The pope chose his name because of San Francisco, not because of St Francis." A man listening for a while yelled, "I am from San Francisco." Rock on! This was a divine appointment for him.

Tracy preached after me. I noticed one cop, so I warned him. I had on normal clothes, not preaching clothes. My Ralph Lauren shirt had "Italy" on the back. I used that later in jail to befriend the cops, letting them know "I love Italy"! I knew God wanted me in that shirt today. Tracy wanted me away from him to hide and protect the camera. Yet, wherever I went there was talking that would interfere with the preaching on the film. I only wanted to get good footage to be a blessing. We were all learning as we went. With these Italian cops, things were so different from America, Friends. I went to get near Dean and when I did a huge Italian man came after me. Rome is known for thieves. This huge Italian with muscles, gold jewelry and a hairy chest said he didn't want his photo on film. I just stepped back away from him to protect the camera. Then he tried to grab the camera. My strong right arm pulled back in force and nailed this Italian in the chest with my fist. Wham! He then grabbed me and the fight began. I stuck the camera down my pants! He got mad. Grabbed me and got his arms behind my back. Then a cop grabbed the other wrist or my arm. The Italian man set me up. He wanted that camera to erase his picture from it. He was an undercover cop and I punched him. No charges for the hit, thank God! They then started grabbing the whole team. No handcuffs, but they were hurting my arms to the point that three finger marks were bruised into my arm. I had a bruise on my left wrist. They took us all upstairs to the police station. They made me go into a bathroom with two female cops. They strip searched me. They took his camera out of my trousers and erased the film. They dumped my bag out. I kept quiet about my bag. They looked again later. I saw the cop look right at my camera bag. He did not open it. Praise God! So I still have my Vatican sermon. A miracle for sure! One of the undercover cops asked me something and didn't like my response. He slapped me across the face and his hand hit my ear. Later, he liked me. Supernaturally God showed him that I forgave him. I showed him my Italy shirt. He smiled at me many times after that. Jesus shined big to him through me. He slapped Jesus, not me. Then we sat in another hot room for hours. Then we got our paperwork. Our charge was "Preaching without permit." Tracy handled all the legalities. They took us in three fast cop cars, with lights on, through Rome, Italy. We saw so many sights as we went. It was too fast and I almost puked. Tracy rode with me in "Alpha Roma" car. I think that is how you say Rome car. Everyone stared at us as we flew through the city. We went in another building. They said "Photos" They had our passports all this time. We got stuck in a dirty, smelly jail cell, with one window for air at top. We could see a few other dudes across the hall in jail. I waved at them trying to give them hope and show them we cared. We sang many songs. Don't ask for a CD, but it was beautiful to God. We bonded as a team in that small cell. We laughed a lot and were all dying for water. They only gave us one bottle of water all day and we passed it around. We were detained over six hours and then still had to get a way home. That was a long time to wait for water. We all got fingerprinted, a photographed and then released when it was almost dark. God put a Rainbow over the jail in the sky. God always loves to comfort in intimate ways. The Holy Ghost was with us all day. We enjoyed singing in jail. I posted the day from my eye view of what happened. I have never been arrested in twelve years of open air preaching. My first time was in Rome, Italy. Now, I can say my trip was walking in the " Footsteps of Apostle Paul." *If God be for us, who can be against us. It was great day."

What did I do the day after going to the Roman jail? I finished writing Rome postcards with a very sore arm from hitting that Italian undercover cop the day before. Of course I was also having my fruit bowl, coffee and morning croissant at a local Roman coffee shop across the street from the Vatican. I called my parents and partners to tell the story of following in the "footsteps of Apostle Paul." Then, later that night I met Pavel and Dean for a final outreach in Rome with our banner raised. We did not have one problem with the police at this outreach, praise the Lord! The outreach was a concert in Rome.

Next day we all had places to go. Dean invited me to Florence because of all the English-speaking people there sightseeing. Dean is the same age as my son. We preached for two nights in the most popular place in Florence we could find, by beautifully painted, crafted historical churches.
People gathered all around to listen and a group of college ate students wanted their photos with me after I finished my message. That night I shared about my former struggles of being an alcoholic and how Jesus totally set me free.

The next night, in Florence, the girl from New Jersey that had cursed me out during the Roman Spanish Steps Crusade, came up to me. She blew my mind by being there and then she told me "I liked what you said last night better then what you said in Rome." I shook my head amazed at how sovereign God is and said "You were here last night?" She began to confess to me her need to stop drinking so much. She was under conviction of the Holy Ghost, because I knew she had a drinking problem when I met her in Rome. God brought her all the way to Florence to hear me speak two more nights. That is God's romance with the human heart. Oh, how He cares so much for people and wants a personal relationship with them. Preaching in Florence was great after spending that long day in the Roman jail. People listened and asked good questions. One guy was from Australia asking me about my great God that I serve. A large crowd of young people asked for a photo with me. Always a happy missionary photo that I enjoy re looking at because it was right after jail in Rome. Freedom is beautiful!

Earlier that day I was waiting on Dean at a fast food place, eating outside with a tray on my lap. I could have eaten inside, but I wanted to make sure Dean spotted me. Again, no cell phones in Europe. Munching away on highly salted French fries, I looked up to see the Jewish guy from Rome that took my testimony tract. He turned around and smiled. He said to me, "I read your pamphlet. You sure did go through a lot, didn't you? Hey, what did you say about the Jews again?" Forget the salty fries, I was in awe of God right then. How did He do that? How did God bring this guy from Rome to Florence and put me right there? I replied, "The gospel is for the Jew first."

"For I am not ashamed of the gospel of Christ; for it is the power of God to salvation to everyone that believes; to the Jew first, and also to the Greek." (Romans 1:16)

The Roman hotel implied that a free shuttle to the airport would be included, but actually offered a very expensive ride to the airport. I don't like liars very much. False advertising makes me pretty upset because I have to be careful and stretch any mission's money I receive. They attempted to make me take a personal car to the airport for the ride. That fired me up the whole time I stayed there. When I looked out the window and saw a taxi, I said, "Is that my ride?" They said no. They had someone coming. What they were saying was you are going to ride in luxury and be forced to pay it because we said so. I went and asked the taxi how much he would charge. He was half the cost of the luxury car. I took the taxi and watched them deal with the letdown. Rome was not going to sucker punch me on my last day. I won by getting in the cheap taxi. Bye, bye Rome!

CHAPTER 9

East Coast Tour

(Mid-August to Mid Oct. 2013)

Traveling north and south, east and west across America in a small car will wear you out. Then add the drama of a trip to a Roman jail to the season of ministry and it spelled "tired woman of God." However, when I looked at the map of America one day on the local news from my father's Lazy boy, I noticed the North East. Doug was scheduling as many Ivy League schools as possible. I thought, "man it sure would be awesome to go up there and preach the gospel." Then the news showed the map of America colored in dark for the states that were legalizing gay marriage. Those states seemed mainly to be neighbors of each other and all up at the north east tip of America. All alone that day, I asked God to send me and I would gladly rebuke all those states for legalizing gay marriages. Nowhere in the Bible will you find two people of the same sex getting married. Jesus set the standard in Matthew 19, in agreement with Genesis, Chapter 3.

My heart increased with a burden to go and so I added Washington DC to my trip. One million Muslims were supposed to show up on 9-11 in DC to march. Being an American and a Christian I was compelled to go confront them with banner "Fear God" "Trust Jesus" banner on a pole.

I parked in a 24 hour guarded parking lot by a coffee shop. The morning of 9-11 I walked to the White House to give my first sermon of the day to President Obama. He didn't come out to listen, of course. It just felt good to have that banner outside his temporary home. A few Muslims, tourists and even Mormons heard my message. Praise the Lord! 9/11 is a day Americans will never forget because of the terrorism attack on 9/11 many years ago. I was in bible school the day it happened and we were all shaken. Many students wept for fear of what would happen next. Its days like this that remind me to take a stand for the Word of God and be a voice in my own country. There are so many Christians in USA. It would great to see an end time army rise up in America and mission's movement be birthed again.

9/11/2013 was a very hot day. I went to Washington Mall in time for the rally. Where are one million Muslims? The leaders that wanted this march were on a small stage talking and maybe fifty people were with them. Some of the people looked like they were anti-government more than marching for Islam. I ran into Ruben and several other street preachers. Some of the men there believed in women preachers, and some didn't. Father God used me that day as a tool to reach several people at the march. As they were preparing in transition to go from stage to street, I belted out as loud as my voice would go, a message the Lord laid on my heart at that moment. A man tried to heckle me and he was almost blown down by the wind. When I watched the video, it made me laugh watching him blown away from me.

Philippians 2:10-11 KJV

"that at the name of Jesus every knee should bow, in heaven and on earth and under the earth, and every tongue acknowledge that Jesus Christ is Lord, to the glory of the Father."

The East Coast Tour started when I preached at University of Delaware. There was a nice small crowd that stayed for the whole three hours. One student wanted my testimony tract when I finished. Another student asked if he could interview me for his radio show. Knowing I was on a schedule, I put him down for October 18, because I knew I would be there again when traveling south. The Baptist student union told me before I preached that I wouldn't draw a crowd on this campus. Never say never! My faith is in God to draw the crowds. My confidence is in the Holy Ghost and crowds were drawn to the net. Praise God!

1 Corinthians 15:34 KJV

"Awake to righteousness, and sin not; for some have not the knowledge of God: I speak this to your shame."

Doug was on tour from California to North East. He was even sleeping in his car at times, showering at truck stops. He has a calling to deep conversations with philosophy students, professors and atheists. He is wired by God to challenge people about the existence of God and the truth of God's Word. We are two totally different people, yet we wanted to team up as the Lord led us to. Later in October, we did meet up in Boston. I needed my car fixed in New Jersey. All that traveling and my car screamed "Fix me now!" A five hundred dollar problem and, bam, back on the road. Rarely has my car given me trouble and I thank God it hasn't. My life is scary enough as it is. I had so many car problems while in bible school. Nice to have a good car because there are plenty other attacks in my life and ministry to deal with daily. Japan is on my schedule for Jan. 2017, so I can preach the gospel and thank the Honda company for my awesome car/home.

Fall colors in New England have always been so beautiful in photos and I was so glad my eyes could view the glory of God as I drove from New Jersey to New York to Penn State to Vermont. As soon as I reached Vermont, I parked my car to enjoy the moment. The quietness at the state line was beautiful but it all changed once I showed up at the University of Vermont.

Vermont is one of the first campuses established in America and one of the first states to legalize gay marriage. When I started preaching I boldly stated I was there to preach the gospel that week and rebuke Vermont for giving in to gay marriage. Several students asked me to please stop. One girl said she was trying to study. When I refused to stop, she took all her clothes off down to her purple underwear and bra. She began slapping her skinny butt next to me. Someone took the photo and it went all over the internet with over 1 million views. I was known as "The crazy preacher." It is easy for me to find my work now on the web. All I have to do is type in "anti-gay" "crazy lady" "crazy preacher" and "Angela Cummings preacher" or "Controversial Evangelist."

Soon the crowd grew to hundreds of students to watch the free stripper. Hecklers can be used to draw crowds. The photo went around school that week and students knew a gospel preacher was there. That helped me all week. Every day there were great meetings. Small, at times, up to 300 or 400 at other times and then back down to a group of students sitting in the grass to listen. The police were always around, but not close enough to interfere or even listen. One day I waved at the police while a huge crowd was around me. They waved back from police car. Days like this, I love America! One day Americans will complain about losing free speech and I will say, "Why didn't you use it while you had a chance?" Students at Vermont put grass in my hair, yelled for me to go home and also clapped for gay marriage. Even with all their devilish ways, I had hope for them. I think it is possible for another preacher to continue working this campus and see many souls saved. They are clueless about the Bible there, which can be a fresh start. Where I was raised in USA in the South are many churches. Many people believe you can live in sin and still go to heaven because you prayed "The Sinners Prayer." Jesus preached repentance, not easy believism. The devil believes in Jesus.

Luke 13:3 KJV "I tell you, Nay: but, except ye repent, ye shall all likewise perish."

This scripture is one reason street preachers can say to people "Turn or Burn!"

James 2:19 KJV "Thou believest there is one God: thou doest well: the devils also believe, and tremble."

This scripture is one reason why there is more to being a Christian than just believing.

Mark 1:15 KJV "And saying, the time is fulfilled, and the Kingdom of God is at hand: repent ye, and believe the gospel."

This is how I preach the gospel. As Jesus did. He called sinners to repent and believe the gospel.

The gospel journey continued with visits to Thomas College, Colby College, University of New Hampshire and University of Maine. Students listened at every campus. The police ran me off from three of those campuses, at least a few heard how to get to Heaven and were warned to flee from the wrath to come. Some of the campuses were public and some private. The police will figure out a reason to run a preacher off when there is a crowd drawing. Police don't always want to get involved, because then they are forced to hear the preaching.

I drove to Boston next and slept outside a coffee shop. Monday I got to see Doug for the first time since we were at the University of Santa Barbara Campus together. He had his banner raised on the sidewalk of Cambridge, Massachusetts by the philosophy department of Harvard Law School. He already had a great one-on-one talk going. I briefly said hello and then carried my red sign throughout the campus. I drew with white letters on the sign, "Jesus Care is Free." Harvard is where President Obama went to school. The hot topic that week was how much Obama Care was going to cost. I did open air preach a few times, even with it being a private campus. Nobody caught me or turned me in to the police either. A group of tourists from Sweden wanted to photograph me with my "Jesus Care" sign. This was an exciting day for sure. I enjoyed all the divine appointments and heavenly assignments for the few days there. Yeah God! I talked to one Harvard student several times. He was a big Obama fan that was totally convinced that abortion has caused crime to decrease in America. What and this is supposed be a smart student at high level school? Liberals are usually abortion endorsers. God hates it!

Proverbs 6:16 to 17 KJV "These six things doth the Lord hate: yea, seven are an abomination unto Him: A proud look, a lying tongue, and hands that shed innocent blood…"

I gave you 3 of the 6 things God hates to make sure the reader understands that God hates Abortion. Before I was a Christian I almost aborted my son. At the clinic I was $100 short and walked out still pregnant. God was merciful to me while I was living the prodigal life running from God. My son was born in Jackson, TN on Dec. 1, 1990 and I decided to raise him. I didn't want to put him up for adoption, because I was adopted. My heart always missed my birth parents, until God saved my soul in the 1990s and healed my broken heart, if you have had an abortion, God wants to forgive you and heal your heart of this sin. Your baby is in heaven. I pray right now for God to comfort you in Jesus name amen. Forgiveness is so wonderful! Praise God!

My next campus was at MIT in Boston. My first evangelism teacher from BRSM named Bert drove all the way down to open air preach with me on the streets. What a dream come true to preach with a professor of mine. He had fire shut up in his bones. We had a great ministry mentor chat after preaching at a nice restaurant. I believe this meeting helped me for the big crusades that were ahead of me. I'm so thankful for those that stop their schedules to minister to the underdogs like me. Some preachers don't have time. Bert made time. God bless him for caring and sharing. He writes for Charisma magazine. Check out his articles, good stuff. Holy Fire Ministries.

Former first lady Hillary Clinton was guest speaker at Yale Law School on a Saturday afternoon in October. Doug manned one entrance with his banner and I got on the other entrance. There were lots of Yale alumni going in to hear Clinton. I used my powerful natural voice to reach this entrance. Doug called and said the former New York Governor caught in a prostitution scandal was right in front of me. Quickly I hung up and brought a focused, direct word for Mr. Politician. This same guy is running for an office again. I just saw him on the news this past week. We had a great outreach at Yale and got to see in person what a police escort for Hillary Clinton looked like.

The last outreach Doug and I were at together was at Rutgers in New Jersey. We had lunch together and just shared the joys of the Lord together.

Princeton University was where I preached next several times on campus and by front gate. I sat in my chair with my banner raised, "Fear God" "Trust Jesus." My seat was one of the best in the city, no doubt, and caught many people going by. Because New Jersey was passing gay marriage that next week, I decided to get my anti-homo t-shirt out, and put it on the banner. I wanted New Jersey to understand real clear, because apparently Hurricane Sandy didn't work in getting their attention.

A short haired blonde lesbian drove by and stared me down. I knew she was coming to chit chat by that angry look. Sure enough, she parked and confronted me. I took my banner down to try to calm her down. Then she stood on it and refused to move. She wanted cops to arrest me for sitting in a chair with a sign. It is America! You can do that. The police came. She was told nicely by Princeton Police that I was NOT breaking the law. Cops told her standing on my banner was "criminal mischief" and she was one breaking the law. Sweet vindication. That completed the New Jersey outreaches. After I left that campus they had a huge outbreak of some disease and students were being sent home. Gay marriage makes God mad. New Jersey can do whatever it wants, but you reap what you sow. America is losing the Fear of God. This is dangerous. God is powerful. 2 years later same sex marriage became legal in all 50 states. I was in total shock that my country had gone to this low of standards.

Psalm 9:17 KJV "The wicked shall be turned into Hell, and all the nations that forget God."

Brown College had a "Nude Week" on their campus. It is a private school; however I wanted to try to reach as many as possible anyway. Several Jewish students talked to me and others asked questions. Then the police came. They were very close to taking me to jail for not having my ID on me. Jail wasn't scary to me. It was the parking ticket that had me concerned if I went to jail. "Nude Week." Yes, they had a room you could go to on campus to do nude body painting and just hang around nude. It was the "bright idea" of two young girl students. Brown College used to be Christian college. Harvard, Yale and Princeton all have great Christian history. This is one reason I wanted to preach there and stir up something for the Kingdom of God and His righteousness.

East Stroudsburg University was a campus that I found by accident. Just like the University of Vermont, this campus had amazing crowds of listeners. One guy dressed as Spiderman, climbed down the campus wall, stole my Christian flag and ran around the campus with it. When he returned, Spiderman put my flag in the school garbage can. On my last day there this young man confessed to being a prodigal. He even told his mother about me preaching there. Her prayers probably got me there. Oh man, that makes me want to cry. How awesome it is to work for God and be able to stand in front of so many people and tell them about Jesus. A few Christians stood by me there, while others chewed me out and walked off. One day the crowd was everywhere; on the top floor and bottom floor, all listening and some heckling. A young student stood up to them and she told the truth about the expectations of the Holy God. I was so impressed by her courage. This is my heart's desire to see other rise to take a stand for righteousness.

When I preached at University of East Stroudsburg in Pennsylvania the LGBT community took advantage of a gospel preacher being there. They thanked me for coming and told me that they raised $400 during my crusade. I got a piece a pizza and free t-shirt from students. This job sure isn't for the money. Only a few campuses have every fed me or thanked me. Reno, Nevada students blessed me with steak. I will never forget them. One student packed me a lunch on that campus.

My final stop on the East Coast Tour was back at University of Delaware to do the radio interview with Alex, a student with a radio show on campus. It was so refreshing to hang out with him. We spent several hours together. The interview went close to 45 minutes. Alex said it was his favorite interview, so far. He had so many dreams in his heart. It was a joy to listen to his dreams and discover who he was on his way to becoming for the rest of his life.

Right before going home for my birthday, I went to Hickory, North Carolina to start a "Bible Belt Tour." Buddy Fisher invited me to stay in his home with his family. It was a great weekend of fellowship, food, laughter, church and an outreach in Charlotte. He gave me an anti-porn button. Since we were preaching at a barbeque festival, a girl misread my button. She thought it said "Anti-pork" and I didn't like Jews. Super funny! I love Jewish people. The Bible belt is where so many "Christians" think it's normal to get drunk and sing for Jesus on Sunday. God bless the street preachers that have to labor in the South. I would rather preach to a lost soul that has no religious background, then a confessing Christian that is having sex with boyfriend, wearing short shorts to class and drinking alcohol. It takes a lot of patience for me to deal with these people. Jesus has a Vomit Ministry!

Revelation 3:16 "So then because thou art lukewarm, and neither cold not hot, I will spue thee out of my mouth."

CHAPTER 10

UTC – Great Awakening in My Home Town

"And the same time there arose no small stir about that way." (Acts 19:23) KJV

What a long year it had been, preaching the gospel on the West Coast, Greece, Italy and then finishing up recently on the East Coast. Now, I was bored after a week of rest in my hometown.

A thought came to me that I should go preach at University of Tennessee, Chattanooga, where my father used to be a professor. I drove down to the campus, parked, walked up to the area of student union and picked a spot. That was on October 29, 2013. Within an hour the crowd grew so large that the Dean of Students showed up in the middle of the crowd to talk to me. He wasn't asking me to leave. All he wanted was to share the guidelines and have me fill out the paperwork. No problem. I asked for only two more days, since I had already made plans to preach in Fort Smith, Arkansas soon. The Dean of Students agreed and when he walked off with the paperwork, the students assumed I was asked to leave. No, I just got legally signed in so I could continue. God bless America. Sweet freedom of speech laws working for this preacher.

Then I moved to a higher spot to stand and began with, "Jesus Christ changed my life!" The chief of police officer was so gentle. He said, "Hold up. Hold up! I'm going to let you guys stand and listen, but you got to back up ten feet." Then I proclaimed, "My dad used to teach at UTC." All of this was documented on video. There are three security guards and one police officer holding back the crowds on day one. After that I immediately shared my testimony of being raised in Chattanooga and how Jesus changed my life. Police gave me a personal ride back to my car that day.

Day two I showed up to preach in the afternoon and a few students were waiting on me as I arrived. UTC Echo News was there and wanted an interview. Then an atheist had questions. I recorded both of them for my own protection and YouTube channel. News reporters can be liars and not care at all if they lied because they want a story. I regret not recording the rest of the reporters after all that was about to happen. I was learning as I went on this journey. After UTC Echo interviewed me, I turned around and saw several hundred students waiting on me to start preaching. Praise the Lord! People accuse street preachers of pushing people away and here, over two hundred people were waiting for me to start my message.

The police were already there too. They began moving the crowds back into a big circle. Then I went into the middle and was preparing for a long day. Usually, I have to start with no listeners and work at drawing in the crowd.

After preaching awhile, a lady nicely broke the circle without security getting upset to tell me quickly, "The news media is on their way. I thought you should know." I answered her, "OK, Thank you." Everything just shifted at that moment, because my UTC gospel crusade just went from campus ministry to city ministry. Shake my hometown, Jesus! Now, I had opportunity to reach my hometown with the gospel. Also, I had a possibility of all the people I used to get drunk and high with seeing me preach the gospel on Television.

Trophy of God's grace! It really doesn't matter what my critics say about me. God was using me to stir up my hometown and put me in the middle of the circle to show off His work of grace in my life. Soon, Channel 9 news that had interviewed me in the 90's about my cleaning business "Compulsive Cleaning" was now asking me about how I felt about the response at UTC. News channel 3 and 12 briefly reported about the gospel meeting as well.

"Evangelist causes campus commotion," was how the news started at 6:00 pm. My friend watched it online in Pensacola on the 5 pm news and again at 5:30. She said the news reported the crowds getting up to a thousand on earlier news reports. My mother heard about me on the news as she got ready for church that night. The news reporters did not balance the story well. They talked primarily to people who opposed me. There was one UTC student that understood my bold approach. Bryan gave me his number. I almost didn't call him because I assumed he was like the rest of them. He was in full support and wanted me to know if I ever came back, that he would stand with me and help.

Every day I would get a ride from the police to my car. Many people were angry at me for having police security. Hey, the campus set up all that security. Not me and as a guest speaker I go with their rules to be able to have my free speech rights. The cops at the campus were amazing people and I will always remember them on my journeys. My last day there, one officer encouraged me that 600, 700, 800 of them will still be talking about this next week. One positive thing about UTC students was that some did open their bibles during my crusades. Glory to God!

My first visit was just the warm up round. I went to my parents' house to tell them good-bye. The news was not too bad to cause problems with family, yet. I wasn't even sure my son, 23, knew I had made all the news channels. He was napping late in the morning still. I went into his room, kissed him on the cheek, then told him I was proud of him and loved him. My final words were, "Hey son, make sure you see me on the news. Google it." My son was a huge part of watching first hand God calling me, equipping me and then sending me. My son is not my best friend, he is my son. Jesus is my best friend and always comes first. Jesus is my Master above all else. That's how disciples of Christ are supposed to be. Family comes 2nd.

A church in Fort Smith, Arkansas helped me get my passport (mine had expired) so I could go to Europe in 2012. God provided a room for me in a hotel that week because I was speaking at that church on Sunday. They did not pay for it; I did from donations because it was too cold in car. I had fellowship with friends, preached to nice size crowds at the University of Fort Smith. They did have one cop present when the crowd grew large, but no fenced cages or orange cones. I preached to the youth on Wednesday. I then returned on Sunday to preach again to the whole church on "Lighthouses." Someone made me a beautiful wooden painted lighthouse with a hole cut out so people could get their photo with it, to remember we are the Light of the world. Just like God had me in the circle for UTC students to listen to, Christians are lighthouses. We are supposed to shine. No one was really interested in getting a photo with their head in the Lighthouse hole though. Just like many Christians have no interest in suffering for the gospel, either. I got Behold the Lamb's photo in Lighthouse.

"You are the light of the world. A city that is set on a hill cannot be hid." (Matthew 5:14)

While I was in Arkansas, I had made this huge schedule for Arkansas, Texas, Louisiana, and ending the tour in Alabama by Christmas. My plans seemed great and I would even get to visit several friends along the path. The problem was the news media in Chattanooga kept contacting me asking about my visit there. What was the big deal? Don't they ever get street preachers there? A few people even assumed because of all the press my hometown was small. What? God can't use a woman to shake a whole city? God can cause nations to hear about my hometown, if He decides to send it worldwide.

Wikipedia has Chattanooga as the fourth largest city in the state of Tennessee, with a population of 167,674 as of 2010 census, and an estimated population of 171, 279 in 2012.

God spoke to me loud and clear while in Arkansas the day after I made my plans. "Go back to UTC!" Oh no, God I don't want to go back there. It took me over 11 years to preach in the open air in my hometown because I never wanted to. My first time was Thanksgiving of 2012 outside some honky-tonks in Hixson, TN where I used to snort cocaine, gamble and get drunk. When I preached on the sidewalk there both bars full of people came out to listen to me. Hey, I had good news! You don't have to be a slave to sin. Jesus will set you free. Those small bars with maybe ten or so people were easy. I was glad I finally told my hometown my testimony. UTC was only supposed to be a pass through campus, not a nine day crusade that made the news. God sure caught me off guard and now I fear Him in a whole new way.

"But Jesus said to them, a prophet is not without honor, but in his own country; and among his own kin, and in his own house." (Mark 6:4)

I came back to stay at my parents' house with the hopes to finish the three weeks at UTC and then enjoy Thanksgiving with my family. They had already seen me on TV so they (and the rest of Chattanooga) were already aware of my ministry at UTC. My hopes were that a Great Awakening would continue and that others would rise to preach during those three weeks. The Dean of students approved for me to come the six days I asked for. We agreed that I didn't need a permit for the day before Thanksgiving, since no one would be on campus.

My first day back to UTC I told the students that I was glad to be back, which was only said because God prepared my heart for those UTC mockers. A student yelled, "FU** You!" I preached from Genesis 1 and then James 4. When I got to "Cleanse your hands ye sinners" I would repeat it over and over with increased volume.

If you are not a sinner, then it shouldn't bother you. The Bible is clear that Christians are saints. I choose not to call myself a sinner anymore. The Word of God refers to me as a New Creature in Christ. Jesus set me free from sin. Jesus lives inside of me and if I sin, it is only because I choose to, not because I have to. The Holy Ghost living inside of me sure doesn't want to sin. Sin separates us from God. Therefore, reading James 4 stirred up the Bible Belt campus.

Many people in the Bible belt believe you can pray a sinner's prayer and then you are sealed for life with God. What? No way! You can't con God with a simple prayer.

54

Luke 3:8 "Bring forth therefore fruits worthy of repentance..."

The campus set up orange cones around the circle and had security guards close by with real police on site too. The crowds got large on my first three day visit to UTC. Campus police and city police were preparing for anything on this visit. The UTC students have a bad reputation, not me. They have caused problems before on the campus without a street preacher calling them to Turn or Burn.

Adulterers and [*adulteresses! Do you not know that friendship with the world is enmity with God? Whoever therefore wants to be a friend of the world makes himself an enemy of God. Or do you think that the Scripture says in vain, "The Spirit who dwells in us yearns jealously"? But He gives more grace. Therefore He says: "God resists the proud, But gives grace to the humble." Therefore submit to God. Resist the devil and he will flee from you. Draw near to God and He will draw near to you. Cleanse your hands, you sinners; and purify your hearts, you double-minded. Lament and mourn and weep! Let your laughter be turned to mourning and your joy to gloom. Humble yourselves in the sight of the Lord, and He will lift you up.* (James 4:4-10)

Seven minutes into the message I said, "God cares about you students. He is not willing that any perish, but that all come to repentance." After I said that a UTC student on a bike named "Cole" rode up to where I was attempting to preach to the whole campus. Cole said, "Ma'am, Ma'am." Then I replied "Yes." The security was blocking him from going past the orange cones to come to me. UTC set up the cones, not my ministry. Cole began to speak to me with the security guard in front of him, making sure he would not go inside the preacher zone. I told him to "go ahead." Which meant talk to me. I am listening. I wasn't saying to come in the circle, because then I would be breaking the campus rules. We went through this my first visit. Students wanted photos with me and I had to say no because they would all come in and cause chaos. Students needed to stay on the outside and I needed to stay in my circle. No other campus has ever had a circle like this. However, I respect these leaders and authorities for what they went through just to allow freedom of speech to be practiced.

Cole then said, "Maybe you shouldn't be telling everyone they are sinners. Maybe you shouldn't be yelling at everyone, ok?" Right after he brought me his advice, he said to the officer and security, "Get your hands off of me right now. Please get your hands off me." Then I just allowed the police to do what they do best. I stopped preaching and just watched how the word of God stirs up rebels. Other students began to curse me and call me names.

After the third security guard showed up to deal with the upset bike guy, I told the students, "I signed up to be here this week students. I will be here tomorrow, Monday and Tuesday unless there is a rapture" Then a fourth security guard showed up and they were still trying to reason with the bike guy. He could have left and gone to class after giving me advice on how to reach lost souls, but he chose not to.

After my comment on the rapture I continued with "Now rapture is when God calls away His church. Then I stopped. Ironically, the UTC bells chimed a religious hymn while the security began trying to calm Cole down. A city policeman put Cole's arms behind his back. He was still fighting them and security began helping to restrain him. Another UTC student videoing the whole incident, yelled at me, "This is all your fu**ing fault, bitch!" My response was, "God's got your number too, sinner!" The head police officer showed up to help with the student. Nine minutes and 32 seconds into the video on YouTube, you see two city police and two security trying to get the bike guy to cooperate. Another security guard that gave me a ride there was on the scene close to me and communicating with others on a walkie-talkie. Bam! They all went to the ground together. Now, a student was on his guitar, coming to sing so students won't have to hear me preach the gospel.

Turning to the younger security lady, I said, "Is your campus always like this?" Then another security guard showed up to help. I said, "Why is he resisting?" The security guard then went to move students back. Cole was now on the ground with officers trying to arrest him. He was yelling at them "You feel big, man? Cops used pepper spray on Cole. What the fu** did I do?" Then another UTC female yells, "What the fu**?" Another student yelled to cops, "Y'all are some real fu**ing police officers." Then they got Cole up and took him to jail on four charges. This was November 2013 and by January 2014, three charges were dropped. He had to go before a jury to prove he didn't resist arrest.

My camera caught the whole meeting and four months later the video had 54,400 hits. That's not that many. However, it made news in Russia, France, and England and all over America. I made Huffington Post now 3 times in the year 2013. This arrest exploded rage in the students and the church of Chattanooga stayed silent. God had to send helpers from Georgia to help me continue the crusade. Except, one student, one brave student named Bryan stood with me to help. As Cole was being taken to the cop car, and students were cursing the preacher, (me), I quoted the word of God to the UTC mockers. As they were booing the Bible was warning them,

But the cowardly, unbelieving, abominable, murderers, sexually immoral, sorcerers, idolaters, and all liars shall have their part in the lake which burns with fire and brimstone, which is the second death." (Rev. 21:8)

No one had ever gotten arrested while I was preaching in all the years of my ministry. I even told the security guard that day that I wanted a calm meeting. A riot zone is what it became. The police need to do their job. My job is to warn the wicked and preach the gospel. I will not interfere with the police.

What a huge test for me. Would I finish the three-week assignment God gave me in prayer time? Or would I stop the UTC awakening for peace with my family? This was a huge test and the Bible tells us this will happen. You must obey God, rather than man.

Acts 5:29 KJV

"Then Peter and the other apostles answered and said "We ought to obey God rather than men."

My father was a former professor of electrical engineering at this UTC. I told him when I got home that someone went to jail when I preached. He was ok with me staying in their home, in my old room, until Thanksgiving. My son lives with them in my brother's former room. News spread quickly about the student's arrest. I made the front page of the newspaper. My first death threat came in while I was sitting at a coffee shop. I called the police to come document it and then I went home to warn my family. Someone found out where my family lived and threatened to show up there. The battle was intense.

My mother and son were very disturbed with me coming to town and causing a riot. I totally understand them not wanting this to backfire on them. God was testing me. I must obey God.

I had previously offered to change my last name legally to Angela Holland to avoid any future problems. I got a lot of press in 2013 and saw where my life was heading. God owns me and uses me many times as a bulldozer. Dutch Sheets said, "Forerunners are bulldozers." When a forerunner shows up there will be digging going on. Those that are comfortable will have their comfort zones disturbed.

UTC Echo reporter asked me on that Monday if I enjoyed the press. Yes, I do. Why? Because I have a message. I want my message to reach the whole world. When France wrote about my ministry and at UTC they used a photo of me wearing a t-shirt "Jesus saves from Hell" I didn't care what they said about me in French. They just promoted my message, "Jesus saves from Hell."

I volunteered to leave my family's home for the sake of peace. I spent money on a hotel for a week. No one in my hometown offered their homes to me. Maybe it would have been like housing a criminal? Hey this was nothing new. I traveled all over USA living in my car to preach the gospel. Most Christians never offered a shower, a sofa or even a driveway to park my home. God trained me to be a warrior, not a compromiser.

I was on the news enough for local churches to have connected with me. Still, nothing opened up so I spend money that I got from the church in Arkansas on housing. Because it was late November, it was too cold to sleep in Motel Honda. I wanted to preach the gospel, honor God and gladly leave for Florida for winter.

Preaching at UTC was the hardest assignment of my whole ministry because it affected my family. There were times I told students during crusades, very broken, "Look, I am only here out of obedience." They would pick on me about my son and family. Then, I would have to pretend I was not hearing it. My heart was so broken. When I checked into the hotel I spent a lot of time in tears and agony wanting this cup of suffering to pass from me. Not my will, but Your Will God.

When I would go to the stores to buy food for my hotel, I wondered how many people had seen me on the news. Sometimes people stared at me and I wanted to go unrecognized. Then on Monday, I got my third death threat and did request security. The police read the death threat on my phone email and took a photo of it. Was I scared? Yes, somewhat, and thought how uncool it would be to be killed in the Bible belt. That is not the way I wanted my legacy to be told. "Angela Cummings killed in Chattanooga by angry students," How boring of a death scenario. I want to die for the gospel in a country like China or Israel.

Hundreds of students skipped class to protest and "occupy the circle." Signs were made and passed out. What a bunch of rebels!. First, I talked to a few students apart from the mob. People began taking pictures and asking questions. Many liked our conversation and wanted me to continue speaking this way. Well, I couldn't, because I needed my voice to reach the thousand that showed up! Most days there were hundreds. A local ministry there called "The House" really came against me. They passed out hot chocolate and used that as a tool to show Jesus cares. The leader approached me and said, "God wants you to stop." Well, that didn't line up with the Bible. I was obeying Mark 16.

Religious people got mad at John the Baptist when he drew crowds too. God knows this leader's heart, if he was jealous of the free media, large crowds and students sitting by me with open Bibles. I will not stop preaching the gospel. UTC gave me permission to be there. Don't shame a Christian that obeys the Great commission. Get out of the way and let the preacher work for heaven's sake. Maybe the street preacher sent to your campus is an answer to your prayers. The problem is many Christians don't like the package that God sends as a Gift. So, they refuse to unwrap it because it is weird. Dutch Sheets said "Forerunners are weird." I know I am weird. God called me to wake UTC up with gospel, not offer than Sugar.

Channel three interviewed me again and they even allowed me to point in their camera and say:

"Chattanooga, wake up! Wake up, please! Get out and spread the good news of Jesus Christ. Get off of your Lazy Boy and go preach the gospel!"

Students screamed, "Get off our campus! We don't want you here!" Jeff Gardner and his wife Carol came from Georgia and helped me on Monday. They went into the crowd of students with a banner that read: "Turning the grace of God into a license to sin."

When I got done with several interviews from the press, I joined them to help. There were no orange cones on Monday. The nice police officer stood right by me and Jeff and Carol were close too. Students held different signs:

"Ban all street preachers like Angela Cummings"

"Your hatred disrupts my education"

"This is our campus"

"LOVE"

"UTC does not need you"

"Free Bike Guy"

Jeff was a fresh, new voice for them and old enough to be their father. Those UTC mockers needed to hear what he had to say. I loved that he preached with a Georgia Tech cone because my father went to that university. A student talked him in to giving her the banner and then she ran off with it. Jeff got it back. In the middle of the protest one of the loudest girls there asked me how to get to Heaven. My goal was to stand there until 4 pm regardless of what UTC mockers did. I whispered to the officer "I plan on standing here like this, quiet, until 4 p.m." He worked with me during my first crusade and knew me well by now. He agreed to just stand with me and let the heathen rage. We both did our jobs.

It worked wonderfully, because my silence and standing there caused them to get bored and lose their interest. Later that day, I preached to a small crowd and also read Romans 13 to a quieter audience. A few well-meaning Christians wanted us to stop and go away.

"Who will rise up for me against the evildoers? Or who will stand up for me against the workers of iniquity?" (Psalm 94:16)

That is what we did. We stood up to them as a beaming light with the Word of God. The Bible tells us to put on the full armor of God because we will be sent into battles. Preaching God's Word in the world stirs up all kinds of demons.

There was a short fenced cage around us at UTC the next day. There were no more orange cones. The cage was nice because I could protect my bag, tripod, pulpit and my friends. It was like being in First Class on a plane ride. Praise God! Greg, Carol and Jeff came back to help again. Security was set up on every corner inside of the cage. Later that day a news reporter from the local paper asked me for an interview. I could tell he really wanted to see "Motel Honda." I finally told him that he could watch my video "How to live in your car." The reporter showed up again on Friday.

Friday was close to the weekend and I didn't dress as nice as usual. I thought the news was done with interviews. The photographer came down from local paper to get shots and I was in jeans and my East Coast Tour T-shirt. The reporter came back for more questions and stayed awhile. He was getting a big story and I didn't know that. Ronald from my Bible school, Jeff and Carol came down to help. I was nervous that day because I was sick of all the press. All I wanted was these students to get saved and Christians to rise up to help. Bryan T., a UTC student, helped every day on my second visit back. He invited me to his church on Sunday, November 24, 2013 in Georgia. Oh how I needed the Body of Christ during all of this.

The news reporter let me know that my interview would be in the Sunday paper. All day Saturday I wondered about the article and if I would be criticized or understood for my heart to help these kids.

My time was up on my weekly hotel so I moved to another one just for a few days. I wasn't going to be able to eat with my family for Thanksgiving now, because of the sword coming down the week before.

"Therefore whoever confesses Me before men, him I will also confess before My Father who is in heaven. But whoever denies Me before men, him I will also deny before My Father who is in heaven. "Do not think that I came to bring peace on earth. I did not come to bring peace but a sword. For I have come to 'set a man against his father, a daughter against her mother, and a daughter-in-law against her mother-in-law'; and 'a man's enemies will be those of his own household. He who loves father or mother more than Me is not worthy of Me. And he

who loves son or daughter more than Me is not worthy of Me. And he who does not take his cross and follow after Me is not worthy of Me. He who finds his life will lose it, and he who loses his life for My sake will find it. (Matthew 10:32-40)

Christianity isn't just about going to church. When the fire of God comes to try the heart, the truth comes out. Are you really a true disciple of Christ? It is easy to be a Christian in America if all you do is go to church. That is not a sacrifice. It is not that big of a sacrifice to give money either for most. Giving of yourselves with the spotlight on you is hard. Look at Jesus. He was crucified and hung publicly naked in humiliation.

I beseech you therefore, brethren, by the mercies of God, that you present your bodies a living sacrifice, holy, acceptable to God, which is your reasonable service. And do not be conformed to this world, but be transformed by the renewing of your mind, that you may prove what is that good and acceptable and perfect will of God. (Romans 12:1-2)

As I began packing to go to the other hotel, I was lonely and saw my neighbor at her door. I began talking to her and she said that she was from Chicago. She didn't think Chattanooga was friendly at all. Even after this incident, I still love my hometown and all of its beauty. Like anywhere, I try to find the good. When my hotel neighbor found out I was the street preacher from the news, she wanted to talk. I even shared the gospel with this woman before I got in the car to pull away. She said, "You have no idea how much you have been on TV." Apparently it was on all the time for days, small clips here and there. She said that even on TV I seemed normal. God used this neutral lady who was not even from the area to share her thoughts. Yep, Bike Guy should have obeyed the rules. He is a grown man and could have gone to class that day.

Sunday morning November 24, 2013 I woke up to go get my morning coffee and free newspaper in the lobby of my hotel. My photo was huge on the front with the title:

"Her Cross to Bear! – The Story Behind the Street Preacher Trying to Save UTC"

This article took up most of the front page and another page in the paper as well. Wow! A woman street preacher made the front page of the Chattanooga newspaper on a Sunday? The first time I read it, I was so overjoyed that I didn't mind the sixteen mistakes Jeff Lafave made in the article. Possibly, some of the mistakes were intentional to hurt my family. No family friend ever molested me as a teen, which was stated as fact in the article. I was molested at age 5 by another boy older visiting the house from a local group home. 16 mistakes are bad journalism. He did great on article other than the mistakes.

With all the excitement and what I had been through, I wept several times that day thanking God for vindication. Thank you God. ***Yes, it was the cross***!!

"No weapon that is formed against you will prosper; And every tongue that accuses you in judgment you will condemn. This is the heritage of the servants of the LORD, *And their vindication is from Me," declares the* LORD. (Isaiah 54:17)

I drove my car in the cold, rainy weather to a small church of my faithful friend's grandpa. My evangelism partner, Bryan, had a birthday that day. I met his wife, son and father-in-law, who was the pastor. When I walked in, this precious family was singing about "going home someday to be with Jesus." The trials of my faith had weighed heavily on my heart. I broke and began to weep out all of the pain.

that I may know Him and the power of His resurrection and the fellowship of His sufferings, being conformed to His death; (Philippians 3:10)

This church was like a family to me. They allowed me to weep and share the story of the "Awakening" at UTC. I shared how it was a cross and death for me to endure. Yet, Jesus asked me to do this for Him despite all of their mocking.

The article on the front page shared how I lived in my car, took baths in sinks and slept outside of fitness centers. That was all true, however I was blessed to have a gym membership then and took baths in real showers. Jeff told the truth saying, if I could get the money that I would go to Miami for Christmas.

Times Free Press writes:

"The 43 year old lives in her car and hopes to make it to Miami by Christmas – if she can find the money."

"College students stop because it's a show." She said. "Some street preachers are boring and it is no wonder why they don't get a crowd. But once I get a crowd, I point to Jesus."

The article was very long and, like I mentioned, it had over sixteen mistakes. Though I met him a few times, I was never personal friends with Dan Martino. Journalists don't always write, thinking of feelings of others, although I felt that Jeff tried his best and truly enjoyed being on the campus to do the interview. He gave the article the perfect title and helped me into my next season of ministry more than he realized.

Let me finish the UTC crusades in this story and then go back to the article.

When I went to the school on Monday, I asked my friends in Georgia to allow me to wrap up the meetings alone. Bryan was there, which was ok. I just needed closure; something between God and them and me. The cage was there for me and I handed out eight "Thank you" cards to the officers that had been helping the crusade. I took my stuffed lamb with me, thinking maybe he could soften the students some. Hecklers were out yapping away and rainbow flags covered all the corners of the cage. One homosexual told me he bought $15 gloves just so he could be there all day. Sad, the homosexuals can stand in the cold all day and the church of Chattanooga is nowhere around to help. Bryan was there. I will always remember his labor of love.

On a good note, a few Christians read about me in the Sunday paper. I received some nice e-mails. A man in Knoxville said that he cried reading my story. A lady showed up to encourage me. Another Christian walked up and handed me an envelope. He smiled and said, "God bless you," and left. It had a $100 bill in it. I was shocked and hoped it was real!

The police all knew I was not coming back the next day. The weather report said it would be very cold and rainy. The head police jokingly told me that I caused him to get a cold. So, I told them I was heading on down the road. The students could wait in the rain for me if they wanted. A few students over the nine days did thank me for coming. One student said, "Thanks to you coming, there has been more religious discussion than ever before here."

Street preachers are made to stir things up and wake up sleepers. We are a unique breed in the Body of Christ. When God calls a street preacher, it is for a special purpose. Street preachers that are called and anointed by God are like the Special Forces. I really question whether some street preachers are called or even true Christians. Some folks just like to scream at people. God wants to save lost souls. Shouting is to awaken them to the Love of God through Jesus Christ's sacrifice on Cross. There is nothing wrong with raising their voices. In Isaiah, God says to raise it like a Trumpet.

If you love, you warn those you love! What kind of preacher would I be if I didn't preach righteousness, judgment, and holiness or warn about Hell? I know the answer; A popular likeable preacher. My calling is to please God and deliver the mail. Some people can't handle the mail, so they attack the mailwoman for bringing the mail. Hey, go to God about it. Don't kill the messenger.

Well, praise God! It was over. The police walked me to the cop car to take me back to my car one last time. As I was leaving, a nice lady that was a friend of my mother gave me a book. Maybe one day I will read it. She seemed very sincere. I forgot to mention I hugged my father good-bye on Saturday. I told him I would be in the newspaper again. He seemed anxious, but his main concern was that this might be the last time that he would ever see me. I hope not. My father stood by me even through preaching at his school caused such a huge stir in city. I never dreamed UTC would explode like this and thousands would hear the gospel. God chose me for that, no doubt in my mind. God wanted my enemies to see me as God's trophy of grace. God took an old crack smoking, drunkard and made her an anointed, booming voice for the Kingdom of God. The police even brought a machine out to test level of my voice. Such an amazing story being there and God allowing me to kick the devil like that for weeks.

When the Chattanooga police and security dropped me off at my car, they all hugged me good-bye. The nice officer that dropped me off at my last crusade in October told me like a concerned father, "Make sure you get your belly full for Thanksgiving, ok?" That was a great way to leave and go to my hotel to rest before driving south towards Florida.

Times Free Press also stated my website ministry title and that I had a Paypal account. Because Jeff added that in the front page article, several donations came in from strangers. That was such a blessing because it helped me to forgive this city.

When I drove out of Chattanooga the next day in the cold rain, I began to cry. For about ten minutes I cried and prayed for the students. Then I became quiet before the Lord, asking Him to lead me and help me. I got a hotel in Birmingham, Alabama and then the next day drove to Pensacola, Florida, where my spiritual family lives and my former church of 7 years. This is the city where God called me to preach and trained me as a preacher. When I go to Pensacola it is like going home.

God, where do you want me to go? This was my prayer on the way. Miami was awesome; however I was only going there for the weather to live in my car. Not long after my prayer, I was behind an 18- wheeler that said, "England."

Long story, short, by the time I walked into my friend's apartment in Pensacola that day, I bought a round-trip ticket from Orlando to Dublin, Ireland. I also bought a round trip ticket from Dublin to London, England. I had better have those tickets before coming to Pensacola or someone would try talking me out of going to Europe in the winter.

Thank you Chattanooga for paying for my plane ticket to leave America! **God bless you**!

Oh, one last funny fact about the UTC awakening. Dr. Joe DiPietro started a petition to try to get me banned from UTC. 3,952 people signed this petition. Just for fun, I even signed it. The petition was: "Stop allowing verbally abusive protestors to scream on the UTC campus."

Barna Group declared in 2014, that Chattanooga, Tennessee was number one list of America's most Bible minded cities.

How did I feel when I read that in January 2014? I felt mad all over again and tried to remember that Chattanooga bought my ticket to Europe to the mission field.

"Father, forgive them for they know not what they do." Jesus.

Student who questioned street preacher gets charges dismissed

Chattanooga News

About 100,000 people got on YouTube to see Cole Montalvo's arrest last year after he questioned street preacher Angela Cummings on the campus of the University of Tennessee at Chattanooga.

Four campus security personnel wrestled the biochemistry student to the ground on Nov. 14, 2013, after he crossed a perimeter marked by orange cones and told the fire-and-brimstone preacher, "If you're trying to spread the good word, maybe you shouldn't be telling everyone they're sinners." Campus police cited Montalvo for resisting arrest, inciting to riot, disorderly conduct and obstruction of justice.

The last of those charges, resisting arrest, was dismissed Monday afternoon -- provided Montalvo stays out of trouble with the law for the next six months.

Hamilton County Criminal Court Judge Rebecca Stern made that ruling after she cut short a bench trial just as Montalvo was going to take the stand after UTC police Sgt. Willie Trueitt ended his testimony.

Stern had a whispered conversation at the bench with Assistant District Attorney Brian Finlay and Montalvo's attorney, Franklin Chancey, of Cleveland, Tenn. She disappeared into her chambers for a 10-minute break, then called court to order and let Montalvo speak about the arrest. Video of it had been played and replayed on a screen in the courtroom, where about a dozen of Montalvo's family and friends came in a show of support.

"Looking at the video now, a year later, it's clear that better choices could have been made," Montalvo said.

Stern said, "Sometimes restraint is the better option."

Attorneys for both sides said afterward they were happy with the outcome.

"I'm pleased that he accepted responsibility," the assistant DA said.

Montalvo won't have any difficulty meeting the requirement to stay out of trouble for six months, his attorney said, after which he will seek to have the arrest cleared from his record. In January, charges of inciting to riot, disorderly conduct and obstruction of justice were dropped against Montalvo.

Contact staff writer Tim Omarzu at tomarzu@timesfreepress.com or www.facebook.com/tim.omarzu or twitter.com/TimOmarzu or 423-757-6651.

When you go on the campus of the University of Tennessee of Chattanooga you will see a seal on the ground right where I preached with a scripture. Let this scripture be a reminder to the city of what God wants from this campus and why He brought preachers of righteousness to wake up the campus.

Philippians 2:15 "That ye may be blameless and harmless, the sons of God, without rebuke, in the midst of a crooked and perverse nation, among whom ye shine as lights in the world."

UTC is called to shine.

"You should practice what you screech."

CHAPTER 11

Twenty Country Gospel Tour

"Ask of Me, and I will surely give the nations as Your inheritance, And the very ends of the earth as Your possession." (Psalm 2:8)

For many years I have heard from different Christian ministers that the day of the "name brand ministries" is over and that God is raising up the nameless, faceless generation. I have always felt that God had something big for me to do for His kingdom with all the training that He has given me. Being famous has never appealed to me, mostly because I don't want to deal with the leadership and responsibility that comes with that. However, I do want to influence as many Christians as possible to be bold for Christ and give their all for Him Also, I want to reach as many people with the gospel as possible in all nations.

*Then I heard the voice of the Lord, saying, "Whom shall I **send**, and who will go for Us?" Then I said, "Here am I. **Send me**!"* (Isaiah 6:8)

A very nice older lady in Florida that enjoys my YouTube channel told me once that if I am ever her way to stop over to stay at her home. I ended up going from Pensacola to her home in Daytona Beach for several weeks. She loves end time prophecy news and just being there got me interested more in the Blood Moons, Antichrist, Israel, signs of the times and urgency of the final hours in history. My heart longed to be in Israel in April for Passover. I thought about it constantly, spent hours looking for tickets and even told friends. Soon, fear set in my heart. I convinced myself that Israel airport would never let me inside the nation because I was arrested outside of the Vatican in Rome, Italy for preaching the gospel. Not only that, I convinced myself that if I got into Israel, as soon as I preached the gospel I would go to jail, banned for life from returning. Then I would have to get a cleaning job to pay back all the people that helped me to get to Israel. Isn't it amazing how fear can keep us from even attempting something great for God? Notice, my desire to go to Israel wasn't to just visit the Holy Land. My dream now was to preach the gospel of the Lamb of God to the Jews of Jerusalem! God put that dream in my heart, not me. Only God could ever make that happen. To make the desire go away, I allowed for the dream to die and focused on my two week trip to Europe.

Two weeks in Europe meant several things to me that were depressing and also like a dream teaser. For fourteen years my desire had been to move to Europe to live as a missionary. The usual normal routine for Christians desiring to be missionaries overseas for long periods of time is to join a missions sending organization. After doing that, they begin going to churches to speak, show videos of their future dream and goals and then ask for people to support them on a monthly basis. Some mission sending groups make you have $2,500 raised a month even if you go to a poor country. What church is going to show any videos of me street preaching in England without a church base there for me to be connected?

God gave me five weeks in 2012 in Europe fully paid going alone without any churches there to greet me or connect with me on outreaches. Thinking about all my victories in the past, I began to think on the 25 states and two nations in 2013 that I visited. Wow, God, what a great adventure! Maybe God could help me fulfill the Great Commission for longer than two weeks in Europe. What if I decided not to get back on the plane on January 30th? What if I planned two months of travel, raised support a different way and then figured out the spring months later? Dreaming big was all I could do over the Christmas holidays, because I sure didn't have any family around or even close friends. Websites with cheap flights were more comforting than laughing with friends.

You can make friends as you go. I have been on the road so much the past few years so it wasn't like I had a set home any way. God custom-made me on His potter's wheel just for His Kingdom purposes. That is why I didn't fit in well with the church, because I was not supposed to. If I fit in well with the local church, I may still be stuck in one with dead unfulfilled dreams.

I decided not to come back in two weeks because America got on my nerves so bad. The most romantic place in the world to be in February was in Paris for Valentine's Day. Where else should I go and preach the gospel? Belfast sounded good; I have a Facebook friend there that I always wanted to meet that has the same name as me. Let's do it!

One more place on the schedule was a train ride from Paris to Nice, France. My plan was to preach the gospel at the carnival in Nice. Over the Christmas break I planned a missions trip from January 16 to March 3rd and then went on a fast. Any time I do a fundraiser I have to fast. One thing I learned about fasting was that it helps you have more faith and pray the will of the Lord more clearly. Just before leaving, the budget was met by someone in Europe that is a missionary. It was a very hard fundraiser but the outcome was victory, victory, victory! Praise the Lord!

Before leaving, Brother Jed asked me to help in his ministry as the warm-up preacher. I went to three campuses in Florida and then when his wife arrived to help him for Spring semester she helped me take my car (my home) to the parking lot to, hopefully, leave it for a year. Sister Cindy, Jed's wife, and I had some good laughs while I parked Motel Honda at the paid storage lot close to Orlando.

Would I be back in three months or a year? My faith was high and I didn't want to ever come back if possible. Not just because America already heard the gospel too many times, but because Europe needed to hear the gospel for the first time. I wanted my dream so badly that I didn't care if I froze in some English storm or was homeless in March. If I can live in a car and travel twenty-five states in 2013, then what will God do with me in 2014?

"Let faith arise, O Lord, let faith arise!" Jason Upton

This happy missionary got her bags weighed in at forty-seven pounds! I packed red and white cowgirl boots and within the first two months of the journey I found someone to please take them. When I got to New York to wait for my Dublin flight, I noticed WTVC news channel 9 had a top story about "Bike Guy in Court." They dropped three out of four of his charges.

My last few minutes in USA were spent alone watching the riot I started in my hometown on the news station on my laptop.

Ireland has the best bacon!

Dublin, here I come with the gospel. I went to the City Hall on the way to a popular shopping street. There was a huge protest going on outside with signs and bullhorns. God had me stop to preach to them and it got rowdy. They didn't expect a preacher to confront their protest. All their signs had the issues of life on them. Sadly, a little boy held one with "Suicide." There was no way I could just walk by this scene. They all got the gospel message and a few had questions. Then I moved on to several other spots to preach. The people of Dublin were voicing their anger at the Catholic perverted priests. Ireland has had a bad curse on their land with priests harming children. They have protested in the streets about it, even in the summer of 2014. My heart hurts for these people. Hurting children is never ok. It is even the worse coming from someone in the clergy.

It was time to go to London and look for a lost sheep named "Clayton." He made major news all the way to USA because he wanted to "lose his anal virginity" for his art project in his art school in London. Before I got to his school I found out he was giving free tickets away to this horribly disturbing event. My friends were praying. My heart for him grew even more when I discovered he was Jewish. The day before the event I took several trains and walked to the art school. Boldly, I began talking to the students outside. They all had a unique way about them; different haircuts and fashionable clothes and they were shocked that I was there. They couldn't believe I came all the way from America to find Clayton. The day God showed me the England 18-Wheeler in Tennessee is the day God called me to go to look for him. Did I find him? No. However, around ten of the students invited me to the pub by the campus. I simply went with my water and sat with them to talk about the gospel. Three of the young men were ticket-holders to the "art project." What? Yes, they were going to watch him have live anal sex. Homosexuality is unnatural, per the New Testament book of Romans Chapter 1.

God cares about these London students regardless of what sins they love the most. These students enjoyed our talk and time together. They wanted a photo with me. They all wanted a "Lamb" sticker. They all took my testimony tract that I wrote about how I was a wicked woman and Jesus changed my life. My trip to London was awesome, especially being with them for a few hours.

Clayton postponed his art project until later and never went through with it. He ate bananas as an art project per Huffington Post. Many of us prayed for him to not do this sex act in front of his class. Praise God, that he changed his mind. Students wanted me to return for 420 day, but I couldn't this year.

London was cold and raining for many of the days I was there. Sunday, though it was pouring rain, I went to preach at famous Hyde Park speaker's square. Not giving up, I waited in the city until the rain died down. Then I went to preach the gospel in the park. There were hundreds of cops everywhere because a man from Hungary was running for prime minister and he was there. He was a Jobbist and controversial. The cops thought I was cute, wanting to preach. They were trying to get me to move to another spot. However, I wanted to speak to that crowd already formed. Lots of rebels were in that crowd and they needed to be warned of the wrath of God if they don't repent and turn to Jesus! Preach? Yes I did, right there and my voice boomed!

Shortly after, I went to another area of Hyde Park to preach. A Christian gladly allowed me to use his ladder. I ended up having a showdown with a Muslim evangelist. No doubt I won the moment. People stopped to watch. He didn't intimidate me. He has no good news to tell. Jesus Christ and His sacrifice on the cross is the good news. I was not getting off of my brother's ladder until I made my point. It was a great outreach. A lady in Wales saw the video and invited me to come to her home at any time. Praise the Lord! God used me in my hostel all week to share the gospel with girls from Brazil, Slovakia, Australia and I even found a girl to give my size 9 red boots to. She cursed a lot in her thanksgiving for those cowgirl boots. I hope that my boots will rub off on her in a good way since they were gospel preaching boots.
After traveling through two nations, I began to down size my bags so I was really happy to give up my boots.

My trip from Ireland to London was only $100 roundtrip. When I went back to Dublin the border patrol gave me a hard time. I was nervous because my return ticket was for the next day. I knew I was not going to board that plane back to USA. My plans were to go to Belfast.

A man saw me walking around with my luggage, lost in Swords, Ireland. I couldn't find my room for the night. He had two small children with bright red hair. He offered to take me out of the cold into his home to check the directions on his computer since I had no phone. When I found the directions, he offered to drive me there. What a sweet man he was! His children just looked at me with such curiosity. As an icebreaker I Googled "Chattanooga, Tennessee" to show them my hometown. These young boys may have never met a country girl from America. I realize my accent is really strong. Sometimes I think people want to talk to me because of my accent. God uses all kinds of ways to stop people for the gospel.

The next day I took a bus to Belfast, Northern Ireland to stay about ten days. I had been praying all winter for some snow to enjoy. Yet it never snowed anywhere on my journey. It sure rained though. Rainy days meant evangelizing indoors to anyone in the hostel. Belfast has produced some great worship songs. My heart was overflowing, being in the church of the writer of many of those songs we sang at the Brownsville Revival. I hitchhiked to make it to church on time. A nice man took me straight there and I sat on the front row. In Belfast I visited two churches and meet a facebook friend.

Walking through Belfast and on the way home from church I learned something. The UK flag is offensive to certain parts of Belfast. There is a Catholic Irish side in the city and a protestant UK flag group on the other side. Hey, I was an alcoholic at seventeen and sleeping in high school. I learned a lot of things I missed while I was in high school. I began to wear the UK hat less because I didn't want to start a riot over a hat. If a riot starts, I wanted it to be because of the proclaimed Word of God.

Several outreaches I did while in Belfast were at City Centre, City hall and then a Saturday morning protest. After being in this city I gave them the nickname "Belfast Bombers." Teens at city hall told me how hard it was growing up there around bombs. My heart really broke for one kid in particular. I visited him before leaving to make sure he knew the gospel and someone cared for his soul. Many of the teens wanted lamb stickers. Their faces are printed in my mind when I recall this mission trip.

The outreach that I remember most was on a Saturday morning. I was in a coffee shop. A guy working there told me a big protest was about to happen. He told me about the Catholics marching and the Protestants opposing them that day. There must have been three hundred cops out there. Most had bulletproof vests and over ten SWAT armored cars. There was even one outside my hostel. It was so cold that day. I was not about to miss this protest though. The cops allowed me to be out there without a problem. I reached both sides with the gospel. A guy from the Netherlands gave me a pair of socks. His pair was my third pair on my cold feet. I still was super cold, but by God's grace I got to reach hundreds with the gospel that day. My videos in Belfast got me an open door to a radio interview with BBC later in my journey, but turned it down due to subject matter being pointless.

My roommate from Spain at my hostel invited me to go with her sightseeing one day. It was something to do, so I went. She gave me the nicest postcard before leaving about how I impacted her life those few days. God set her up one day to see my preaching in City Centre. The message didn't change. Sometimes open air preaching is easier because they don't feel like the message is directly for them. People usually think they are good enough for Heaven. Addressing the crowd with truth can be easier. Personally, I enjoy "net-fishing."

There was a guy in my hostel that I picked on in a fun way about him being an atheist. Several of us discussed my plans for staying in Europe a year. A couple people told me about the 180 day rule in UK and 90 day rule in European Union. This came as a shock to me and I knew that by April sixteenth I needed to go somewhere out of UK and Europe. The couple suggested Turkey and the atheist suggested Israel. The atheist said he lived there for years and it was safe. Israel was way more appealing to me then Turkey. Anyway, I wanted to go where Jesus lived, walked and is coming back to soon. I have been arrested for preaching outside the Vatican. Again, my fears came and they were real. I didn't want Israel turning me away at the border for being a religious fanatic. This guy convinced me that I could get into Israel. Thanks for the encouragement! God sure used him to re-water a seed that I thought was dead in my heart.

I arrived at the Belfast airport, where I waited all day to go to Paris. I was reading the Holy Bible in the airport when all of a sudden God spoke!

"For the Jews require a sign, and the Greeks seek after wisdom:"(I Corinthians 1:22 KJV)

When I read that, the fire of God came on me in the Belfast airport so strong that I had to shut the Bible and catch my breath. "God, are You sending me to Israel to preach the gospel and tell them about the Blood Moon on April 15?" That was powerful! I posted on Facebook that I wanted to go and gave the price for the roundtrip ticket from London, England. Within an hour a Texas man I never met that enjoys my mission's efforts wrote to offer to buy that ticket. I soon received $346 to cover my airfare. I had no clue where I would stay or even how I would eat. Now, a faith walk has begun for the Middle East.

Praise the Lord! Brother Scott had been reading the Four Blood Moon book too. He volunteered to buy my ticket within the hour I posted my desire to go and preach in Israel. I would not necessarily see the Blood Moon, yet I knew I was supposed to talk about it to many people there. My #1 goal was the gospel, not the Blood Moon.

There was no time to worry about Israel. It was February 9, 2014 and I was heading to France to preach the gospel. I couldn't think of a more romantic place to be on Valentine's Day then Paris, France. God is so awesome to allow me to make my own schedule. Thank You Jesus! Because I am so busy in ministry, I don't have time for a relationship. Maybe someday I will meet my soul mate and we can change the world together. Until then, my life is for the gospel; cold, rainy, dangerous, unknown, violent, wars, protests… This is a great life God has given me, tasting of the Bible as I go. Suffering is normal for a real disciple of Christ.

A few years ago I was talking to a guy on Facebook named Brad. He had left Florida over twenty years ago to move, by faith, to France to be a missionary. Brad's life really inspired me. One day he posted a photo of him preaching the gospel by the Arc De Triomphe. I was the only person that commented on the photo. My mind couldn't understand why no one else could see the beauty in this photo. This man left everything for the gospel. Last year Brad died of Cancer. Although I never met him, I felt that he was my friend and brother in Christ. I knew I had to go stand in the spot of this picture and honor his legacy. The day I did go there to preach, the joy of the Lord was like a river. Anyone that got near me began to be joyful as well. Over fifty people that day wanted their photos with me and "Behold the Lamb." They didn't know me. They just saw a woman in love with Jesus. One guy got his photo with me about three times. He enjoyed jumping up and down with me. The police came a few hours later to run me off. They pointed to some building saying they have been watching me up there. I think it was the Embassy. Well, isn't that special! Brad, you rock brother! See you in Heaven, love sister Angela.

Back at the hostel I was enjoying French croissants. My cleaning lady in my hostel came in my room while I was praising God and we ended up singing "Alleluia" together. We both lifted our hands and worshiped for about twenty minutes. The Spirit of God came on us and then we hugged. I don't know French, but we know God together. Wow, that was so awesome.

The day that I got ready for my big Valentine's Day outreach to the Eiffel Tower, my hostel workers gave me a blinking heart with a rose. Then they gave me heart-shaped balloons. I put two balloons on my hat with my **"Trust Jesus"** T-shirt. It was a perfect day to talk about the greatest love story ever told. When I walked out the door to go preach, the staff stopped me for a photo. After I got back, I noticed it was on their Facebook page. That is why wearing Jesus T-shirts is awesome. They just promoted the gospel on their page for me.

"You are more exciting than the Eiffel Tower." Mark and Sarah

<u>Here is my post from Facebook 2/14/2014.</u>

"What a day in Paris. I looked for a spot to preach and finally after about four spots I finally felt peace about a spot right in front where everyone was walking in and getting photos by the main road. Cops walked by me for hours and even had huge guns. They said nothing. Thank you for prayers. Yesterday cops told me I had the Embassy upset with me. God really touched lives today. A huge group of teens from London flocked to me and all had questions. I felt like a mama bird trying to feed them all. It was a pretty nice size crowd, for a police to not say a word.

Again, it is the prayers of the saints. I stood on a platform the whole time and lifted my Bible in one hand and Behold the Lamb in the other hand. I had red balloons with me as well. The two people that blew my mind the most were Mark and Sarah. They sat and listened for hours. That is their confession. They insisted on taking me out to eat. This is Valentine's Day and they chose to spend it with a street preacher. Mark said he had never in his life talked this much about religion. Sarah is from Canada and Mark is from London. They live together and were in Paris for romance. Yet, they said I was more exciting than the Eiffel Tower. We spent hours together and I tried to answer their questions. I must say that our waiter was gorgeous. For me, being a single woman, I had to say, "Thank You Jesus!" Hey, I didn't' want to go the whole day without seeing a cutie pie in Paris. Mark and Sarah hugged me good-bye. They both took a testimony tract and allowed me to show them scriptures about sin and how to get to Heaven. What an amazing divine appointment! The human heart cries out for unfailing love. Only God can make that happen. The Eiffel Tower can't do it. I had a great day and was thankful that so many heard the gospel of Jesus Christ and his cruel death on a cross to demonstrate the Father's love."

Paris was great, even if it was February. God used me to preach at a few other places in the city, plan my Israel trip some more and visit Montparnasse to overlook the city. While up there, I had French coffee and salmon salad. Goodbye, Paris!

Nice, France was having a big carnival. It was time for me to take the train from Paris to Nice on the French Rivera.

Gay French Riviera! Hey, I didn't know that, ok? Two men holding hands and walking around will never be normal to me. The city was all decorated nicely and had a great hostel room. The hostel manager taught me a simple French recipe; peas, bacon, cream and pasta. My roommate was from Chile and worked in Monte Carlo, Monaco. My fundraiser was only on until March third. When I went to the bank the next day, I only had enough money for the hostel and food for two weeks.

Before any ministry begins I wanted to take a quick day trip over to Monte Carlo, Monaco. The wealthiest people in the world live there; Zillionaires. My daydream was to meet some rich person to fund my ministry so I wouldn't have to fundraise anymore. Well, it didn't happen. God wants to get glory for all of this and huge reason I had to write this book. God made all this happen, because He wants more workers in the harvest field. A rich person is not the answer to my faith walk, its trusting God one day at a time in my faith walk. I have had to learn this. God rarely uses rich people in my life. Usually, it is the simple average people that just love God that help fund world missions.

Monaco was almost the same as France. There was nothing super special about it. When I got back to the hostel, I taught my hostel roommate from the country of Chile. The church song, "If you're happy and you know it shout amen, stomp your feet, clap your hands…" She wanted to learn English, so I was her crazy teacher and possibly first missionary.

My plans were to stay in Nice, France for two weeks. Then I would fly to England and take a bus to Wales to preach with my Facebook friend. However, plans changed quickly when I felt my life was in danger. Remember, I was only a 5'2" woman alone in France. I didn't even have a phone with me. My life is a huge faith walk, trusting in the Lord and His angels to watch over me. Strangely, people started giving to the ministry during that week and I couldn't figure out why. I thought I was all right for two weeks, so why have money in my account if I didn't need it. How many preachers say that? I asked God what this money was for. The answer came in about 24 hours. One of my Facebook friends suggested a month ago that I should go visit his unsaved sister in Italy. I looked several times at my schedule and finances, only to tell him, "Brother, I can't. I don't even have Italy on my schedule." Italy was 2013 and there are other places I needed to reach. Then, after my first and only outreach to Nice, France, everything shifted. Here is my post from Facebook 2/20/2014.

"Angry Muslims in Nice, France"

"There have only been a handful of times in thirteen years of open air preaching where I have almost been beaten up. Today was one of those days. I left for a tram to get back to the hostel quickly. A Muslim was in my face and I could feel the warfare. Another Muslim already had stolen my bag and threw it into a tree. What happened? I preached at two locations on the campus of Pole Universitair St. Jean d Angely in Nice, France. It was a beautiful day and I felt the Lord leading me there. The cops drove by and saw me preaching. I told them about Paris and how I preached there. They never even got out of the car. They waved good-bye to me. Praise God! That was good news. The first spot I preached drew crowds everywhere. People were on roofs and windows were opened. People stood on bridges to listen. I will admit not everyone spoke English. Great reason to wear a Christian T-shirt. They can Google my T-shirt message! Anything to get their attention. One guy stole my hat and brought it back later. Students there were fun and light-hearted and just wanted a good show. They even clapped once. Later a professor came out to demand I leave. I stayed with camera off about 20 minutes praying. Then I went to a small group. Muslims. I gave them the gospel and they were angered. I left and went to another part of the school. This crowd got angry. Because some of them were at the other place and knew I was saying "Jesus was the Word made flesh and the only way to Heaven." I even sang a song about spiritual warfare. I felt enemies of the cross rage. Soon the bag was stolen and thrown in the tree. I began praying for help. It was my fault for taking the backpack off. A student went and retrieved it. My only set of car keys was in that bag. Thank

You Jesus! After thirty minutes, several men ganged up on me. I wasn't scared of most of them. Then a man came out that the Muslim students had summoned. This man would beat his wife. I know he would. It was in his eyes. He came to me and a mob of about five were around me. A man was recording me and even with all that craziness I gave him a simple gospel message. He asked me and I stood in confidence while others appeared dangerous standing so close. Praise the Lord! I got on the tram and was glad he didn't get on with me. Just not sure what is next. That campus is stirred up. Riot mode is not a good thing alone and in France surrounded by Muslims. I'm not going back there again. My hands are clean of their blood, referring to a scripture in Ezekiel about when you warn someone, and then their blood is no longer on your hands."

My hostel manager gave me a full refund and my plans shifted to Italy. I ended up in Genoa, Italy. While there I preached at a soccer game to hundreds of people walking by. Someone almost touched my camera, but I yelled at him with a mother's voice. Praise God I got there in time to stop him from touching it.

Meanwhile, somebody named Michael that I don't even know gave me $71 in my PayPal account. He left me a note that read, "You have more balls than I will ever have." That is so embarrassing when a man says this to me. I have lost count of the times hearing comments like this about my bravery.

God sent me from Genoa to Milan. Milan is 45 minutes from Brescia. This is the city where my Facebook friend's unsaved sister lived. Her family invited me over for the weekend. Milan is a big university city and has an international school with 2,000 professors.

Milan, Italy Facebook post 2/25/2014 – "Catholic named Paul answered the altar call today! Today was great! Milan, Italy has a hunger like Florence, Italy had last year. I preached two places today. First I started ministry in the open air at University of Milan and then by the HUGE Catholic church in the city center. At the University, I had a long talk with a young guy named Benjamin. He had so many questions. His friends yelled at me, "Hey Preacher!" They wanted me to come over there to talk. Ben talked with me close to an hour. I almost picked the fruit by trying to lead them to the Lord. However, I felt he was not ready yet. He was close, but just decided to pray for the spirit of truth and conviction to come. I don't like having false converts on my conscience, just for a number. Then I went to City Center. It was one of the easiest preaching crusades I have had in a long time. No one heckled and people stood and listened. I gave an altar call and Paul, a big Italian Catholic, raised his hand. He came and held my hand. He prayed to repent and believe in Jesus and make Jesus Lord. He stayed another hour and bought me dinner. He had so much on his heart and wanted so badly to know God closely. He hated all the money making tactics of the church. He had a really pure heart. When he prayed with me I started crying and it was hard to preach. People lined up everywhere to listen. People stayed so long, I ran out of evangelism messages and started giving testimonies. People still wouldn't leave. God is moving in Milan! Glad that he brought me here. I wanted to go to about four other cities. I obeyed the Lord to come to a city I knew nothing about. Milan was very open to the message. Cops never bothered me. Thank you saints for prayers. God bless you."

Forty-two thumbs up!

Brescia, Italy was my next city. I had a Facebook friend's sister living there. He wanted me to go stay with her and share the gospel. Praise God this family opened their home to me.

I went to Italy out of obedience. I had the money in the bank at this time to choose where to go next before going back to Nice to catch the plane to London. I wanted to go to Spain, Holland, Hungary and Norway. It just wasn't the right time for those countries.

The Brescia trip was a fun time hanging out with my Facebook friend's family and friends. We ate great food and went to a friend's son's soccer game in the rain. Then she and I went to see the city. She got a phone call that a close friend of hers had just died from cancer. That is when I knew I was in God's perfect will again by being a comfort to her in her loss. As a missionary I am still an ambassador to speak the Word of God in some way. Some people accuse me of cramming the Bible down people's throats. That is just someone saying "Hey, you are bold." I felt like I needed to address eternity with her in a light way and still make it real. A church in America was praying for God to use me. After the day out, we went back to eat with an Italian family before she drove me to Milan hotel. Grandma cooked all kinds of good stuff. I have always wanted a home cooked meal in Italy. While sitting at the table with all the family looking at me while eating good home cooked Italian food, one of them said "So tell us, how do you know Mark?" I said "He is my Facebook friend." Italian Grandmother said "Oh, you never met him?" I said, "No." Awkward moment and quiet. My sense of humor loves moments like these because they are classics. God sent me to stay in this home because of their souls. I am not randomly just going places. The Bible says "My steps are ordered of the Lord."

The steps of a good man are ordered by the LORD*: and he delighteth in his way.* (Psalm 37:23 KJV)

Wales! How exciting to stand in the rain at the church where the Welsh revival was in 1904 in Swansea Wales. Evan Roberts was used of God to spark a revival that ended up spreading to Los Angeles. He didn't stay in the ministry. His story has a sad ending with him going into hiding and not preaching again his entire life.

My plans were to take a bus to Glasgow, Scotland after Wales. Then ride down to London and board a plane for Israel. I ordered a backpack and great walking shoes (shipped to my friend's home in Wales). Sometimes, I admit my ideas can get too radical and I try to push the limits on my faith walk. My journey with God has been very intense and colorful with mountains, oceans, sunsets and many sidewalks across the world.

I was thinking a lot about my pastor in Texas, Steve Hill, while in Wales, because he was very sick and no one has impacted my ministry more than him. He had become my favorite preacher since the first time I heard him speak, January 1997. Then in February of 1999, he pointed at me through a small crowd, telling me to come to him for prayer. I have no doubt that impartation came on me that day, because so many of his godly characteristics are now in my life and ministry. My last time seeing him was a few years ago in Texas. The Lord told me to drive all the way from California to honor him at church Sunday morning. He had not been there for about eighteen months because of cancer attacking him so badly. It was great to see him and his family on Christmas morning. He even came to give me a father's hug. He was my spiritual father for a long time. Then, I went back to California, not knowing that was my final time to see my hero in the faith. God had plans for me to go to the nations. I put a picture of Steve weeping for souls on my Facebook page while in Wales.

I went to preach the gospel with the mother/daughter team that took me into their home. Oh yea, I forgot to finish my crazy idea with the backpack. Jesus was homeless, so I will be homeless too. I have wanted to be homeless so bad to get that scratched off of my bucket list. God won't let me. So my faith had to rise up! God will you help me with housing in Israel? My faith was being stretched because I was to be there seventy days. Sometimes I try to "help God out." He doesn't need my help. He wants me to bring my desires to Him. When God stamps "approval" then the blessings begin to flow. I usually don't know how I will see those blessings, though sometimes I do have an idea. God has hand selected a few givers to help me over the years; Two awesome women of God that are former Catholics. They love me so much and enjoy the journey with me. Praise God! They get excited when they see others help and have prayers increase for this mission. They love Jesus!

The outreaches in Wales were pretty awesome. We preached outside Cardiff University and a Muslim evangelist came over to talk. I stuck "Behold" the Lamb to his cheek to kiss him and he smiled. A student wanted his photo with me. We also preached in the City Centre with a few others that are clocked for a one hour outreach and then they go have coffee. I wanted to stir it up a little. Some liked it and one lady was nervous with my bold approach. Hey, I came a long way to start a revival or a riot. One guy started singing "Highway to Hell" to try to make me mad. Later, he changed the song to "Halleluiah." That was weird, but the power of the preached Word of God was there.

The second church I spoke in on my March trip to Wales was a night I will never forget. I was talking about how my pastor influenced me so much and trying to reach a guy in the front row with the gospel. Right before I went up to speak I went to the bathroom. I saw three young men outside. I tried to get them to come inside to hear my message. One did come in and after I was done, they wanted me and Brother James to talk to them outside about God.

That night my pastor died. Finally, he is not in pain any more from cancer. The sad part is that a huge void is now on planet Earth because he was such a great Evangelist. Sometimes, I wondered if God was saying "Come on church, you can preach the same gospel Steve Hill did. Go church, go!"

People say that Steve Hill inspired them all the time. He is inspiring. People have also on a lower scale, said to me, "Angela, you inspire me." If we inspire you, what do we inspire you to do, is my question.

Merrian-Webster.com's definition of inspire:
1. To make (someone) want to do something; to give (someone) an idea about what to do or create.
2. To cause (something) to happen or be created.

3. To cause someone to have (a feeling or emotion)

Well, I needed to grieve over my pastor's death. My trip to Scotland was cancelled. Thank God I was with friends when the news came. I was very grateful that Julie allowed me to have my own room in her home. I had a long, good cry on Monday. Within a few days I was in a hostel in London for one night. I believe I was there to witness to one lady because she said, "Let me think of all my God questions for you." That night around 3 am, in my hostel room, I watched my favorite preacher's funeral at Brownsville Assembly of God on-line. The next morning the lady said to me, "When you came in this room I thought 'who is this whirlwind coming in?'" That was the most comforting thing she could say to me. Not knowing how much I loved the story of Elijah and Elisha in 2 Kings 2:11.

I went to a dorm room of my own in London. I only preached once that week. My goal was to rest, refuel and prepare for seventy days in Israel. Life was nice that week with no schedule and just resting. I listened to teachers on YouTube and Johnny Cash read the Bible to me. The peace of God was amazing and I was so glad to have learned that God is a God that allows His servants to rest.

ISRAEL Passover 2014

C T Studd, "Had I cared for the comments of people, I should never have been a missionary."

Istanbul, Turkey has free dark chocolate spoons in the coffee shop in their airport. It is a really nice airport. I took a nap upstairs on the children's playground equipment, out of desperation for rest. I was there for ten long hours. No way was I going to the city and risking my Israel assignment. My goal was to wait for Israel. After my nap I went back for my coffee and free chocolate. A twenty-five-year-old Indian from Canada and a couple from Amsterdam sat by me. The lady mentioned that she spoke Hebrew, so I got to witness to them because of the open door.

In Hebrew, Strong's #5774 means "Year of the open door."

March 26, 2014
"Israel did let me in! Praise the Lord! They held me in a room for fifteen minutes asking questions. Then they said, "Merry, here's your passport." I am so glad my preaching name is my middle name. Woot Woot! Having tuna and weird coffee at the Tel Aviv International Airport."

My first morning awake in Israel was spent getting the biggest Israeli breakfast available. I took leftovers with me for lunch later. I found Behold the Lamb a camo Israel Defense Force Kippah. When I went to a place to eat leftovers, the Jews freaked out on me. They said that if the Rabbi finds out non-Kosher food was in their restaurant, they would be shut down. I guess the Rabbi was ok with cigarettes though. They were allowing a man to smoke. That shocked me!

I went back to the hostel to give Behold the Lamb his super cool kippah. My roommate was Jewish from Australia. She cleans houses in Tel Aviv and stayed at the hostel for cleaning exchange. She like me.

"You're the funniest missionary I have ever met." Jewish Roomie.

She even said, "Praise the Lord!" one day after our talks. I gave her my testimony tract and she read it. She told me I was a "normal Christian and keep spreading the Words of Jesus, Honey."

Tel Aviv was known for being like a little New York City. There is always a party going on and sadly it is also a big, gay party city. I didn't always sleep well, due to the noise outside. Friday at sunset the city gets quieter, though to celebrate Shabbat Shalom.

My Jewish roomy wanted to show me Jaffa. We went for a nice chat/walk by the Mediterranean Sea on a sunny Saturday in March. We talked about one day going to the Dead Sea. Neither of us had ever been there. She taught me about Yeshua the King of the Jews. She decided to go back home after pointing out how to get to the top of the hill in Jaffa.

After lunch I saw a few Christians passing out invitations to a coffee shop. I asked the one of them if they ever share the gospel. He didn't want to complain, but said "Yeah. I was wondering that too." Right then and there, since he was far away from his organized group, I began to open air preach in Israel to a small crowd on a hill. A local Israeli named Michael came to talk with me about what I had just shared. So far, so good. I was getting myself ready for the upcoming preaching at the Jerusalem Passover.

My backpack was killing me and people suggested that I buy a bag with wheels. Good deal! My backpack was ripped any way from the flight over. I found a Red Swiss 4-wheeler for $76 US. I choose to wait until my father's birthday on March 31st to step onto the ground of Jerusalem to honor him.

Jerusalem was a culture shock to me and I didn't even want to stay there. The first night Muslims praying on loud speakers spooked me out the most and I felt awakened to the fact that I was in the Middle East. I knew I was not in Kansas anymore and was scared at times. I ate my first meal by the station in Old City where Jesus, after being sentenced to crucifixion, was exhausted and Simeon was told to carry His cross. It was a great day of reflection and getting myself used to the culture. Jerusalem Old City is where I stayed in hostels.

My Jewish roommate from Tel Aviv sent me an e-mail telling me how much she enjoyed my testimony tract. I missed her fellowship, but had to go to Jerusalem for my big mission from God.

Later that day I sang "Jesus Messiah" from my pink notebook to see how reactions would be just from singing about Jesus. Many Jews walked past me that day. I even talked to one Jewish lady that lived there for over fifty years.

My favorite place to hang out in Jerusalem is by the Western Wall where the Jews are praying. My first day there I saw so many young Jewish soldiers and even a bride dressed modestly. I quickly began to record and capture the moment. Christians are called to be a spotless bride waiting on Jesus (bridegroom) to return for us (church). My first prayer and only prayer at Western Wall was for my son. Other days I visited and prayed for other things. I wanted my first Western Wall prayer to be for my arrow of the Lord, Nicholas.

April 3, 2014 I rode an Arab bus up the Mount of Olives. I spent a lot of time in prayer and reflection of the power of the historic ground overlooking Jerusalem. A couple of Palestinian boys climbed under a fence to get into the city. Every young man I met up there wanted me to know they were Palestinian kids. I guess it didn't cross my mind if I was in danger or not walking around alone up there. As I rode back down the mountain in the bus full of Muslims the joy of the Lord came on me. I was listening to DC Talk on my IPod and head banging to "Jesus Freak." The bus riders seemed to enjoy that I was happy about something. I tried to get a couple of teens to listen to my ear piece.

My hostel is in the Old City with great window view. The business owners are always bugging me and others as we walk through. One day they asked what I was looking for and I said "Jesus!" He didn't understand I was referring to the Second Coming. A business owner pushed me one day for no reason and told me to leave. One day another business owner asked me where my little lamb was? The one annoying part of this hostel was the loud call to prayer every day for the Muslims. Being that I am a Christian it is not an attractive sound to hear over a loud speaker. That sound puts an uneasy, evil feeling into the atmosphere in Jerusalem. There are Christian, Muslim and Jewish quarters in the Old City where I was staying. The Christian quarter is more of a Catholic or Orthodox area than Christian.

My first hostel had many divine appointments set up by the Holy Ghost. A man from Oregon and I talked awhile. He even went to the Garden of Gethsemane with me to watch me make my video there. He wasn't a Christian, yet loved coming to Israel all the time. He would go sit at the empty tomb for hours watching people. I ran into him at my next hostel too. God brought Christians from Washington State to this hostel. They reached out to him as well. The nice lady joined me for an adventure in Tiberius. This is where Jordan River is and also the sea of Galilee.

April 7, 2014
"Behold the Lamb got baptized in the Jordan river while a group of Jewish boys listened to me preach on the hill. I held Behold up in the air and a boy said, "Your lamb is peeing." My flip flops were getting stuck in the mud and little fish nibbled at my leg while I was preaching. Donna and I preached to two Jews on the way to Jordan River and two more after the baptism. We didn't pay the money for the white robes at the normal tourist attraction. I wanted something free and unforgettable. When I got out I was covered in mud to my knees. I went in the bathroom to clean off. When I came out I found two more Jews by a dove on the walkway tourist spot. I'm not joking people. Those unconverted Jews were at the John the Baptist baptismal tourist attraction. I showed these college age Jews in the New Testament scriptures where a dove showed up at the baptism of Jesus. After that, I boldly declared, "Jews require a sign." There is your sign. It's time to get saved. God gave us divine appointments almost every hour that day with Jews. I can't even post all the stories. God did it. We just shared the good

news. I haven't had this many divine appointments in one day in a while. Holy Ghost is fishing for Jews. We had a great time at the Sea of Galilee. A Muslim named Mohammed, stood by me for my video. He wanted to hear my message. All glory to God. I'm so thankful for Jesus and you prayer warriors. God bless you."

One other place that I wanted to visit before open air preaching during Passover began was Mt. Carmel where Elijah called the fire down from Heaven. I went by myself walking from the top of the mountain to his cave. His cave was filled with Catholicism, which was disgusting. Elijah wasn't a Roman Catholic, blind guide priest. Elijah was a man of God that connected with God's power.

The trip to the Garden of Gethsemane with Brian was cool. I told the gardener that I liked the great job he was doing on the garden. Shortly after that he walked to the fence and whispered for me to come over to talk. He wanted to know if I wanted a branch from an olive tree in the garden where Jesus cried out for God to take the Father's cup away if possible. Wow! Of course, I want a piece of it! He saw me by the huge olive tree and clipped a branch off a smaller one. He stuck it in his work bucket with weeds and came to the fence. He handed it to me when no crowds of tourist were watching. Later, I gave a piece to Andy in New York City and Dr. Sandy. Then I glued mine to my preaching Bible and left it in my childhood room. If I get martyred someday I want my Bible to remain in my room where I grew up in Chattanooga, Tennessee.

My first Shabbat Shalom meal in Jerusalem was with the needy. I had met a Russian Jew at my hostel that showed me where the poor eat for free every day. When I was seated on that first Friday the view I got with the Jewish women surrounding me was of the Western Wall. I felt God's presence so strongly that night. It was truly life changing. I continued going for the free meal. The food was awesome. Every day I sat with a Russian Jew or would at least wave at her. She was homeless and always carried her suitcase with a winter coat. My friends from the hostel came the next Friday. One was a Christian from Germany and the other girl was a Jewish scientist from Sweden. She didn't like me at first, but then changed her mind. I got to give her my testimony tract and share about Jesus being the Lamb of God.

April 12, 2014
"Shabbat Shalom, @ Rabbi's home with about 80 people! Woot, woot Jesus! First meal was at usual place by the Western Wall. Then, I was invited to next meal. My hostel friend from Germany is a Christian. A man at the first meal insisted we both come. We followed Rabbi Mordechai all the way to his home, maybe a two mile walk. We walked through the Via Dolorosa with him and a group behind us. We ate a lot of good food. Then, he had an open discussion. He encouraged people that spoke English to talk. I asked him what he thought about the coming blood moon, April 15 on Passover and the book of Joel? He was very respectful. He felt maybe God would see the red in the blood moon the same as the red on the doorposts, then, Passover many people and good would happen. He did not see it as a warning of some kind. Interesting. I made sure to thank him. I learned a lot today about Jews. They try to care for the poor from their heart. I like that. One part I loved was him talking about how they look for people hungry to feed. It made me think of when Jesus stood up, "All those thirsty come to me and drink!" This Rabbi has a son named Yeshua. I asked him what is his English name. I said

your name sounds like Jesus in English. Young college age Rabbi's son snapped at me. 'We don't use that name in this house. We don't believe in that.' Shabbat Shalom."

Check this out. After I left the Rabbi's home I did some research. Let me show you what I found out about the blood moon.

www.theopenscroll.com

"The meaning of an eclipse
According to Jewish Rabbinic tradition, an eclipse should be interpreted according to the following: (Talmud-Mas. Sukkah 299)
- Solar: a bad omen for idolaters
- Lunar: a bad omen for Israel
- Red Moon at lunar eclipse: a sword is coming for the whole world.
- Black moon at lunar eclipse: the arrows of famine are coming to the world.

"The sign of the blood red moon:

A blood red moon is noted in a number of scriptures pertaining to these last days. Sometimes this striking visual phenomenon is produced by a lunar eclipse. The rabbinic tradition identifies a lunar eclipse as a bad omen for Israel. They interpret a red moon to mean a sword is coming for the whole world. The tetrad of blood red moons in 2014 and 2015 should be seen as a sign or series of signs. Joel 2:28-32."

There is more to say about it on above website or you could read John Hagee's book, Four Blood Moons like I did to learn before going to Israel. You don't have to know about blood moons. It is just interesting why Jews require signs.

Aprils 13, 2014
"My voice was as loud as I could get it tonight as I stood on a concrete bench in the Old City by Jaffa Gate. Crowds did gather, with even a few Jews. No problem with the police. Maybe because after about 45 minutes I stopped to talk to someone. Then another guy from Florida just had to talk to me. College kid and former Assembly of God, now into Judaism. After 40 minutes of his yapping about why he left Jesus, I was so grieved. I told him 'Look, you deny Jesus, He will deny you. OK!" He tried to follow me, telling me all the flaws in the Bible; that I should give him my camera because he asked. He was a yapper and tried my patience, which was good for me to prepare for Passover. I gave him the bottom lines, because I know the Word of God is truth. His name is David from the University of Florida. He now lives in Israel. Two people tried to buy Behold the Lamb. No way! This is my preaching buddy. One man gave me five pounds from Egypt. Pretty cool. Great night, getting my voice ready for Passover. God drew a nice crowd of close to 70 people in Jerusalem. Going during the day tomorrow. It got cold and windy late in the night. Thanks for prayers friends. Many people said Hallelujah with me."

April 14, 2014

"Jonathan the Jew day 2 outreach in Jerusalem. Right as I started, a man from another country said, 'I wish you all the best.' Then, I told him I was going to preach the gospel. He changed his mind. He said I shouldn't do it right here. Go to where Christians were and preach. It is Passover week and not a good time to do this. My voice was stronger, bolder, clearer and louder than yesterday. The police saw me, heard me and did nothing. Yeah saints and Team Jesus. Jewish children cheered for me. Muslims were ok with me, even. Several Christians said, 'Shhhhhhhh!' Not surprised. I preached harder. Many people listened, filmed, took photos and a man from Egypt asked me about Jesus. Many stories…

Jonathan came to help with Muslim children, to make sure they didn't pick on me or steal my camera. His name is pronounced with a "y". He was named after David's best friend. He was the perfect friend at the moment and 100% Jewish. He had been to Israel eight times. His mother was from Arkansas. I told him about the Arkansas church I speak at sometimes. Then he warned me to be super careful where I preach; that I could get hurt. He didn't want me to hush, like those Christians a few minutes before. There were many Christians that did cheer and sing with me. There were only a few ashamed of Jesus. A guy brought me a water as I left. A lady from Egypt blew me a kiss. She was a believer. Several Egyptians liked my preaching the past two days. Praise the Lord! Almost time for Passover! Worthy is the Lamb!"

Went to Passover Seder at the usual place I eat for free with the needy. The whole service was in Hebrew. My Russian Jewish friend insisted that I stay, even with the meeting being almost three hours. I kept leaning my head on the wall about to fall asleep. It was awesome being there, but it was just waiting that long on even a cracker to eat that was hard. I got hungry. The fish was great.

April 16, 2014

"Day 3, Passover outreach - South African Christians: Preaching the gospel in Jerusalem on Passover, wow! God is awesome. My voice was full blast loud. I used Behold the Lamb all night. Hundreds of Jews walked by me and not one cursed me out. Not one threw a stone. A few stopped to listen. Praise the Lord! God brought several Christians from South Africa to sit down and be the "Amen" corner. They even blew the shofar. They gave me Pentecostal hand shake, which means I got an offering while they shook my hand. This always helps, but I never expect it. Because they sat down it caused several more people to get in line to listen. A German sat down to listen, but didn't want the gospel. Jesus is watching all this. That is constantly in my thoughts. Great night, no cops. A girl started filming me. I didn't recognize her. Later she told me that I preached with her years ago in Dallas. Yes! She is so cool and her mom drove an RV. Her mom is a preacher and her dad was there too. She gave me a DVD of Kevin preaching years ago. Interesting because watching Kevin preach on YouTube in Jerusalem is the very reason I chose Jaffa Gate. I wish everybody could have seen how many Jews walked by and heard the gospel. Glory to the risen Lamb! Thank you for prayers, friends.

Back at the hostel, my Danish roommates talked me into going to a huge concert. I knew I wouldn't go inside, yet the crowds in the photos caused me to put this on my schedule for evangelism. Also, I began planning a trip to south Israel to get out of Jerusalem after Passover. I knew that it would be wise to cool off the area after plowing it during Passover all week.

April 18, 2014
"Outreach went great. God brought a weeping intercessor from South Africa. God returned the three friends tonight that were in ministry. All three of us women preached. Demons got stirred up tonight. A Christian man from Miami in USA military became like a body guard. So many Jews heard the gospel today. A few mocked. A few asked questions. Great footage coming soon. Acts 4 came alive when a Jewish lawyer told me I couldn't do this here. He told me his friend was a judge. I said, 'Judge? Let's all wave at Jesus. Let's wave to the biggest Judge.' The crowd loved it. His yapping stopped. Anointing was strong on the team. Praise God."

Christian Quarters is so full of Catholic stuff that it's hard to find something legit Christian. Catholics go nuts every year trying to light a candle in Jerusalem during the Holy week. Some even have died being trampled on in the crowd. There are huge posters of the pope in Christian Quarters. I know he is coming soon. I need a vacation before dealing with the pope coming to the Holy Land while I am there. People in my hostel talking about Greek islands got me thinking. Religion stresses me out. Jerusalem isn't a place for rest. It is #1 most spiritually attacked place on the map because of Redemption. Why? Because Jesus defeated the enemy when He shed His blood on the cross in Jerusalem and arose again. Thank you God for the Lamb! IT IS FINISHED!!!!

A Jewish college student from New York contacted me about my Israel videos. He wanted to know more about Jesus. That was worth all the hard week of preaching during Passover.

Gaza sometimes likes to send missiles over to Israel. Hello! Don't do that! I need to preach to Eilat now and then to the pope lovers in a few weeks.

April 24, 2014, "Outreach in Eilat"
I was praying about why I came all the way down here. Then, within thirty minutes a Jewish University student from Beer Sheva tells me that thousands of university students are coming here to party all weekend. He even wanted me to see the lustfest short promo clip on YouTube. I didn't even watch the full minute and turned it off.

April 26, 2014, "Eilat Israel Outreach"
"Jesus walked on water!" Jewish teenager said as he mockingly attempted to walk on water. I chose to preach in a popular mall area by the Red Sea. No problems with police there. I preached a couple of spots tonight. I came home soaking wet with sweat. Many people stopped to listen at different times. Many mockers were out tonight and people laughing at Jesus. Some people thanked me for my courage and shook hands with me. Some had no problem with Jesus. People told me if I preached in Israel I would get stoned with rocks. Finally, a Moroccan guy threw some small rocks. I had to wait a long time for this promise. Praise the Lord! He was drunk on Vodka. I blame the Vodka not the culture. Vodka made me whacko too. He passed out asleep when I left the outreach. Possibly four hundred people were reached in a few hours with the gospel. Thank you for your prayers. I am going back tomorrow to the same place and it will be packed. Shabbat Shalom from the Israeli mission field."

Back at the hostel God was using me with one-on-one chats. This happens all over the world. God brings people to me and other missionaries for us to share the good news. I just had an hour chat with Bar. He's the Jewish University student from Beersheba here in Eilat to party through Spring break. Bar had questions for me about politics, Christianity supporting Israel, Mormons, Catholics and asked, "Can anyone become a Christian?" His name has many meanings. Bar means "harvest" and "wild." God gave me a University student to share Jesus with all the way from the Red Sea. God is awesome. This is one happy missionary, for sure!

April 27, 2014
"Jesus haters were out tonight in Eilat! These teenage boys spit and told me they hated Jesus. Then they kicked my water. They almost got my camera. Not once, but twice tonight they came after me while I stood on an orange plastic soap box. Others sat to listen and even offered me their water. They watched the meanie pants harass me. One girl said in perfect English, "I don't understand English." She and her friends pushed the benches together to sit and listen for the next thirty minutes. They asked why the drunks and potheads don't go to Heaven? I am the bible answer woman now. Praise God!

Next day I traveled for hours all the way back to Tel Aviv on a bus while riding with an Israeli soldier's machine gun touching my leg. Normal life in Israel is to see young people in Israel Army carrying weapons.

April 29, 2014 – Huge airport drama in Israel!
"Praise the Lord! I am in Athens, Greece waiting for a flight that leaves six hours from now for the island to rest, write and read. My morning started at 4 a.m. with a bus driver insisting that I get on his bus because he would take me to the train station. I showed the girl on the bus the piece of paper with the correct name of the train station. She lied; the bus driver lied and took me to the closed train station. The 5 a.m. train station (wrong one) opened and I waited until 5:52 a.m. to get the train. The other train would have had me there on time at 5 a.m. Trust no one! I was wearing my 'Trust Jesus' t-shirt. Jesus is trust worthy. I got to the line for plane check in at 6:15 a.m. My plane was at 7 a.m. They asked me too many questions. Then they informed me that I can't go on this plane. I was too late. Thanks bus driver! They wasted a few more minutes and took me to the ticket counter. When I got there they informed me that I would be forced to wait a day. I would be forced to buy a new ticket. What? No way! I knew I didn't have any money. I couldn't fight it and began to cry and fold my hands in prayer. I begged them to let me on the plane. With tears I sobbed in the Israeli airport to God. "God help me! God help me!" I had a return ticket already paid for. I knew I was supposed to get out of Israel to rest. The enemy was mad and trying to send me backlash for preaching the gospel in Israel. My tears caused the guy on the phone to panic. He called a manager of the airport. I told them they had 25 minutes to get me on that plane. **Please**! They took me somewhere to talk. People were watching me cry. This warrior was tired and breaking down publicly. I was at their mercy. Wearing the "Trust Jesus" t-shirt, crying, frazzled; it is kind of funny now. They brought me to another group to talk. New airport staff said, "OK, we will help you. You will receive your bags another day though." The favor of God came and they started tagging my bag. I was escorted to customs next. So many people helped me! Thank You, Jesus! Then I got stuck at customs. My flight was leaving in five minutes. My tears instantly came because of stress. I couldn't help it.

Three hours of sleep, then epic bus driver failure. Not enough money for the taxi because I needed all of the money I had to eat when I went to Greece for three weeks. Customs waited for that same manager. Then my change all spilled out of my bag. They helped me pick it up. Customs went through my bags and time was ticking away. When customs finally got done, I was put on an airport shuttle. They zoomed me through Tel Aviv airport to make that plane. They even called my plane for me. My customs stamp said 6:57 a.m. with 7 a.m. flight. The lady shuttle driver was mad and running her mouth about the drama all in Hebrew. I cried again. I was so tired. The airline workers were mad when I walked on the plane. All I could do was humbly go to my seat and cry again. My head bowed in my hands with pure worship to God and with Thanksgiving. Trusting Jesus works. Glory to God! Romans 1:16 – "To the Jews first, then the Greeks." Hello Greece!

My bag came the next day. I tried to hitchhike to the airport to save money. A few friends gave me some extra for me to enjoy my vacation. I rented a 4-wheeler very cheap to drive to see the whole island and sunset several nights. Santorini, Greece has the most beautiful white churches with blue tops. I really enjoyed riding around the island just taking pictures and going fast.

May 9, 2014
"Four-wheeler ride was awesome to Oia. I have ridden almost every part of this island now. Hundreds of sunset chasing lovers were there. The castle was full of people sitting on top watching the sunset. I took out "Behold the Lamb" for his vacation photo. People began looking at my lamb like he was famous. Praise God! One dude wanted my photo holding Behold. Quick moment for me to explain Jesus is the Lamb of God.

I ate some meatballs, drank a fresh watermelon juice and had coffee, but not Greek coffee! Yuk! I went into a cute shop that was a spa. You stick your feet in a water tank and toothless fish eat your dead skin. I only paid for ten minutes. The fish munched on my leg more than my toes. My feet sure felt soft after that. Cross that off the bucket list! It was a great day with God and that was the best part. This week I have struggled in prayer. Tonight's hour bike ride home was refreshing. I love being a daughter of God. Bless you friends." You know, people at that sunset clapped. It was such a beautiful moment to hear people not curse, but simply applaud an act of God. Sad, so many people don't know God. My island trip was a blessing. I wish I had just stayed there the whole time, but I forced myself to go to Athens thinking I needed to preach. Nope. I needed to rest. God is trying to teach me balance.

May 20, 2014 Airport Post:

"That was so easy! I am in Israel again. Praise the Lord! It is 1 a.m. and I'm taking a taxi to my hostel. Thursday I go to Jerusalem. I hope to preach Friday, Saturday and Sunday. I'm praying about plans and trying to hear the heart of God. No hope in the pope!"

May 22, 2014

Personal invite to protest against the pope with the Jews tonight in Jerusalem, Israel

"Protest of the pope in Jerusalem was a concert. However, the Jews were really there to protest the Pope and used concert as the excuse. They had singing, prayers, speakers and flyers. I talked to a police officer that said she deals with this 24/7. Police have been called in from other cities for backup tonight with the pope coming to the city. My crazy night started with a teenage girl coming up to me with a clipboard. She asked me to sign it if I was against the pope taking their property (Upper Room). I signed it. Then she asked my occupation. This was the final question. So far so good with me, blending in with Jews. She found out I was a missionary and not even a Jew. She got mad and scratched out everything we accomplished on the clipboard. She began telling all the teenage girls around her that I was a missionary. God opened the door. 5774 on the Jewish calendar is "year of open door." Perfect timing and here comes the Jewish teenagers flooding me with questions. They were mad that I believed in Yeshua, yet still wanted a photo with me. They even tried to tell security I was evangelizing to get me kicked out but it didn't work. The girls wanted to know; why I was there, why I like Jews, what was I praying about? Did I live there? Do I want to live there? Do you know Jesus was a Jew? They called me crazy for believing Jesus was alive. When I began blowing kisses toward Heaven they got even more angry . Rebekah began to help me. They started to pick on her. One girl acted like she would chest-butt her. We talked to those girls for 30 minutes. Later I got my photo with the Rabbi from YouTube. I told him that I saw his video and wanted a photo. Rock on!"

When I first got to Jerusalem my original plan was to stay all week at a hostel. Instead I got there and saw rainbow stickers. That changed my mind quickly. I only stayed two days. The only problem was that I had planned the whole seven month trip in this hostel. A few girls wanted the fan on and a few wanted it off. "Fans off girls" won. No big deal. My dream was to stay with real Jews, until I left again. My new place was a three bedroom apartment with a balcony in the new city Jerusalem with my own room. I even got free pick up from my gay-friendly hostel. Great room to rent and the roommates were born and raised in Jerusalem. I got to share a lot of the gospel several times with the chess teacher. I can come back at any time when I go back to Jerusalem.

May 23, 2014
"Just got home from outreach. Short version: My friends came, because they were still in Israel. They helped me preach. Israeli soldiers got fired up. Two soldiers got on a concrete block to shout their thoughts on life back at us. Brenda noticed Secret Service with police driving up Jaffa gate restricted drive in Old City. Her discernment was right on. Huge leaders from around the world were arriving for the visit with the pope. We ran over to get in the middle and end of the trail to see them. Orthodox looking men began to unload from cars with tinted windows in the Christian quarter by the pope posters. Cameras were snapping. Without even thinking too long I began to preach, "Repent! Woe to you blind guides."… and other strong statements. A lady called me "cuckoo." I am not sure so many people respect the Catholic Church or the pope. There are over three huge posters of him there. Here is a quote from Brenda that day while we looked at a poster of the pope together.

"Is this man being presented as a man of peace? Angela and I disagree. He has come to take a spoil. That spoil includes the separation of Jerusalem, and the ownership of my Zion and the unification with all the denominations under the Catholic Church. Are you ready to kiss his ring and pray to idols? Sorry, I am a Protestant that still sees a reason to continue to protest after hundreds of years of persecution to all true believers." May 25, 2014.

Back at my awesome, private room in New Jerusalem, I am preparing the rest of my schedule from June 4, 2014 to August 3, 2014. A complete stranger game me $500 and now I can reach more nations thanks to his obedience in giving. My roommates know I am going to protest the pope and that I may even go to jail. No big deal. Jerusalem is an exciting city for religious drama. The problem with all the religious is that there is only one real Star. Jesus Christ is the only way to the Father. Pope Francis said atheists can go to heaven if they are good. He makes me very angry with his unbiblical lies always coming out of his mouth. Many Christians believe the pope is the Antichrist. He definitely has a spirit of antichrist. He isn't concerned with true biblical Christianity. The pope wants a New World Order and is combining all religions. People are following right into this trap too.

"For there shall arise false christs and false prophets and shall show great signs and wonders; in so much that, if it were possible, they shall deceive the very elect." (Matthew 24:24)

May 26, 2014 – The pope declared Muslims as "brothers" to the Christian faith at Dome in Jerusalem today. Helicopters are flying all over the place today. I hear them above my apartment. If I don't go preach then I will regret it the rest of my life. Fear hit me hard because of the police beating up people yesterday and so many arrests being made. Let me tell you what Jesus, the real leader of Christianity said about who is our brothers:

"And He answered and said unto them, my mother and my brethren are these which hear the word of God and do it." (Luke 8:21)

"For whosoever shall do the will of My Father which is in heaven, the same is my brother and sister and mother." (Matthew 12:50)

May 27, 2014 was Jerusalem day and I didn't even know it. Here is my journal from today. Great memories!

"Favorite Jerusalem Outreach was today! I walked all the way to where the pope was having mass in the Upper Room. Cops were everywhere and mostly Israeli soldiers. I walked all the way back to Jaffa Gate. I saw about twenty Israeli soldiers. I ignored my fears, stood up and preached any way. After hearing about all the people that went to jail and were beaten by cops, it took the conviction of the Holy Ghost to still get me to preach. God made me His weapon. Praise Jesus! I started with Proverbs 1 about the fear of the Lord and Wisdom crying out in the main square. No one ran towards me with handcuffs. God had me preach on Philippians 5:2 and the beauty of Jesus. I also addressed Timothy 4 about people having itching ears. I preached very hard on Psalm 5:5, David's tomb. David hates evil. The pope is liberal. The pope doesn't fear God or hate evil. Roman TV crew showed up to film me. I pointed into the camera very directly with my words. I said the pope was a liar. Then I gave the true gospel from I Corinthians 15. Many Jews stopped today; more than other days. I made it plain. "You won't get another Messiah. Jesus is your Messiah." My favorite part of the day besides upsetting the pope-worshipers was when a huge group of Jewish tourists showed up. The tour guide was trying to talk about Jaffa gate. I was too loud. He smiled and asked me to come to him. I was wearing my Jesus hat and Israel shirt. He let me speak in his microphone to them. He translated it. The Holy Ghost gave me the greatest gift of the year: to preach in Jerusalem against the pope during his Catholic mass. I got to explain why the upper room for me was special as a Christian. The crowd wanted to know. Not one police issue. God is amazing. Thank you all for prayers and holding my arms up to minister blessings!"

By the way, I made a D in Jewish roots class at BRSM and for God to call me to preach in Israel is the favor of God. Hopefully, more will go preach over there without fear. Praise God!

After the pope left for Rome I went to the Upper Room to clean out all the evil spirits in Jesus name and sang "Send the fire" by William Booth. I also found out a small fire came to Bethlehem after pope left. I decided that I needed to go over there and preach the gospel. Behold the Lamb needed his photo taken in the spot baby Jesus, the Lamb of God was born. Yippee! Crazy how I need a passport to go 45 minutes away. Oh, it's because they call it Palestine. I still call it Israel.

Bethlehem street preacher upsets local nuns
Posted on May 29, 2014

Sometimes when the Pope speaks, I say, "No way, not again. No he didn't just say that." Even the media and other priests have said he was liberal and goes off the book sometimes. Yes, that is the problem with the man that is a leader of the Catholic church of a billion people. Anybody that has a ministry title and a following needs to feel the weight of the responsibility of speaking for God. The leader should always have the Word of God as their final authority, not another book. God's Word is God speaking. You will know a false prophet/teacher by weighing their words next to God's Word. If the two don't match up, then there is a serious problem.

When the Pope entered the Holy Land, Israel had an earthquake and The World Trade tower was hit by lighting. When the Pope left Holy Land the church where Jesus was born had a small fire (not arson) and fights broke out on the Temple Mount to where it needed to close for the day. The Pope said Muslims were Christian brothers. The Bible does not say that. Jesus said his brothers are his disciples, the ones that do the will of his father. The Pope blessed Bethlehem as a Palestinian state. That is wrong as well. Any believer and follower of Christ knows not to split the land of Israel.

Being only an hour away, I decided to go visit Bethlehem, Israel today. There were Pope signs everywhere, even more there than in Jerusalem. A taxi driver insisted he be my driver. He went from fifty shekels to a reduced fare of twenty. I used to sell cars, so I knew how to talk him down; Just keep walking away until he chases me begging for business. It worked. The best part was he volunteered to stay an hour. That way he could give me a ride back. Twenty shekels is only about $6.50. I explained to him I was going to preach. He didn't understand what I was saying. God gave me favor with him. He waited while the police had me in their office. The story begins....

I went downstairs in a church, to the spot where Jesus was born. Everyone was in line and bowing to kiss the spot. I nicely butted in to stick Behold the Lamb in the spot for his photo. If my stuffed Lamb had a bucket list then this would be it for him. A Lamb should be born in a a manger in a barn. It had a lot of Catholic stuff around it all, so I hurried up to preach.

I set my camera up and tied it to something. I was in an open square by the church hosting birth of Jesus. Muslims were everywhere. I suppose cab drivers or had other businesses were occupied by them. They just stood on the wall across from me. Catholic groups came in and out. Plus several nuns walked by me. After I begin preaching a man started to say "SHHHHH!" His "shhh" only made me get louder. I preached, according to my camera twelve minutes. That is all I got. What did I expect? There is a huge Muslim tower in the backdrop of the video. My two Jewish roommates can't even come to Bethlehem because it is too dangerous.

I made a comment quoting the Pope and it upset somebody, so soon after my comment the cops came. Nuns became angry at me. Security and police showed up. I was wise in taking my American flag purse. Ruben Israel told me as I travel, have the American flag. It helps street preachers. The cop was very careful with my camera. He allowed me to take it off my tripod. I had to follow him to his office with the other cops.

There I sat wondering if I was going to jail, wondering if they would slap me like the Roman police officer did and wondering if they would destroy my camera. Let me say these guys were very nervous of hurting my camera or offending me somehow. I told them I spent a lot of money to get there; that I didn't plan on ever coming back. They made phone calls and also copied my passport. They tried to look at my camera several times and even passed it from cop to cop. I kept reminding them to please not hurt my camera. They finally asked me what I said. I didn't tell them everything, just that I quoted the Pope. Oh, ok they understood then. They thought I said something bad about Muslims. NO WAY!! I was very careful. I did bring up Dearborn, Michigan to see if they heard of the city.

90

They offered for me to watch their TV and have some coffee. We talked about the song "O little town of Bethlehem" and I shared that I loved Jesus and He changed my life. One cop was mad that I said Catholics were not Christians. My taxi cab driver saw the whole thing and I told them he was waiting on me. Please let me go back to Jerusalem. After they finished with phone calls, they handed my stuff back. They told me not to speak there again. I said "no problem. I am gone. Thank you." (Twenty minutes at the police department.) The police officer that didn't like that Christmas tune about his city said to me "Jesus be with you."

One security cop walked me out to my taxi cab. He stopped me and asked about my message; why I felt Christians were so different. I explained the blood of the Lamb and that Jesus Christ's blood was the only way to heaven.(John 14:6) This is the guy guarding that church for a living. He may have heard the gospel for the first time. I feel like God sent me for him, mainly, because he asked me to tell him. No one else was around and this happens all over the world. When someone is under conviction of the Holy Ghost, they don't care if I am a woman. They want to hear. He wanted *fresh bread*. Praise the Lord!

As the taxi driver took the visiting preacher (me) back to the bus stop, people starting coming to the window wanting to see me. I think a small stir started. I said "Shalom!" Taxi driver laughed because that is a Jewish word for hello. It was worth the trouble and all the shekels it took to achieve the small outreach. Now, to upload the videos. I am amazed the police didn't ask me to erase the footage. WOW!!

Praise the Lord God of Israel! Thank you Bethlehem for giving me and the world a *Jewish Messiah*.

May 31, 2014

My Jewish roommate just watched the video of me preaching in Bethlehem. I am so glad that gospel message was on the video. After watching, the apartment became very quiet. Looks like I will be leaving Jerusalem on Tuesday morning. A major Jewish holiday begins Tuesday night and no public transportation. I'm flying to Budapest, Hungary on June 4, England, Wales, Denmark, Germany, Netherlands and Sweden. The rest of my time in Israel will be just waiting on the Lord for any divine appointments that He wants to bring my way.
Interesting how God used me to stir up Bethlehem and the next day a suicide bomber was stopped trying to get into Jerusalem from over there. ABC, Huffington Post and LA Times all covered it. My final words as I drove off with taxi driver to the young men trying to talk to us was "Shalom!" The cab driver laughed. The taxi was surrounded by young Arabs trying to talk

to us about what just happened. Yet, I needed to go because police almost arrested me and wanted me to go back to Jerusalem.

Budapest, Hungary adventure

June 5, 2014.

"God used me at hostel to open the with the 18-year-old Hungarian staff worker to hear the gospel."

A couple of reasons I always wanted to visit Hungary: First is because of a young couple I met in Munich Germany at Oktoberfest 2012. They were very interested in our God conversation. Second is because of a man called "Grandpa." For 18 months I lived in a backroom garage apartment of my friend's grandpa's home in Texas. I got free rent in exchange for cleaning his home. He was a nice Catholic Hungarian man that appreciated being in America. I thought of him often as I walked around Budapest. Some people mark your life with amazing kindness and Grandpa was that Hungarian man.

Now, I needed to go preach in Budapest. The easiest way for me to reach the city was to buy the All-Day Hop on Hop Off City Tour. I preached outside the second largest Jewish synagogue in the world. After getting done, I saw a lady walking her pug. I ran to get a photo. God is so awesome. Then I preached outside a big Budapest Castle by a Catholic Church. The city was beautiful and perfect weather. The crowds I reached were fairly calm with only a few stopping to listen. Budapest was one of the cheapest flights leaving Israel. Wizz Air is a new airline and uses very small planes. My evangelism outreaches that day were not in vain and never are because people need Jesus. However, it became clear to me in the next few days that my trip to Budapest was more about getting to Slovakia then Czech Republic to join my friend in reaching his nation. My friend may be the only street preacher in Czech Republic. We were arrested together in Rome in 2013 at Vatican.

"From my blog, Happy Heavenly Messenger", June 16, 2014

"Because I flew from Israel to Budapest, Hungary so cheaply it put me only four and a half hours from my preaching buddy. He invited me over on the perfect weekend. Fireworks show with huge attendance of beer-drinkers, would be there. Then there was a sold out Iron Maiden concert with 10,000 attendees. I had already preached at several spots in Budapest. I decided to go on over for a $30 round trip and stay at his cottage, while he slept in his car for the second night at his friend's house. It was a new faith walk to be in a cottage in Czech Republic with no phone, no shower, no electricity, no Wifi, no car or anyone else around in yelling distance. God allowed me to have this moment for some reason in the future. I love the pioneer life. Giving all for the gospel and worrying about where to shower later. Missions is burning in my heart. Give me souls or I die. Iron Maiden Concert had many hecklers, men pulling pants down to show their butts (mooning), pushing, kicking preacher's soapbox, stealing soapbox, throwing beer, using their hands to signal the signs of the devil, flipping birds with middle finger, cursing, hailing Satan. A man that loved Hitler slammed his forehead into a new street preacher that only came because I was there. He wanted to meet me. My friend told him about me. Welcome to the team, Bro. This is front lines. Next time don't wear a brand new nice white shirt. It was covered in blood and so was his Bible. Unforgettable and I would say on this outreach for sure "no small stir." He went to the hospital to get stitches and his nose seems to be ok now. We made the newspaper in Brno, CZ. The paper said no one listened. Really? I got the impression that they were very aware we were there shining in the darkness with the gospel. Demons didn't invite us. Jesus did. Pentecost Sunday in Czech Republic: classic."

That week on my YouTube thousands began to watch the videos and my account documented most of the viewers from CZ. They were still thinking about the three bright lights they saw that day in their darkness.

Because of my winter clothes and laptop being in my friend's home in Wales, I needed to go back and grab my things. I flew to Luton, England and found a place to stay in an apartment for $20 a night. The man was a very nice Arab and non-practicing Muslim. He was renting out his mother's apartment while she was in America. She didn't know and I was just happy to get free airport pickup. I had my own room and planned out the rest of my European tour in my quiet apartment an hour from London. Luton is full of Muslims and supposed to be a "no go zone" for non-Muslims. I had no clue and briefly preached there one day after eating at a local carvery. There were Muslims everywhere, but no one told me it was a No-Go Zone for non-Muslims. I meet Christians sharing gospel there that day as well. Just not the British First group that gets attacked a lot in England by the radical Muslims. I would love to have meet this group of Christians.

I took the bus up to Birmingham, England to preach the gospel. I accidentally walked the wrong way looking for my hostel. However, a short man my age offered to walk with me. He said he had hardly ever left this city and began to tell me his life story upon my patient approval. He had almost died from brain problems and lost his wife and kids because of her affairs. His heart was so broken and he needed a listening compassionate ear to hear his cries for hope again. He even boldly told me how long it had been since being intimate with a woman. As a minister, people have shared all kinds of stories in the past twenty years. I just view times like these as bringing the church to him. He thanked me for listening and wanted to hear about my travels. He didn't realize we were by my hostel. I just waited for him to feel peace, so I could pray for him and share Jesus. This man hopefully is serving Jesus now. It was obvious God saw his brokenness.

I went to preach in Birmingham and had several small crowds listen. Then, the next day I went to Coventry, England to preach with two brothers from Facebook. We worked hard and preached hours that day in five different spots in town. We had different reactions at all the places. We were impossible to ignore. Man, I enjoyed those guys a lot. We were on the same page with the messages.

One spot got great crowds and children even enjoyed listening. One boy waved at Jesus in the sky with me. I love that! Christians lined up to thank me for coming that day to preach. One lady was a Jewish believer in Yeshua and even sent an e-mail to thank me. Now we are Facebook friends and talk almost daily through Social Media. I wore Israel shirt that day and a

Muslim cursed me out, grabbed his privates and then flipped me a bird. Christians and Muslims do not have the same God. Pope Lies!

I was tired, going back to Birmingham. I saw an open square where I had preached the day before. There was a Muslim table with Koran, on loud speakers and Muslims praying on a carpet. One smiled as if I was interested. I was exhausted and let them know I didn't appreciate their religion at all.

After these outreaches I went to Wales. I decided to give most of my clothes away. It is not worth dragging them around and paying for check in at airport. I was going to mail the stuff home and it was way too much money. It's better to just give clothes away. My family was always doing this growing up and I have never gone without nice clothes in my life. I headed to Belgium by bus and preached there. There were lots of Muslims in Belgium and not a place to enjoy too long. It's not even a big tourism stop for visitors. After preaching, I headed to Amsterdam to preach before going to Denmark to reach that huge concert I heard about while in Israel. God gave me favor with a Christian bookstore owner in Amsterdam that allowed me to give him a small amount of money to hold my bag while I did some traveling. Praise God!

I went to preach on that Monday at Dam's Square and ran into Christians I met two years ago. Also, I met two other guys on fire for God reaching out to people in the area. Small crowds gathered that day and then I had a nice long talk with a guy from Russia.

Next, Copenhagen, Denmark; here I come. I love this city. Most people speak English. Copenhagen has a beautiful postcard snapshot of their colored, bright buildings on the water in promoting their country online. My idea was to pursue this place to preach for an excellent back drop for the video. Upon arrival, a tour guide was taking her break eating sushi. She said she had never seen a street preacher there before. People sat outside eating, drinking and riding bikes by the canal, picture-perfect spot. I began to preach the gospel and immediately a few people yelled back at me in perfect English confessing to be proud of their sins. When I finished speaking, a man a little older than me wanted to talk to me about his depression and how he needed a breakthrough. Gladly, I helped point the way for him and pray for his breakthrough by bringing the Kingdom of God to earth. Next, I went to a huge outdoor concert with some other missionaries in Rockslide, Denmark. They enjoyed watching people's reactions to my bold Jesus shirts. We stayed right on site there in their camper and had many divine appointments. Some of our best talks happened at the Burger King with young people. All I did was knock on the window and tell the young people to come in. They did and sat down. Holy Ghost made fishing there very easy. Thousands of youth were going to this rock concert and would take breaks there. We found several spots to share the Lord Jesus. Vice Magazine even interviewed me, glory to God!

Off to Berlin, Germany! My airline took my one bag that I had on the plane and told me I would get it in Berlin. Never again will I trust an airline. My lamb, money, computer and clothes were in there. For three days, I didn't have my things because they didn't put my bag in the storage compartment under the plane. They took it back in the airport in Copenhagen. I was so thankful to have a missionary pick me up, feed me and give me a home. Without her I would have been stranded at the airport for three days with no money. When we finally got my bag at the airport,

I cried a few tears hugging Behold the Lamb. I thought I would never see my travel and preaching buddy again.

"Berlin: USA college student joins Team Jesus." July 12, 2014
"The other day I was only working camera in Berlin, Germany for a local ministry. A lady on the team that was a local German wanted me to speak and not just run a camera. When I got up to speak this young man with a guitar just happened to be there. His dad is German and mom is American. He speaks both languages great. He told me if I ever needed an interpreter he would help. We ended up doing a song together. The next thing I knew we were talking to four youth about eternity. Today he is coming back to the streets with his Bible study group. Praise the Lord! Spreading revival fires in the nations."

My visit was pretty short in Berlin and it was a lot of fun riding in a car with a missionary that had been there in Germany for 25 years over to Poland. She agreed that my testimony needed to be twenty nations in 2014. We both looked at the map of Poland and she picked a place for us to go evangelize for the day. Amazing how God was so involved in this simple choice.

"The steps of a good man are ordered by the Lord: and He delighteth in his way." (Psalm 37:23)

My blog from July 12, 2014 "Revival on the streets of Poland!"

"Two people on the streets heard me shouting Revival in Poland! They ended up joining in praising the Lord with me. The older man stayed about an hour. Then Jacob came. He heard me and came over. He had never heard the gospel. Jacob was so happy he could be forgiven and said "I am going to pray every day." God moved in spite of Mormons and Jehovah's Witnesses on the streets with their lies. Jacob is receiving my testimony tract here (in photo) and hope he stays in contact with me."

That day was great and it took me some prayer as we drove the streets looking for the spot I felt God calling me to stop to lift up my voice. God truly sent us there to impact that area with the Kingdom of God. Sometimes people over-pray, when they need to stop praying and go preaching. Prayer is a must or there won't be any power behind the words. However, many hide in prayer closets when God is calling them to go standup and speak. Hanging out with God is so much more comfortable. Just don't forget the Great Commission is a command to be obeyed. Oh! The soaking Christians always wanted more of God. For what? What did you do with the last touch from God He gave you? Christians in America can be annoying at times with how they complain while other are getting their heads chopped off for God in other countries. Talking to myself, reader. I like my coffee, Facebook and nice clothes too. God has trained me to be a warrior. So any good thing or strength anyone may see comes from God. He shaped me through fire to be a warrior for Him. *Then the word of the LORD came to me. ⁶ He said, "Can I not do with you, Israel, as this potter does?" declares the LORD. "Like clay in the hand of the potter, so are you in my hand, Israel."* (Jeremiah 18:5,6)

Germany Wins World Cup!

I was staying at a hotel for a few days before leaving again for Denmark. Berlin is known for Hitler and killing Jews. That is one huge reason that I don't even like sleeping in this wicked city. The night of the World Cup I put on "Jesus Saves from Hell" t-shirt and my "America/Israel" hat. The war between Gaza and Israel was going around the clock at the time. I wanted Germany to know this five foot two woman, Jesus-lover stood by Israel. Maybe I should have done that early that day and not after 10:00 pm at night alone in Berlin. Sometimes I can be too risky and God sends more angels. I went to the main train station where hundreds of people gathered to watch the World Cup on a massive screen outside. It was cool being there because ever since 2000 I thought one day God will made me a missionary in Germany. My first mission trip was to Essen, Germany with "Together in the Harvest Ministries." This night was unforgettable and the Holy Ghost spoke to me in the midnight hour after Germany won the World Cup.

Walking through the people I briefly talked to a lesbian couple about my Jesus shirt and then talked to some others. Mainly, letting some guys know I wasn't interested in drinking. I am a preacher. Then I stepped into a crowded zone of fans. A young man with a Palestinian wrap around his head noticed me and Israeli hat. He pointed at me and yelled "Palestine!" Next thing I knew four people who looked like Muslims surrounded me. They were Israel haters!

I slowly turned the camera off. I spoke peace to the moment, took my hat off and protected my camera, hat and me while backing away slowly. No one hurt me. Then my risky radical self went home to the hotel. Father God protected me and I learned a lesson about late night evangelism and wisdom in timing. The German football team's hat is my first souvenir I ever bought on my first mission trip and it is hanging in Motel Honda. When I see it now it will make me smile, knowing I was there on a day of victory for the team.

That night God spoke to me and told me to stop beating myself up for not being a missionary in Germany. My calling is to the nations, not just Germany. The Lord wanted me to stop asking when I was moving to Germany. I asked God for over fourteen years to go to Germany as a missionary. God let me know Germany won and is now number one. My number one missions trip that birthed nations in my heart was Germany. That Germany will always be special to me because it was my first trip. I was just not to assume that I failed by not being there as a missionary. Father God really released me from a burden that night. Now, I understand Germany was just the first of many nations to come.

Somehow I got a plane ticket back to Denmark from Germany and not straight to Amsterdam. I had one day in Copenhagen and WOW what a divine appointment at the single mom's home by the airport. It was not a travel mistake; it was a divine appointment. She needed Jesus comfort. Testimony of Copenhagen home: When I arrived, a different name was on the door. Thankfully, she saw me coming and let me inside her home to my room, where I quickly went. She left a snack-pack with chips, banana and cookies. The room was decorated nicely and I felt a bright warm feeling being there. Her young son didn't speak English and had a cold. He had a backpack with Denmark Viking cartoon characters hanging in the kitchen. Later that night, my host shared her story with me. She had just gotten a divorce because the boy's father was an abusive alcoholic. Deep sigh. Yes, this was a divine appointment. This woman needed a stranger to share with and someone to encourage her on her journey. She was renting out the room to pay attorney bills and had an alias name to protect her from this wicked man stalking them. My heart hurt for her and I shared my story. I also let her know that I was going to immediately pray for her and then encouraged her of God's love for both of them. Single moms don't always get applause. I know because I was and still am a single mom. My son happens to be 23 now. He's my favorite person on earth. This woman was a great host and a mother that protected her child with all her might. The next day, she left a note and went to work. In the afternoon, I walked to the airport admiring all of the homes in the neighborhood, dreaming of one day owning a home in Europe. As I crossed the bridge I saw a billboard advertising visiting Sweden. Right there I stopped to take a photo. Soon I would be in Sweden. Then the twenty nation tour would be over and I would be going back to America. Good-bye, Denmark! Hello Amsterdam, again.

Upon arriving in Amsterdam I found myself staring at the balloons in the flower shop. Especially the airplane balloon, caught my eye. I went to get on the shuttle bus to my hotel for the night. Relaxing in my room, happy to be back in my favorite European city, I began to watch the news. Oh no! Another plane crisis! This time a plane leaving Amsterdam airport full of passengers from the Netherlands was shot down and the plane crashed in the open fields of Ukraine. This was really huge! I needed to find out if preaching at the airport would get me in jail or not. A few seasoned street preachers gave me the thumbs up so I boldly went down there to preach on the property.

Amsterdam airport has a great tourist outdoor sitting area with a large sign that people get photos next to. What a perfect place for an open air crusade! First, I found a luggage cart to tie my scarf to and then tie my tripod camera to. My biggest concern was if I would get arrested. Some drunken Irish man began to heckle me right away and soon others joined for photos. One Middle Eastern man got very upset by my preaching and he cursed me, flipped me a bird and kicked over my camera stand. Thankfully it didn't hit the ground because it was tied to the luggage buggy. The security guard came towards me. They sent me a cute blonde motorcycle cop. He was very handsome and he told me to "behave" and that I needed to lower my voice because of the airport security in the building "up there" (he pointed up) didn't know what I was saying. People called them to complain. We talked about rules between us all. He smiled, got back on his motorcycle, his dimples showing. His blue eyes caught my eye and he gave me a wink. Then, off he drove into the sunset of the Amsterdam airport. I fell in love for a brief moment. Rarely am I distracted by men on my journey. Thank You, Jesus for this grace to not have men issues. Preacher woman had more work to do that day for King Jesus, so I moved across the airport outdoor plaza to a new spot. I parked my tripod and began to open-air preach to those coming and going out the doors of the airport, plus those taking a cigarette break. Coming towards me, about fifteen minutes into my message, was a Russian that appeared to be drunk. He showed me his demon tattoo. I thought it strange as the Russians were being accused of shooting down the Amsterdam flight the day before, where hundreds were killed. This man got it too stirred up and I agreed with airport security to go bring peace to the moment. Hundreds were reached with the glorious gospel. I'm so glad I took the risk that day because it was a hot topic.

Billy Graham once said, "Preach with the Bible in one hand and the newspaper in the other hand." That inspired me to hold up the Netherlands newspaper as I preached.

I took a break to go to the city to get my bags and leave some things at the Christian bookstore on my way to my new room in Amsterdam. I gave up on the camping after my first trip in 2014 to Amsterdam and prayerfully found a new place to stay. A student needed money for his dorm room outside of the city. It was a perfect price and very quiet. I rented it immediately. The place rocked! Free washing machine, which is a rare luxury anywhere. I always research several websites, because some things are too good to be true only because God is setting you and I up for a blessing.

Every good gift and every perfect gift is from above, and cometh down from the Father of lights...(James 1:17 **KJV**)

When I was visiting the bookstore, I bumped into an older, blonde lady buying something. We looked at each other and revival broke out. Ahhhh! My friend from two years ago was right in front of me. This nice lady preached with me and even bought me a gift from this bookstore for my birthday. God is awesome! She said that after I left in October 2012, she became bolder, sharing her faith and she missed me. She didn't want me to leave. What a great testimony of my mission work. Thank You, Jesus, that the Body of Christ is encouraged and challenged. Glory to God!

The next day I preached at Amsterdam Central Station with her and her friend. They helped with videos and pictures. Also, I chatted with some locals. A few stoners talked to me and a woman from Turkey with a nose ring had a conversation. My visit was then spent in my room working on this book and also watching the news about the airline crash on my breaks. I was there for the Netherlands National day of mourning. I cried and grieved with the nation. On my way to Oslo, Norway, I took photos at the airport of flowers, teddy bears, notes, shirts and cards, covering yards and yards of the upstairs, outdoor airport. It was just another reminder why my job as a full-time missionary is important. I want to reach as many souls as I can in all the nations of the world.

Oslo, Norway is no doubt one of the most expensive cities in the world. God graciously helped me find a place for under $25 a night. Again, research is so important. Normally, everything is $40 and up there especially for summer months. My place was an apartment with rented out rooms with dorms all over the building. My first roommate was a Jewish young lady from New York. We enjoyed sharing stories and I especially enjoyed sharing the gospel of her Jewish King with her. She mainly ate Pringles (chips) to save money. Once she said she paid over $30 for a salad. It's true and daily I am careful with budget.

July 26, 2014

"Norway terrorist watch! Right now there is a possible terrorist coming and cops are on standby with guns. News is covering my city, Oslo. The second big issue is as I was walking through the city looking for the Oslo Cathedral, all of a sudden I found another church with Palestinians. The church is supporting them. They have anti-Israel stickers and were selling Palestinian shawls. In 45 minutes, at 4 pm, they were going to be marching against Israel at 4 pm and ending at that church at 5 pm."

I decided not to go preach at the Palestinian protest. I then realized how risky it was wearing the Israel shirt on the plane, then walking with it on, alone after midnight to my hotel. God has His hand on me, no doubt about it. While all the craziness in Oslo was going on and all the newspapers had headlines of terrorism on their covers, God brought me a different Chinese pug two days in a row. The photo I have of a pug in my lap is so beautiful. The pug is smiling so big.

My Jewish roommate left early and then two college-age, Bavarian Germans showed up to be my new roomies. There was a street preachers in Oslo that many of my friends knew, but I couldn't connect with him. He didn't believe in women preachers. I couldn't avoid his nation or city just because he didn't agree. Obviously, I believe in what I am doing or wouldn't be doing it. So, there I went!
Here is my Facebook post from the outreach that day in Oslo.

July 26, 2014
"Will you submit to me?" an Oslo man asked me today while preaching. "No, I am busy trying to reach all the lost souls, sir." Jesus came to seek and save that which was lost.

One girl hugged me and cried, thanking me for coming. One man came out of his comfortable outdoor bar to shove me. One lady turned off my camera and one guy said amen. Many make-up professionals lined up to listen from inside a store in the mall.

One man asked if I believed in fasting because I drank some water after preaching in the hot sun. I said "yes, but I am not a Muslim and not fasting on your fasts." He was mad about the message and stormed off saying "Jesus is not God in the flesh." That is when the Christian young man showed up to stop me from preaching. Later at the second spot, which was private property, several cops showed up to make me leave. Also, because I upset people the police wanted me to stop. The cop said, "There is a terrorist threat right now. We are using caution." I said, "all the more reason people need Jesus."

20 YEARS CRACK/COCAINE FREE!!!!!

Before leaving Oslo, I got a good-bye note from the Bavarian girls and met some dudes from Spain dressed in Spanish clothes. They reminded me that I had written on Facebook in February of 2014 "I want to go to Spain, Holland, Hungary or Norway." God told me to go to Italy. Later Father God sent me to Holland, Hungary and now Norway. 2015 I will be in Spain to preach in February. I already have my ticket, praise God!

Allow me to take you back in time for a few minutes so you will understand and appreciate my victory. Some readers may even cry at the goodness of God and how kind He has been to me. God has made me a trophy of his grace.

July 31, 1994, Chattanooga, Tennessee on Hwy 58, I drove to a bar, sixteen days clean and sober, knowing that my sobriety was going to be given away for a long night of partying with the gang. We all listened to a country music singer with shoulder length, blond hair and blue eyes, dressed like a cowboy. He sang out the latest country hits from his Karaoke machine, hoping one day to become a star. Later, God saved this Karaoke Cowboy and made him a preacher. Praise the Lord! Back to the story… We all began to drink to the point of getting drunk. The shame of failing was huge because sixteen days before that I was so humble. I was on my knees by my father's chair, broken crying before God for freedom. Crying, pulling my hair and feeling demons trying to take me to hell. My skin felt as bugs were marching inside my arms, up and down. My teeth would grind and I couldn't find any peace. I was only twenty-three years old and my son was three. He was asleep in his room while his mommy was in the living room, warring with demons all around me. I had allowed these demons into my life the very moment I walked away from Jesus at fourteen years old. Demons invite more demons and their goal is to destroy God's creation. It is a way of mocking God, when Satan attacks what God values.

Sixteen days before, after wrestling with demons and crying to God for freedom, my failure caused me to not trust myself. After 3 am I woke my parents to tell them that I was not just alcoholic. "Mom and Dad, I am also a crack/cocaine addict."

The next day I went to rehab. I was kicked out for cursing on the fifth day. I got a job at a bar. I remained sober until July 31, 1994 and then, there I was with a bottle in my hand, wondering why I was back in this darkness, knowing it would destroy me.

Addiction is a horrible Hell on earth. When you do something that you don't want to do, it is because you are a slave to sin. I had no willpower. So many people assume you can just stop and go back to normal. If it was that easy, rehabs would not be so popular, even with the rich and famous. Some people never make peace with God and take their own lives, trying to end the demons attacking in the head, soul and body. Suicide won't end the demons. It is just a guarantee to spend eternity with them, if someone chooses that route.

That night after the bar closed I craved a crack rock. So did three of my guy friends. They drove us down to where popular crack houses could be found in the area. At 4 am we walked into a house of three men I had never seen before. Now I was the only girl among six men. All I had left of my paycheck was $10.00. The black young man placed a small, white rock in my white hand. Then, I just stared at it. The moment was deep for me because I began hating crack and hating what it had done to me. Crack wasn't my friend. Crack was destroying my life, causing me to steal food and steal gas. I was hanging out in an abandoned house with a dealer in the dark, while he cooked more. I was lying to my family and it almost made me become a prostitute. I had already sold myself to a few people I knew in cheap ways, just never complete strangers. This crack was about to take me into deeper sins that might jail me or kill me. That night God was in the crack house with me. I knew God, by His Holy Spirit, was dealing with my conscience and was the good voice I heard reasoning with me to let this be the last one. July 31, 1994, after 4 am, I smoked my last crack cocaine rock. Did I know that it was my last? No, because it took six months for me to stop thinking, almost daily, about it. It was a hard walk, changing my lifestyle, when partying was all that I had known since seventeen years old. August 1, 1994 I entered "Another Chance Recovery Program" and stayed in it for eight weeks. I continued with recovery at AA meetings for two years. One and a half years after being sober I yielded to the kindness of God that leads to repentance. I was born again at a Geoff Moore concert. On March 1996, in Rome, Georgia, I truly became a new creature in Christ and the old things passed away. Pretty cool that my first place to go to jail for preaching was in Rome, Italy. I was saved in Rome and jailed in Rome. Praise God! It's nice how God buys me plane tickets and all the devil did was give me drugs, alcohol and abuse.

Does this make more sense now, why I am grateful? I must tell you something that may shock you. The churches I went to didn't teach me the meaning of "gratitude." Do you know where I learned about gratitude? Alcoholics Anonymous taught me about gratitude. "If you are grateful, then do something. Gratitude is an action word," said Lance, an old timer, when I was six months clean and sober. His words changed my life. When I was born again, I continued with my gratitude. That is why I don't wait for a church to send me. The Bible tells me to go preach to the nations. I don't wait for an evangelism partner either because the woman at the well was so thankful for her encounter with Jesus. She ran into the city to tell the men what just happened. Zeal can be a good thing, when wisdom is leading the Way.

The woman then left her water pot, and went her way into the city, and saith to the men, Come, see a man, which told me all things that ever I did: is not this the Christ? Then they went out of the city, and came unto him. (John 4:28-30 KJV)

Twenty years crack-free and traveling to twenty nations was my way of saying "Thank You, God." I didn't know God was going to send me to twenty nations until I got to sixteen nations. That is when I knew God was building a testimony for me for His glory!

Again, I prayed to God, "Where do you want me to preach on my twenty year anniversary of being crack-free?" The answer came quickly and made me smile: "Amsterdam, red light district where marijuana and prostitution are legal."

William Booth (founder of Salvation Army) said, "Go for souls and go for the worst." My pastor used to quote that around Christmas, when he would talk about the Salvation Army bell-ringers. Steve Hill now has this quote on his grave site in Texas. He also mentioned two years ago that when David Wilkerson went in the Red Light District he ran out of there sick. I can't get my courage from my pastor or my pastor's pastor. If I am going to boldly walk through the Red Light District, preaching again, then my strength must come from the Holy Ghost.

I can do all things through Christ which strengtheneth me. (Philippians 4:13 KJV)

My plan for my third visit in 2014 to Amsterdam was to stay only two days in a hotel by the airport and after preaching the gospel on my twentieth anniversary date, grab my bag from the Christian bookstore. From there I would go to the hotel to wait for my flight to Sweden on August first. I didn't want to stay in any hostels in the city because it was Amsterdam's gay pride week. That made my upcoming crusade even more challenging. Amsterdam has canals and I had a few thoughts of being thrown into the water. In 2012 a man grabbed my "Fear God" banner and tried to pull it out of my hands in the Red Light District. I like danger, like salt on potato chips. It makes things more exciting if there is a chance my life is in danger. There sure were a lot of riots and preachers suffering for Christ in the Word of God. As an ambassador of Christ I expect the same when I step out into the darkness.

<u>July 31, 2014</u>

Red Light Revival! Tonight in Amsterdam was one of the best crusades all year. Twenty years ago today I smoked my last crack rock. I felt the Lord leading me to make sure I was here July 31st to share my powerful testimony of freedom that Jesus gave to me. My T-shirt said, "Jesus saves from Hell" and I walked boldly in a legal pot smoking bar and gave my testimony while they were toking on doobies. Then I walked into the gay district with rainbow flags all around. The crowd got so big that over eight people were recording. People everywhere were listening. Holy Ghost invaded their gay/sodomite pride with the good news of the gospel. The message went out that they needed to repent!

Then I preached by a tattoo parlor and the crowd grew to about seventy-five people. A worker even got me water. I had none and really appreciated it. After that, I went to another bar and preached. I was at an outdoor bar talking to a small group that was drinking. I noticed a magazine and said, "Is that a gay magazine?" The guy said, "yes". My response was the same as with cult literature. "I would like to rip it up," I told him. After that bold statement, behind me were the Amsterdam police officers. They let me know they were there. We stepped away from the bar about seven feet to talk about what I was doing, because people called to complain about me upsetting people. They have a hate crime law and no doubt I was guilty for breaking it. The Amsterdam police said, "If we get another complaint against you, you will miss your flight tomorrow. You will go to jail." I couldn't carry my normal cameral on a tripod with me because some of the hookers don't want people filming them. I wore my spy camera glasses like I did in Jerusalem the day the pope was in the Upper Room. No one ever notices they are being recorded. The quality is not as good, but if I got wrongfully arrested, it is on film. When they were done giving me my super strict "no, no's" I went to my next spot to preach. As a woman on a mission for God, I wasn't done yet. Time to go reach some hookers! Four of them came out of their work booths to laugh and listen. I told them that they didn't have to be whoring anymore. I stopped whoring. "You can let Jesus change your life. You girls can become a preacher like me. I am a good role model. We need more preachers." There were other points from the Word of God I made in this area to the hookers, drunks, potheads, pimps and whosoever's. A few people even yelled at me from windows in the upper buildings. I made my rounds from spot to spot in the Red Light District shouting for people to repent and believe the gospel! New cops came again just as I was close to my goal spot in the area to complete the circle. They wrote down my passport information, then left. Thank You, Jesus, their threat was only a threat. I needed to finish my crusade and God is in control, not the Mafia of Amsterdam. Glory to God! I finished by talking to a couple of guys in the area that had sincere questions. They seemed inspired that I would confront sin in Red Light District. As I walked off, some man yelled about hating my orange shoes. Several people yelled, "Shut up!" Well I can't shut up because I have Good News! Thank You God for getting me off crack twenty years ago today! Bless Your Holy name Lord Jesus!

I went into the Christian bookstore to get my final bag of things to take to my airport hotel to wait for the next day trip to Sweden. I gave him my tent and sleeping bag to bless someone with.

He asked me to pray for him. I did right there in his store. I looked down to notice rings that seemed to be wedding rings for sale for only ten Euros with "Jesus" on it going around the band. I wore one for years until it broke. I always wanted a new one. Happy anniversary, Angela! I felt the Holy Spirit wanting me to buy it to remember my twenty year anniversary, crack free and the three crusades in Amsterdam in 2014. Amsterdam is my favorite and God is so thoughtful to me with His perfect gifts. Being single and alone most of the time is one reason I am so love struck with God. He is always being a hero and a good husband to me. I promised one of my mentors when I returned to the states to never marry a poor man. Jesus buys me plane tickets to Paris for Valentine's Day. A man would have to be pretty amazing for me to stop traveling and preaching to settle down in one city and live in same zip code more than 2 weeks.

"For thy maker is thine husband..." (Isaiah 54:5)

Country #20 is Sweden! I picked Sweden because it was one of the places I really wanted to go the most. Also, it was one of the cheapest flights back to Florida. Months before I got there I found a very unique hotel/hostel in Stockholm with free shuttle to the airport. I knew there was only one day I could go to the city and preach anyway. I was grasped with excitement upon finding an old, retired airplane with attached deck, sitting in a huge parking lot near the airport. My room had four beds. One night a girl stayed from Korea, then left. The next night an older lady from USA stayed and left very early. So, my last day in the airplane/hostel before checkout felt like my own room. I sat there looking out the airplane window on my bed, with such thankfulness. God allowed me to travel to twenty nations in 2014 in 7 months.

A local Sweden street preacher from facebook joined me to preach. We started noticing rainbow flags on buildings and buses. Oh no! I hope it is not Gay Pride Weekend, because I just left Amsterdam. They have had gay pride days over the years. I had preached at eleven gay pride marches, but it is not something that I volunteer for, believe me. Jesus said, "Follow Me and I will make you fishers of men." When I preach with teams (only teams) at gay pride marches, I compare it to fishing for piranhas. The Bible lists about 25 characteristics about the sodomites in Romans chapter one. A girl told me in Arizona once, "You are just jealous because we are special." I would agree; sodomites are special. God says their sin is "worthy of death," in Romans 1:32. Christians that say "Don't judge me because I sin differently." Who came up with that wicked quote? Jesus said "Go and sin no more." We are not even supposed to be sinning. Christians are supposed to be saints. That is why Jesus said for us to Shine. The reason many Christians don't want to do evangelism is because they are still sinning every day in thought, word and deed. If that is you, stop it. Let Jesus be Lord of your life and walk in holiness.

And whosoever was not found written in the book of life was cast into the lake of fire.
(Revelation 20:15 KJV)

Chapter 12

20 State USA Gospel Tour

August 3, 2014 my plane landed back in America with rainbow lights going back and forth across the ceiling of the plane, with pouring down rain on the outside of the small windows. My friends that I ran into while preaching in Jerusalem now were in Fort Lauderdale picking me up to take me to their family's home for rest from the long seven-month mission trip.

First thing I bought was an eight-wheeler Swiss carry-on suitcase because I had my heart set on going back to Europe as soon as possible. Then, I went to get a pedicure with royal blue for Greece and Israel.

Now, we were about to drive to Orlando. Everybody wanted to go to Disney World. My host family wanted to take grandma to TBN Holy Land. They invited me to come and rest in the room there while they all went. My car was parked close to Orlando, so this was the perfect plan.

While I was in Europe traveling around from place to place, a man in his fifties asked, "What will you do when you get back and your car doesn't start?" That comment put me in a bad mood. I was kind of hoping the same God that helped me get to 20 countries would now help me in America. Motel Honda didn't start. My sister in Christ jumped it and off I went to preach in Bonifay, Fl. Bonifay, Florida church was the first church to ever ask me to speak after nine years of open air preaching. Now, they were the first church to open their pulpit after I returned from long victorious mission for kingdom of God. It was great to see so many faces and share about what God did overseas.

Time to go visit my family for the first time since UTC drama. All I wanted to do was cook them a huge meal with my own ministry money from the nations. They all came together for a meal and tried new food; humus, pita bread, Greek salad, Italian cheesecake, peach tea and pasta with peas and bacon that I discovered in Nice, France from my hostel manager. It was lots of fun watching my family try new food My mind would drift back to Greece, Italy, France, Germany and Israel as we had this meal. The fellowship was sweet and nothing was said about the past. Praise the Lord!

However, time to get back on the American mission's gospel tour. I hugged them all and we said our good-byes. I slept in a hotel and arose to drive to Indiana. Monday, back with the Smocks for campus ministry. They have done it 35 and 40 years each. I was caught off guard when Brother Jed asked me to be the first preacher on campus. He was getting me ready right away for USA missions.

There the students were all walking by to class on the first day of school in Illinois. I began to lift my voice and ride the waves of campus ministry again. By the end of the week, I was tired yet, hooked again. Those college kids need Jesus so bad. They need someone to tell it like it is.

Immodesty seemed to be a bigger problem than usual. So many girls wear short-shorts. They are supposed to be getting an education, not going to the beach for a tan. This was so embarrassing, but I had to address the issue a lot. As an older woman of God my role is to teach younger women some good basic life skills. I am on campuses for hours. My number one goal is to make sure they understand the gospel. When you are preaching for hours you need to have some knowledge on various topics. Students will ask you questions. God gives me grace to deal with them.

An Indiana State University student asked me one day, when it was 105 degrees, "Do you love us?" He may have asked because I had only been in America for three weeks and was talking a lot about Europe. My response was that of a compassionate mother. "Group hug, everybody!" I told them we needed to bond. Several of them wanted a hug. Cindy got the photo for me. I do love college kids, but don't need to prove it. God doesn't have to prove He loves anyone either. God demonstrated His love through the Cross of Jesus.

My journey took me state to state, campus to campus and I preached in a new church in Illinois while in the area. The youth enjoyed so much. I could have preached that night and no doubt the youth would have come back to hear more stories.

Students blew cigarette smoke in my face, mooned me, spit on my shoes, threw tater tots at me, clapped for bestiality, gay lifestyle, marijuana, yelled in my face, cursed me, flipped birds at me and played "Highway to Hell" while I was preaching. Just another day in the office in America. Some of these kids are like wild animals. I would hate to see who gave birth to some of them. Students dumped buckets of water on me, threw ice at me and sent me hate mail about burning Bibles.

Let me pause right here. I must tell you that when I got to Ohio to rest, every day I was daydreaming and praying about when I could leave America again. Oh, I was in compete obedience to share the message with the college students. Yet, when the Illinois church gave me an offering I quickly went to the bank to buy a plane ticket to Finland, leaving February 7, 2015. I wanted to go there, to Spain, and to UK to preach a full circle around their colleges and universities.

Quickly after the purchase of my Finland ticket more tickets were bought. A dream was being built for the next season, as I was still actively preaching in this current twenty state tour. Spain, England and Netherlands were added to the schedule. For several years I have wanted to be in the Netherlands for tulip season. There will be many people in the Netherlands during that season, yet how many of them even know the God that invented the tulip?

Daily Eastern news: August 26, 2014
"Preacher Sparks Controversy on Campus" by Stephanie Markham new editor. "Angela Cummings of Highways and Hedges Ministries was preaching religious salvation and having heated conversations with students about two to four pm Monday on the South Quad…"

"Cummings responded that she was only preaching out of concern. 'I love you enough to help you get right with God,' she said. 'My job is to plant a seed,' she said. 'What is that seed? It is the Word of God.' She plans to visit Western Illinois University on Tuesday."

I only used a few quotes from the article. My website has several news articles from over the past few years. Even bad press can be good. It shows that I haven't been ignored. Lots of press comments have been lies and their isn't much I can do about that.

When I decided to go back to the University of Vermont this year the family I was going to stay with got nervous about persecution. The nice Christian lady contacted two churches. Neither one were interested in my "confrontational evangelism service to their community." My host home was afraid someone would find out they were housing me and she would lose her job. By God's grace I just paid for a hotel three nights because it was the week of the 9/11 anniversary. Being in my car wasn't an option because I needed to stay up to date with possible terrorist attacks on America from Islam.

My host family ended up home all week with sick children. Not everyone is happy when an evangelist comes to town that will challenge status quo. A lot of Christians will fall apart when persecution comes full force into America. I bless these people and wish them well. I went to this liberal, high-rape-stats school anyway, because last year very large crowds came for days to hear the gospel. I am going to share with you two days of Facebook posts from the University of Vermont outreach 2014, then a small clip from the school paper. Remember, I am alone on this campus. No Christians came to help me.

September 11, 2014
"Tyler is a girl! University of Vermont Outreach day two. How to start this update when so many things happened on campus today. So many lost sheep without a shepherd. Students looking over my shoulder waiting to look at what I had circled in my Bible and why I circled it. It was like they never met a Christian. A few of them read out loud what I had circled. Then, read that I had Hell Fire written at the top of the page. Yes, Hell, it is in there and both pages were red letters. I explained 'red letters' today. Tyler is a cutter that gets angry when I call her ma'am and has forced her friends to call her Tyler. I honestly couldn't figure what she/he was yesterday, but showed compassion towards her, seeing her pain in all that cutting up and down her arms. She allowed me yesterday to hold her hand and pray. Today she came for most of the meeting. She even brought a gay friend to campus church. Praise the Lord! She looked beautiful today with a feminine hair tie and girl clothes. I affirmed her lady likeness. She seemed ok with it because she wanted to get her picture with me three times. These kids were not behaving well.

The police showed up in the suburban and began videoing the meeting out of his window. Students were sodomizing one another with kisses and showing porn to each other on cell phones. They tried to stick a camera in my face. I wouldn't tolerate it. The Jew that mooned me yesterday came back to campus church. Today he let me put oil from Israel on his head. I sincerely prayed for him. God brought so many Jews. My "Jew radar" was at an all-time high. I wore my Israel shirt and hat today since it was 9/11. I read Isaiah 66 and did a pop quiz with the Jew in front of a large crowd. I said, "Where is the Lord? Where is His Footstool? "He wasn't focused at first, but then he got right answers. Some of these students are starting to seriously quote me. Things I have taught for two days. It is not easy because they are cruel. They constantly say how much they hate me. Yet they stay. I gave them the gospel several times throughout the day. I enjoyed sharing on Ishmael and Isaac on Mt. Moriah, explaining who the Passover Lamb is: Yeshua. Jesus is the Lamb of God! I studied that today before going to campus church. Holy Ghost brought the Jews to hear. I asked who was a Jew and they began to raise their hands all across the audience in front of me. I told them they are the apple of God's eye. They still need Jesus, like everyone else, however. One student said, "How do you do that? How do you get 43 people to listen to you?" I said, "You counted?" "Yes," he says. I told him that Holy Ghost draws the people to hear the message. At 4 pm I walked away to do my promised interview with Jake from University of Vermont newspaper. After the crowd left, the police drove away. Just another day in the office.

The very next day was horrible! It was my last day before going to Maine to rest three weeks and work on the book in silence. My cabin was paid for. I was in a good mood, ready to go rest from all the ministry and traveling in 2014. When I got done with the outreach I called my teacher from Bible school. She said, "I told you to rest." This was my last day and thought it would just breeze by without too many problems. This campus is full of demon children though. They stripped down and begged to be filmed. The only girl I met in three days that said out loud she was a Christian was a lesbian that took off her shirt and bra for the crowd. Jesus came to call sinners to repentance.

It got wild. While I was preaching on top of a concrete bench at UVM a student laid down next to me on top of a girl. He begins kissing her and purposely bumping me with his shoulder. Then, I was forced to the side of the bench. He then attempted to rub my leg while he was on top of her kissing and stuck his hand around my ankles. My next reflex was to protect myself from falling off face first on the concrete ground. He did not have permission to touch me and it was disgusting the way he was rubbing my leg. Their cameras were rolling and so was my camera. It was tied down on the bike rack to protect me. I hit him in the back twice to get him off my ankles and to quit touching my leg sexually. He got up quick and checked his lip for blood. The girl was not even his real girlfriend that day. The police came and walked me off campus. I was banned for 6 months and have decided to dust my feet off from this campus.

Here are some comments from my Facebook friends; most of them are active in evangelism, so they could empathize.

KS "Be encouraged woman of God."
DT "Sister Angela is not crazy. She loves Jesus with all of her heart."
JJH "Proverbs 23:13-14 – Do not withhold correction from a child, for if you beat him with a rod, he will not die. You shall beat him with a rod. And deliver his soul from Hell."
EK "The fist of fury."
AC "Glad you are ok."
CZM "Wow Angela. That is really intense. John the Baptist Cummings."
DR "You did just fine sister Angela. I fully agree with Brother Ruben."
EN "I love that crazy Jesus Lady!!!"

LCF "Wow! We are definitely living in the days of Sodom and Gomorrah! I don't judge you sister. I pray for you!"

JW "Praying for you sister! May the Word of God being proclaimed run swiftly through this campus and everywhere the Lord allows your foot to tread. America is lost. So, so sad the hardness of hearts.

DA – "Only the strong survive."

JG "Nothing like a couple of kidney punches to ward off sexual perverts!"

EG "Wow, those people need to keep their filthy hands to themselves! And to have the nerve to then be offended when you defend yourself."

KV "He deserved that. I've had to push people off of me and have come close to laying someone out. I wouldn't think anyone, man or woman would put up with some perv feeling on them. You did nothing wrong.

DC Angela, I would have don't the same thing. But not as nice. Continue preaching to these lost dying students.

JG – "Good for you. Jesus would have used a whip way before they grabbed your leg. Hell fire awaits them. Thank you for serving the Lord in a blue state demonic stronghold."

Ruben Israel (my California pastor) "You have the right to defend yourself and that shirt does not say welcome as per door mat. If you allowed that today expect worse tomorrow. You did fine."

My interview with Jacob was partly used in the three articles written that week. However, the campus police banned me for six months from coming back. As I was escorted by police woman off campus, Jacob wanted an interview. The police wouldn't let me. I am not the only campus preacher this semester that has been lied about in the press and made to look like a hater. When I read articles now, I always read with caution, waiting on some lies in print to slap me from the page.

The Vermont Cynic - September 16, 2014 by Jacob Holzman
"At our Shabbat dinner that Friday (she) was one of the main topics of discussion, with everyone wondering how something like this could even happen on our campus." Vogel said.
"There are multiple outlets for students who felt hurt or need help because of Cummings' presence. These options include the all-inclusive spiritual and religious life council," he said.

That is all I am going to quote from that article. It isn't important for you to read what I said. Read the ridiculous statements from the school offering these pervert strippers, mooners, spitters and mockers counseling because of me, somehow wounding their dirty little hearts. Repent Vermont! What a bunch of crybabies saying they were hurt somehow. I was the one molested and grabbed on the ankles. It was nice to have on video, the pervert checking his lip for blood after my two strong punches. Hopefully he will not be another rapist on campus. The very next day this city marched against sexual crimes. What a bunch of hypocrites. I can dust my feet off from Vermont now. The school even posted a photo of two lesbians kissing each other with me preaching with Christian flag in the background. Vermont is an unreached people group in America. God bless you students and may He show you mercy.

When I left, my GPS took me to the Canadian border to cross through Canada to get to my Maine cabin. I attempted to back out, but it was too late. Four Canadian border patrols ran after me forcing me into Canada. They took everything out of my car. I live in my car, so that made me even madder. They didn't put anything back right and my bed was a complete mess. When I got out of Canada I was crying from the stress. The Vermont cops forced me to give them my camera. Now, some college brat was posting videos all over social media of me punching that student. I haven't even gotten a chance to tell Facebook yet what happened.

I drove all the way back to UVM to get my camera. The cops were embarrassed. They knew they were wrong. They should have arrested the pervert. This will reap a harvest. My stress level was high and I had a long way till the Maine cabin. My bed was messed up, thanks to Canadian police, so I slept somewhere in Maine in my car for a few hours.

Perhaps quitting the ministry for a job would be convenient right about now. I even saw "Now Hiring" signs in Maine. Sometimes I dream while awake on bad days about quitting the ministry to live in Maine or Finland. Then God reminds me that He owns me and that life outside His will would be horrible. My cabin was so nice and it took me a few days to enter the full rest of the Lord.

Hollywood contacted me again with three e-mails offering me a job on a TV reality show. Some people wanted me to take it but I knew preaching the gospel was my calling. When I open-air preach, I feel like I am doing my greatest act of worship toward the Lamb on His throne. My voice lifted up, shouting Jesus name makes me feel the most alive. Go away to Hollywood for a year to live possibly 100 cameras on me in the wilderness, just because I only have $30? This is a test, not an open door from God. People that don't value open air preaching are the ones that tried to push me into taking job. I love preaching the gospel. Also, the people that maybe jealous of my travels and being supported are the ones encouraging me to take the job. One thing I know about being a traveling evangelist is not all Christians are happy for me. Jealous spirits can blind the love for the lost souls being given the gospel.

There I sat in that cabin with $30, tired and needing the comfort of God Almighty to run this race with patience. When I rested in the Lord with full trust that God was in control, then blessings begin to come in. Several people began to give as I rested for the next assignment. My biggest blessing came on Rosh Hashanah (Jewish New Year) when a church in California put me on their monthly mission's support list. This is my first church to give monthly. I'm glad I trusted God. An invitation came for me to come be a part of the SOAPA (Southeast Open Air Preacher's Association) Conference in Atlanta. At first I was like, "no way, I am in Maine." Then when Ruben posted it, the Holy Spirit confirmed that I needed to go to the "John the Baptist Support Group." This kind of fellowship is needed for me, like vitamins and water. Maine cabin sure was a blessing. I did not give into Hollywood. My mind was focused on preaching the gospel around the world by faith. My gift is not for sale. Hollywood seemed to want a controversial evangelist on their Fox show. God had a greater plan, than a TV reality show. I already have my own reality show on YouTube. Praise God!

Before going to Atlanta, I needed to stop by Atlantic City and New York City to preach with the team there. All my plans changed because of needing to be in Atlanta by October 8th, 2014.

New York City firefighters for Jesus! I will never forget my trip to New York City in 10/4/2014.

"Back at host home after long day preaching the gospel of Jesus Christ. The team was an amazing group to be with. Day started with just my sister in Christ. We tried to preach by 9/11 twin towers memorial. The cop told me very nicely to move to somewhere else; this was a place of silence. He asked if I would preach outside St. Patrick's Church. Yes, I would. He looked shocked. Then he told me that a lot of foot traffic was by the fire station 9/11 memorial spot as well.

I went with my new friend to the New York Fire Station. The two police officers there were informed that I was going to practice my freedom of speech rights on that sidewalk by the station. What a great backdrop for the video. I had on my royal blue Israel shirt with red and white striped skirt, with my Israel and USA hat on with a backdrop of American Flag on the fire station. My outfit matched the video. That was not planned. The main reason I wore the outfit was because it was Yom Kippur. My heart is for the Jewish people and New York City is full of Jews. When I told the police that I was going to preach, his response was "Sound professional." The New York City policeman acted like a woman with PMS. He said, "I don't have time for this."

Seriously? These cops dealt with 9/11 and a woman preacher is more stressful? As soon as I began the crusade I started with a song all the politicians sang after 9/11, "God Bless America." However, I changed the words to the song. A man that was connected with the fire department asked me to stop. He didn't like my revival fire outside but no way I would stop preaching. New York City needs Jesus!

The New York Fire Department opened their doors. They turned on their lights and sirens to drown me out. They honked all throughout my message. By God's grace my natural voice still could be heard over their horns. Glory to God! I told the people that I was just as much a firefighter as they were. Firefighters for Jesus! This video has gone viral since that day and one blogger wrote about it.

I preached by the ferry dock and a lady got so stirred up. She started preaching too. Spit was flying and she was giving so many altar calls. It was awesome! We preached John 3:16 together. God sent me a Jew and I enjoyed picking on him about his Messiah. He started the conversation, then hated my answer. He walked off mad with his pink umbrella into the city.

Later that night the team was all together having a showdown in the subway station with Harry Krishna's cult members. We all gave them the gospel. I rebuked them for wearing pajamas at 6 pm in the evening. I brought them a strong reality check that they only have a ponytail and are in a cult. Time to get a new life. Maybe no one has ever told them how silly they appear. God doesn't want these young people wasting their life away in pajamas in a New York Subway singing the same cult song over and over again. The conviction of the Holy Spirit was resting on them. The leader of the cult became miserable and angry. That is a sign of a sleeping cult member coming awake.

Before going to Atlanta I stopped by Rabbi Cahn's church on Sunday in New Jersey. Monday I went back to ESU (East Stroudsburg University) in Pennsylvania and had nice crowds that day to preach to. Several students asked questions and a Muslim called me "Extreme."

Soon, I arrived for the night service in Atlanta for SOAPA. I immediately gave Ruben a pin from Israel that I had bought him. He wore it as he preached that night. Truly wonderful to be in a room full of street preachers, many whom I have worked with across America. Some, I was honored to meet for the first time. A couple of men there didn't believe in women preachers, but changed their minds for just the weekend. One told me to my face and Ruben told me about the other guy. We preached together at a few campuses and then at the Atlanta gay pride march on Sunday. SOAPA gave me a slot to share my journey with others of God sending me to the Nations with gospel. Praise the Lord!

Well, God opened three more churches for me to preach at in October and November, 2014. I certainly have enjoyed being with all these believers after a long, lonely season in Europe. Then I went to two more states to preach and made it twenty states when I got to North Carolina. The fellowship was great there, as well.

My forty-fourth birthday was special this year, being with my family. My son and his girlfriend got me a card with Jesus on it with a twitter account and a lamb. It was very thoughtful and fit me perfectly.

My next mission was originally scheduled for February 7, 2015 to Finland. Plans have changed so I could preach the gospel at the Christmas Markets in Europe. I saw the photos in July and have a strong desire to be there. Yet, I knew God had me in America. I changed my ticket to go on December 10, 2014 and found a family to watch my car for free for five months while I am gone.

Why street preach?

Now, this goes for future men and women street preachers. This also applies to all of you that still are not convinced in open air preaching being a Biblical method for reaching lost souls:

Mark 16:15 And he said unto them, go ye into all the world, and preach the gospel to every creature.

16 He that believeth and is baptized shall be saved; but he that believeth not shall be damned.

Jesus said "GO." Jesus said "PREACH." Where did Jesus say to go preach? Jesus said "Preach the gospel to every creature in all the world." I shouldn't have to explain the world part. What does "PREACH" mean? I am choosing to give you Noah Webster's definition of "preach" because he was a great man of God.

http;webstersdictionary1828.com

"Preach, verb intransitive (Latin proeco, a crier: precor.)

1. To pronounce a public discourse on a religious subject or from a subject, or from a text of scripture...

2. To discourse on the gospel way salvation and exhort to repentance. To discourse on evangelical truths and exhort to belief of them and acceptance of terms of salvation. This was the extemporaneous manner of preaching pursued by Christ and his apostles.

Matthew 4:10 and Acts 10:14

Preach, very transitive: To proclaim, to publish in religious discourse. What ye hear in the ear, that preach ye on the housetops. Matt. 10:7

How many church folk are guilty of telling street preachers to disobey the Great Commission to try a new and improved way of reaching this generation?

Repent if you are guilty of stopping a preacher that is proclaiming God's Word to the lost! I have had Christians stop me while I am reading the Bible aloud. Shame on you, if you have done that. I forgive you. Please don't get in the way of those of us trying to reach the lost.

United States

113

Europe

Australia

Israel

Asia

This was my third free cross made in Asia.

"I was told I couldn't carry a cross in China, but I did anyway"

Praise God!!

Chapter 13

30 countries in 14 months! Glory to God!

December 10, 2014 to February 15, 2016

Welcome back readers. My goal was to end the book by letting everyone know that I was heading back to Europe and UK on a five month missions adventure, but after twelve days into the adventure, God added Asia to the schedule for the whole summer of 2015. I never wanted to go to Asia, however plans changed and now I want to share the journey with you.

December 10, 2014 – I left my car in Fort Lauderdale, Florida and a Jewish believer in Jesus took me to the airport with my one full suitcase. Copenhagen, Denmark has one of my favorite coffee shops called "Joe and the Juice." As soon as I arrived I got an Immunity drink with an avocado sandwich.

My first roommate of the European Christmas Market Tour was from China. She worked and went to school so the place was quiet for me to recover from jetlag. As much as I had hoped to avoid a cold, it happened. My body went from warm Miami, Florida weather to freezing cold in Denmark. My roommate heard me sneeze and cough a lot. She never complained about it. Her kindness made me want to go to China. I had never thought about Asia much. Meeting her was a divine appointment and hearing her sad story of parents divorcing filled me with compassion.

Europe Christmas preaching begins with Copenhagen, reaching many people waiting to enter the markets outside the train station and then a thirty minute train ride across to Malmo, Sweden. My health was still not so good, but I felt compelled to go anyway. My time was limited in every city. It was St. Lucy's day and I had hoped to see some Swedish culture that night. Apparently, Malmo isn't a big St. Lucy party animal city. I only saw a few people with candles on their heads. The huge line for the church having a Christmas program helped me reach many people with the gospel. When the last person in line was inside the church, that is when I walked the streets of Malmo. Suddenly, I ran into a group of Satanists. They were such good listeners and asked many questions. At this point I was so thankful I had chosen to leave American in December instead of waiting until February of 2015 for the original ticket.

Prague, Czech Republic is one of the most romantic cities in the world for Christmas. Oh my goodness, when I got to my room, my window opened to the city. My original plan was to stay with a lady on airbnb but, I felt like I should cancel it. The location was too complicated to get to from the airport. My new place, a four-star hotel, was $25 a night with breakfast. There was one of the largest and oldest castles outside my window to the left. Right in front of me was a mini-Eiffel Tower that lights up at night. This was just the beginning of the greatest Christmas of my whole life. When I was making my Christmas Market Tour, the photos of Prague were so amazing that I had to go see it for myself. Wow! How do I even put into words how beautiful it was? The atmosphere of Christmas in Europe was glorious with all the colors and lights. Growing up at the Cummings house, I always put the angel on the top of the tree, possibly because my name means "Angel". Outreaches in Prague were great and Pavel joined me one night speaking their language. I did reach people that spoke English all over the city.

The beauty of the place and being away from everyone I knew got me thinking about what to do in 2015. Did I really want to return to America in May of 2015? What if I went somewhere cheap and preached the gospel all summer? Soon I was watching blogs on YouTube that teach you how to live cheaply. One video that impacted me the hardest was some tall, skinny guy blogging about living in India for $10 a day. I don't want to go to India, but I didn't want to go back to America either. There was also another video I watched that changed my plans and mission schedule for 2015. A street preacher in Bangkok, Thailand said on the video "Come to Bangkok. The world is here." Without asking any one's advice, I went to Norwegian airlines and changed my plane ticket from going to Florida in May 2015 to flying to Bangkok, Thailand. This was how the Asia Gospel Tour was birthed, only ten days after leaving America. My Copenhagen roommate from China made a big impression on me.

While I was in Oslo, Norway these Thai women told me "You should go to Thailand and get a $5 foot massage. Amazing what God uses to help me get interested in a place, because it sure wasn't rice. Asia is full of rice. I would rather eat French fries.

As soon as Thailand was booked I began thinking about where else to go in Asia. The next place was Hong Kong and then Singapore. While I was in Prague eating right after an outreach, a couple in the restaurant said "You should come to Singapore. We will celebrate fifty years as a country in August of 2015." I kept the invite in my mind and was thinking, "Where in the world is Singapore anyway?"

Twelve days gone from America I had discovered that China declared 2015 as the "Year of the Sheep." How could I ignore this knowing I carry a stuffed sheep all over the world with me. Behold the Lamb and I needed to go to China in 2015. This was Behold's big chance to reach China. Someday maybe Behold the Lamb will have a cartoon show on Christian TV as world traveler. I try to help make him famous. He has over 300 fans on his facebook page.

It is almost Christmas now and I am enjoying Salzburg, Austria. My dream was to come here for Christmas to ride a sleigh on Christmas day. Because of my preaching a few church services in America I pre-paid for this out of my own money.   That way no one would stone the preacher for spending $100 for fun. Because of the preachers that abuse finances, its hard sometimes to have a fun day. Someone might throw a fit. Preachers need to have fun days, just like everyone else. God doesn't mind. It's the abuse of finances that is wrong.   Two days before Christmas I added Chiang Mia, Thailand to my schedule for $48.00. Stop planning 2015 Angela and go enjoy Austria! I have loved Europe for fourteen years! This was a dream come true being there for Christmas.

Silent Night was written in Austria at a small chapel in a village close to Salzburg. This was on my list of fun things to do. The sunset was so beautiful on the water and was packed with thousands of people. I drank some non-alcoholic hot cider and I enjoyed hearing the song in German.

Christmas day my hostel had three girls from China in the room. They encouraged me to not be afraid and that many young people will speak English when I go to China. God usually sends strangers to encourage me on new things. Some believers only can believe so much and then they put limits on God. God is amazing. We shouldn't limit God. Stop right now and pray for more faith. Ask God to show you where doubt and unbelief are in your heart.

Christmas day I walked to the bus stop to wait for the tour bus driver to pick me up. Australians were inside the bus. They explained how it was summer in December so they came all the way to Austria for some snow. There wasn't much snow and my entire year of 2014 I wanted snow and prayed for it. One time I saw snow from a bus in Italy, but it was never anywhere on my whole journey. Now, December 25 we got up to a city in Austria to ride a sleigh in the snow. As soon as the bus parked the snow began to fall from heaven. Christmas was a huge part of my childhood, so seeing snow made me feel like God's favorite girl. Thanks Daddy God! Riding the carriage, eating alone with a view and then going into an old church where no one was so I could worship God, was just a great day. It was time to take a train from Salzburg to Vienna. The day after Christmas and snow was now on the ground in Salzburg and a lot in Vienna. It was so cold! My heart was so full of joy being in Austria with snow.

My outreaches in Vienna, Austria were filled with many lost souls. I preached outside a large Catholic Church and had an outreach in the city center where many teenagers gathered to ask questions about having faith in God. Matthew from Poland has been writing a lot and is excited about my month in Poland coming up. When I booked Poland it was because it was one of the cheapest places in Europe for a month and a great place to rest. Also, I needed to plan the year in prayer and some fasting.

My train ride from Vienna to Warsaw was filled with several divine appointments. One girl had never heard the gospel and suggested I come to her city some day in Austria. Comments like that are encouraging and then sad at the same time. Another reminder that a Catholic filled country doesn't mean they are born again followers of Jesus. Many people will follow a religion to the grave even if it is even because it is how they were raised. I have added Graz, Austria to my 2017 schedule. I didn't forget her request. Not sure it is her city, but I am going anyway because she asked me to come back to Austria.

My room in Warsaw was like a home to me. I had a bed, desk, window, balcony, washing machine, bathroom and kitchen all on my floor. I was lost in the middle of the night trying to find the house and a big Polish taxi driver followed beside me making sure I got there safely. I was too cheap to give him twenty Polish dollars. My room was only $326 for December 30, 2014 to January 30, 2015, by the way.

My short one day visit to Poland in the summer of 2014 was another reason I wanted to revisit Poland. Matthew was my son's age and met me at the big mall in Warsaw on New Year's Eve. I had some supper, while he sat waiting on me to finish. He gave me a small note that he had prayed over and gave to me. I knew this was a special man of God that was in front of me, not just a rebel wanting to tell sinners how much God hated them. Matthew may have been a young believer, but he was seeking to be inspired and encouraged.

January was a month of planning. My dream was to start in London and go to Wales and do a full circle around the UK in a two month period. This got booked during the month. My Israel ticket for the fourth Blood Moon outreach in September was booked during this month. I saw that a Russian cruise went to four countries cheap and Visa free from Finland in February. I did a quick fundraiser and four women of God chipped in to cover this outreach. I even got interested in a man on YouTube from the UK during the cold winter month of January. My heart was open to the possibilities. Maybe this Scottish man will meet me on the UK gospel tour and we will fall in love. That didn't happen and he disappeared after two month of Skype calls.

Matthew, however wanted to travel and preach the gospel like I was doing. He didn't even have a passport or any money. I knew, however, that God wanted me to continue encouraging him. The Holy Ghost told me to even pay for him to come to Finland a few days. That wasn't easy for me. I barely get enough for my own travel expenses. He was so happy when I told him that he was going with me to Finland. He wanted to come to Spain as well. I suggested that he pay for that one. He showed up in Spain to preach the gospel with me. While we were in Poland we preached in Old City University, outside the Catholic churches and inside a Catholic church as the service ended. We had a great laugh that night. I suggested we RUN to avoid possible arrests. His English wasn't very good but, his heart was pure gold. I accidently got on the wrong train one day that had no machine to pay for tickets. After this a man asked for my money. I wasn't sure who he was and I did something stupid. I let a stranger hold my passport when I got off of the train. He was holding my passport and trying to get me to give him lots of money out of an ATM to get it back. Just like a Hollywood movie, I grabbed the passport and took off running for the nearest exit. I ran as fast as I could to make sure he didn't follow me. I got to Starbucks completely freaked out to share the drama with Matthew. He didn't understand my story and what happened. The Starbucks cashier understood and explained it to Matthew in Polish. We all laughed at how I escaped with the passport and no written fine. Never again did I board that green Polish train.

My last night in Poland was spent talking to the guy renting a room next door to my room. The first time I met Thomas he had on a "Mary, Mother of Jesus" tee shirt with wild graphics on over it that were scary looking. When I shook his hand, I felt compassion for his soul. He asked where I was going next. Then I shared with him my hopes of him getting saved because I didn't want him to go to Hell. When I gave him my personal testimony tract he held it to his heart and asked for another one. Praise the Lord! That was a happy ending to my Poland visit! My flight was at 4 AM and Matthew was going to meet me there. My landlord drove me there that early in the morning. I miss that place. She made me feel at home. I rarely stay anywhere a month in my journey. This place is special in my memories.

Matthew and I were now in Finland to preach the gospel. God was stirring something in Matthew to believe God for provision in missions, just like God taught me to trust Him years before. He didn't have a passport yet. He couldn't come with me to Russia in a few days. I sure wanted him too, though. He continued seeking God to be a traveling evangelist and for the money to come in for a passport. We sure did have fun preaching all over Finland.

January 31, 2015 Helsinki, Finland

Matthew and I used a 24 hour pass to go into the city looking for lost souls. We had a man show us cocaine and marijuana after we brought up Jesus. Demons were stirred up in so many people. One girl came to us twice for help and prayer. She admitted mental problems and Jesus knows how to heal a messed up mind. She asked Jesus to forgive her and save her the second time. She does have a bible. The girl, Annalise seemed to have some more hope after prayer. Another man hadn't slept in months and was ok with prayer. He didn't want to get saved though. I told him he wouldn't find rest until he surrendered to Jesus. Teenagers in small groups stopped to listen and even sit down. We spent time with them and they wanted my testimony tract. Some teens standing far off walked all the way over to ask for a tract too. That is a blessing. Europe has always enjoyed my tracts. I remember Florida State University students sticking my tracts down their pants and ripping them up. I put up with whatever place God sends me to, even if they treat me like that. They are treating Jesus like that, not me. I try not to take it personally. I just prefer overseas work. We got on a bus with a group of gothic-looking teens all LGBT. We talked with them, though we didn't even know where the bus was going. The Holy Ghost just said "get on the bus and help them." One girl almost cried, telling me about her childhood. She was under conviction. They all were. First they said they were living in Hell. Then they all boasted that they were happy. Heartbreaking seeing these lost souls on bus. We shared with them awhile and then got off to go find more lost souls. Next, we went on a few trams and metros preaching as we went. It was a great night and we found the university station. We preached there briefly as well. Finland is full of interesting people and we recognize that the human heart is the same wherever you go; undone… without God's love making a lost soul whole. We will go back out in the morning, then the afternoon. Thank you for prayers everyone. To God be the glory!"

We ran into some Hell's Angels bikers from Holland as we went preaching in the freezing cold the next morning. I confronted them with gospel and they told me to F off. The famous cathedral is Helsinki despite the cold and snow was a great place to reach the tourists. Hey, you must figure out how to reach people somehow in the cold months. I am glad not all my videos are in summer clothes. This missionary journey around the world is to inspire believers how to reach lost souls in all seasons. Praise God!

Feb. 1st, 2015 Helsinki, Finland "Demons and angels in Helsinki well, what story to tell first? The middle aged man on the tram pulling sweater over one eye talking to me. Then, him his pistol. This was after we preached to nice size crowds in the metro. Crazy eye guy with pistol even mentioned "Spain and Poland." His demons knew my schedule and knew Matthew wants to go to Spain with me from Poland. Next story of the night was about the showdown in the Metro and started with a magic man. I decided to invade this area with gospel and drive out the darkness. Crowds begin to leave magic man's show to visit the gospel light show. 2 security police came to tell me to stop! Apparently, my preaching disturbed Finnish people. Asked them what law I was breaking after no response I continued my gospel preaching to lost souls. Crowds stayed. Skinny jeans magic man left defeated by the preacher woman with REAL power. Holy Ghost POWER! Muslims were in the crowd listening attempting to praise Allah. A hippie stuck in the 70's shows up with long dreadlocks full of demons. His constant harassment only increased the Metro crowds. I opened the Word of God to Isaiah chapter 9 to teach on character of the coming messiah, Jesus Christ. Hippie demon man hated the words spoken. I told him "If I cast the devil out of you that green slime maybe in the garbage can from all his demons." Matthew was quietly hidden filming the showdown. Suddenly, "Angel Grandma" shows up in the metro crusade. She was glowing and started a chat with her to shift focus on growing potential riot at hand. Hippie man was dangerous. She came at right time and when she saw my Jesus t-shirt things shifted to more on Team Jesus. This new older lady with red hair and kind blue eyes says to me "I will be right back." She had a praise egg that she shook in praise to God for her tunes. In the meanwhile, I had to escape into the candy store to protect my camera from Demon man because he spotted Matthew with it. Since Matthew was new at revival or riots kind of meetings I had to help him, me and camera. I handed the camera on the tripod to cashier of Candy store to hide under cash register. Funny because she didn't know me or him but, sided with me. Candy store clerk forced demon man to buy candy. While he was in his pockets getting change I quickly grabbed tripod back and detached camera to stick safely in my backpack. Now, the tripod was like my police belly stick. Go ahead make my day! Looked out the door of Candy store to see "Angel Grandma" with a microphone, amp and singing to Jesus. YES! That is what we need to do to silence the enemy raging right now. Let's worship the Lord together and it worked. Dreadlock demon man left back into his darkness. He didn't want free yet, so I was not going to cast any demons out. He liked his demons. We continued to worship God and left in victory!

Bye Matthew! See you again in Spain. The Russian Cruise was my next adventure and under $200 for 4 nights with 3 buffets in price. Cheap way to get to Russia without a visa and visit 2 other countries on the cold winter cruise. First stop, Stockholm, Sweden and extremely cold with snow everywhere and more coming down throughout the afternoon. I preached the gospel several hours at the large University without too much hassle from security on campus. Praise God! I had a great meal as well with fish next door. My next stop was Tallinn, Estonia. The gospel was proclaimed in the city center drawing the attention of 3 young teenage boys that were atheists. They were very interested and allowed me to challenge their doubts. Praise the Lord! My third day, St. Petersburg, Russia and I was nervous about this outreach because when Ruben came to Russia to preach at Olympics he was arrested. His photo with snow on him in Russia with Jesus t-shirt inspired me to want to go as well. Photos are powerful like that. I wore several jackets and t-shirts, but leaving my last t-shirt for the outside of clothes to be my banner to reach people with to get message out even more as I walk alone through the streets of Russia. Before my outreaches even begun I noticed a pug and got to stop for hug with photo of it kissing me. That was nice token from God. I went inside the Russian Orthodox church shocked by all the people I saw in lines to kiss picture of Mary and surrounding pictures of dead saints to pray too. The place reminded me of Polish Catholic churches and the culture that is there as well. I wanted so bad to preach inside, but held my fire. One reason is because not everyone would know what I was saying. I am mature enough to know this, plus it could get me in jail quickly too. My plan was to see what God sent me there to do and do it. Then get back to the boat in time to go back to Finland. It was hard to stay silent watching people wipe pictures of Mary with hankies so they can kiss it. I went outside and preached close by church. Several other places throughout I gave messages of the gospel. A few people during the day did speak to me in English. One girl had a very upset grandmother at home scared USA would invade Russia one day. Interesting talk we had close to the onion dome shaped beautiful cathedrals. Everything went fine and mission was over. 3 countries in 3 days were reached with gospel for under $200.00 Good investment and when I arrived back in Helsinki, Finland the next day I was broke because skype automatically withdrew money from my account for phone bill. I called my Pastor for advice about Russia on skype phone and forgot to turn off auto pay for Feb. GREAT! Now, I have to ask a stranger for 3 euros just to get me to my room for a few days. There stood a young Chinese guy my son's age named Jack from Beijing that had just got off Cruise to visit his first day in Finland. He was a student in Russia and loved Americans. God used his love for USA to start a chat with me first. Next thing I know I was showing him Behold the Lamb telling him 2015 was "The Year of the Sheep" in China. I gave him my testimony tract. We became friends that day. He gave me 3 euros and I gave him change from other countries that were leftovers in case he ever needed change in those countries. I was so thirsty and didn't pay for a buffet on boat in pre booking. Thankfully he was kind enough to get us both waters. I was dehydrated and begin to get relief from water instantly. All that preaching drained me. Jack told me his sister was getting married in June in China. My eyes got big as I quickly asked 'WHAT CITY?" I invited myself to this new friend's sister's wedding in China because I knew I would be in China in June, well if Hong Kong approves me a visa I will go for sure. Tickets were already bought as an act of my faith in God's favor. We stayed in touch by Skype and Facebook after that day. His family welcomed me to come to wedding in China. God is awesome! Sometimes being broke causes divine appointments, but I still don't like living that way. Being broke is horrible feeling. Everyone can say amen.

My new room was incredible with white wallpaper listing popular cities all over the world. Great place to make some videos with unique backdrop. I had reindeer soup there and another Finnish sauna with pine flavor in this sauna. My original plan on this mission's trip was to leave USA on Feb. 8, 2015 to start an adventure, but a friend got me all worked up over possible terrorist's attack in Dec. 2014 on USA leaving boarders closed from leaving country awhile. This thought bomb made me quickly rethink my plan and changed this ticket bought in Sept. 2014 to leave Dec. 10, 2014 to add a Christmas markets tour before Finland. My month is Poland was only because it was one of the cheapest places in Europe to stay not knowing God had a young preacher named Matthew there ready to be launched into full time ministry. God is incredible in all His ways. Instead of original date of Feb. 8, 2015 of my arrival into Finland that very date became a day that a Pastor from Ghana picks me up in his station wagon in the snow to come preach to his congregation of believers. Altars for filled with saints wanting prayer and the spirit of prophesy came on me as I ministered at Living Word church. Pastor took me to my hostel after church across town because it was cheaper than the other place. Finland is not a cheap country.

New hostel was full of Romanians and tourists from other countries. I felt uncomfortable there, but had to make it through the night. The next day I had a flight to North Finland very cheap in attempts to see northern lights. My dorm was a mixed dorm with men and women. Cheapest place in the city so I had it paid for several days to hold my bed and bags. That night late as I was resting from victorious night speaking at church a Huge giant man walks in dorm. He looks for an empty bed. There was one above me and 2 empty across from me. I laid there wondering what was about to happen. He picks the bed across from me and turns on his bed light. The fumes from his clothes and body hit my nose. It was the worst smell of a homeless man I have ever smelled up to this point. His hair was curly. His hands were rough. Feet covered with old rugged socks with no color to them. He looked at me and begin to eat his chocolate. My stomach hurt from the smell. Soon he left again. I choose to fix his bed so the staff would know someone snuck in to stay there. Maybe I should have not messed with it. Woops! He came back at about 3 am noticed his bed was messed up. This giant looked angry and hit his pillow. Within 15 minutes I was packed. I left extra things in my locker that was prepaid. Do I contact the staff to say this man snuck in to steal a bed? Or do I just on to airport to sleep to wait for my next flight. Because I lived in my car and have spilt my own urine on me by accident trying to pour it out the car door in the middle of the night. My heart choose compassion. He needed this bed, more than this preacher needed her rights to enjoy her bunk for night. I went out into the winter cold air with snow covering the streets at 3:30 a.m. I didn't get settled in at airport until 6 am for sleep. God's love is beyond the beauty of words.

Rovaniemi, Finland is way up by the arctic circle. You can pay 50 cents to get Artic Circle stamped on passport, but I choose not to spend the money. I hitchhiked my first ride from airport and then several times throughout this trip too. Even the good looking middle aged blonde police gave me a free lift to look for Northern Lights one night. They informed me it was really cloudy and possibly would never see them that night. They were right. I tried. There was some serious fun for me in snow. Wooo hoooo! I found a place for $20 USA at Santa Claus village to see an Ice Restaurant, Ice Hotel and a place in the back to ride a sled. Time for the missionary to have some FUN. I really enjoyed it and reminded me of my childhood riding snow with my brother down our hills in Chattanooga, Tn. My next day I went to University of Lapland to preach the gospel. No one was outside, so I boldly walked into cafeteria to give a message. My voice was loud enough to reach them all. Some students continued talking ignoring that a preacher was sharing the glorious gospel all the way from USA. When, I left I walked through the snow talking one on one with a nursing student from Iran. I gave him my testimony tract. He had never heard the gospel. Praise the Lord! His soul was worth the $100 plane ticket. I doubt I will ever preach in Iran, but I can reach Iran in North Finland. After this trip I returned to Helsinki briefly

128

to await my next trip to warm coastal Spain. I love you Finland! You are beautiful. Sledding at the Santa Claus village was fun. It was cheap and since I hitchhiked so much there. $20 was in budget to have fun day. Someday, somewhere God will show me the Northern Lights. I will wait in anticipation for the light show of heaven.

Barcelona, Spain is a cheap European city. My hostel was full of wickedness. They found out quick I was a preacher of righteousness and tried to upset me with playing music about Sodomy. I called my booking company on Skype for permission to leave with refund. They allowed me to go. It took a month from this hostel to return the money though. Spiritual warfare! I wrote an honest review of place and it affected my money return. My next hostel is where Matthew from Poland had rented. I liked being there. My roommates were from Ireland and became Facebook friends. God brought me 5 pugs during my Spain missions trip. Matthew mentioned to me his greatest heart's desire was to go to Israel to preach the gospel. Just like a mother to a son I stayed on him about getting a passport. We preached all over this city together and had nice crowds listening at big Catholic church in city center.

Valentine's Day I meet a man with a broken heart over losing several family members. He ended up crying telling me about his pain and he was only waiting for his employer to pick him up. The Holy Bible declares "God is near the brokenhearted." This was a divine appointment of Love for his soul. Precious Lamb of God.

Matthew and I went to the famous football stadium for our last outreach. Thousands of people were there for game and we took turns preaching. He had a divine appointment with Jews from Israel. We had a huge last laugh together when I jumped in the back of a family photo of an Asian family with big smile with Barcelona stadium in backdrop.

Matthew left for airport back to Poland. I decided that night to go sleep at airport because of my early flight to the United Kingdom. This is a night to remember because the airport was too cold, so I attempted to go to sleep in the women's bathroom by the toilet a few hours. I simply got my Greece beach towel to lay on floor, the laid on it. Around 4 am I woke up feeling that I better get out of there before the cleaning lady finds me to kick me out. When I heard "Ola" from above my stall then it confirmed for me to get my stuff quick and go. She walked out to tell security on me. I got up and quickly got stuff together. Calmly walked out looking like a woman that just used the WC. Security came in looking for a crazy woman on floor. She wasn't there. Oh yeah, I slept free in the bathroom in Spain. Bye Bye Amigo, hello United Kingdom.

United Kingdom let me in without any questions except "Where are you going?" My passport was not overwhelmed with stamps, yet. Which made it easy to get in the country. I am glad he let me in because my rent was paid for 2 months everywhere including plane ticket to leave in April to Amsterdam. I waited awhile at coffee shop chatting with locals until my bus ride was ready for Wales. I came to do a full circle around the UK starting in Wales. My guest house in Wales was not there for my first night there because of her own ministry schedule. I went ahead and paid for a hostel in Cardiff. The problem is the hostel worker was new and didn't think I had really paid because of the website booking company. Cardiff was cold and raining that night. It was after 10 p.m. and I almost had to go outside to sleep because I no extra money in bank. 2 months of rent was prepaid, but the life expenses were low at moment.

It was a week where I was really empty in my bank account and waiting on an offering to come. Desperate for help I asked a college age young man on sofa drinking beer for help. Maybe because he was with a girl he wanted to impress her or he really was this giving. He stood up to cover me and paid the bill. He gave him extra for my key deposit even. I thanked him. Then went to my room feeling like a loser. The next morning, I went downstairs for breakfast to eat. That desk clerk was still there and looked humbled. However, his pride stayed silent. It took the female manager working to do his apology. She said "We owe you an apology." They were new with this booking company and yes, I really did prepay. They refunded me money. Praise God, I wasn't broke anymore. This is a huge example of the power of a $20 offering. Some people are too embarrassed to give a $20 and so they chose to not give at all. Imagine if someone had of gave $20 and it was just sitting in my account. I could have still gotten a refund. It was just humbling to ask a young man having a date to help me is all. Think about it, don't be afraid to give just $20.00 to a ministry. It doesn't have to be me. I used to give $20 to missionaries monthly. My giving to other ministries was not only to help them. It was sowing into my future. God says "You reap what you sow." I wanted to be a full time missionary. Now, I am one. Praise God!

Wales didn't turn out like I thought it would, but ended up a great blessing to speak on Gospel Ralph show on St. David's Day in the capital of Wales. I spoke about revival. Steve Hill died while I was in Wales the year before and now I am talking about his legacy on this radio show. God gave me new friends in Wales to add to friends already there. Next city on my UK circle was Birmingham, England.

March 5, 2015 "Demon at store knows my hotel!!!" Praise God, my Muslim run hotel has not shut off my free Wi-Fi yet. I just thanked them for the nice room. Now, let me tell you what just happened. I just got to Birmingham, England like 28 or 29 hours ago. I haven't been talking to anyone or wearing Jesus t-shirts. I have been in my room and getting ready for my trip to preach in Coventry with friend the following day. Because I need to eat I walked to a store blocks away from hotel. As I reach for a meal deal on the shelf a homosexual starts manifesting demons next to me. My response was to ignore him, get food and go eat the meal. When I got to trash can to throw away garbage he walks outside and starts talking crazy to me. "Are you that lady preacher talking about God staying at _____ hotel? I was shocked. How did he know I was a preacher? How did he know where I was living for the next few days? Demons told him. He had some strongholds. I admitted to be a preacher, but would not confirm to him my hotel. He says next that he is a Roman Catholic Pagan and begin to name gods he worshipped. He said that his gods were more powerful than Jesus. That comment offended me, because Jesus is King of Kings and Lord or Lords. I pointed at his demon in his eyes and begin to pray for his soul. He went nuts on me. He got in my face telling me about how he will get his sisters of some local Coven. He told me next that he was a wiccan. I laughed at his demons. I told him he needed Jesus. That the blood of Jesus would set him free. That is when he couldn't take anymore of me and pranced off like a girl on a runway model show. My hotel was too far for him to have seen me come out of it. The enemy was trying to spook me before I begin preaching in England. Welcome to the Home of Harry Potter Witchcraft."

Coventry, England outreach went really good with Deborah. She is a Jewish lady that follows Jesus that I meet the year before there while preaching the gospel. We became friends and stayed friends. Cops tried to move me from several spots throughout the day. There were good crowds at every spot we went to along with individual talks with seekers. After the outreach I came to her home for Italian meal with her family, watched Elvis and went back to Birmingham. She bought me a card with dog on it, that I still have with me.

Birmingham outreach drew hundreds of listeners throughout the day. My intention was to go to the bullring to preach. That is where the Muslims openly worship on rugs and play Koran on speakers. I never made it there because crowds drew somewhere else. Praise God! Open heavens over this city and God was bringing the souls to the feet of Jesus. Someone got a great photo of a 14 year Muslim listening to me on one side while an angry middle aged Jewish women debated me on other side. There I stood in the middle of it all with USA bandana and Jesus saves from Hell t-shirt on with my banner. One heckler stayed hours with me and he was a lot of fun. His armpits stunk bad, but he was a good spirited young lad. A girl told her father to please buy her a bible after talking to me. That was smartest girl all day. A Christian bought me a horrible cheese sandwich with drink, but loved her heart. She thanked me for coming and a college aged girl interviewed me for school project.

Liverpool, England was next on UK circle tour. Home of the Beatles. University of Liverpool had Islam awareness week at University. Sounds like a great week for me to bring an awareness to how horribly cruel and wicked this religion is and expose it. After I begin preaching I meet a Christian passing out gospel tracts. Normally he doesn't work up there. He suggested for me to preach in city center. I stirred up too much trouble with my Islam awareness speech and overheard someone mention the police were coming. England has a hate crime law and no doubt I just broke it. I slowly walked off heading in direction of my hostel many blocks away. A Van pulled up with 3 men dressed in black that got out and slowly followed me. I went into a Turkish food store and told the lady I was being followed, please help. She showed me the way out the back door, just like an action movie. I changed my Jesus t-shirt and walked home appearing to be a normal college student. When I got home I downloaded my video, recharged everything and thanked God for safety. I went back down there later and preached to many people in line for a rock concert. Ate curry chips with a new Christian brother wanting to be a Doctor someday.

Next morning, I wanted an adventure. I decided to go to train stations and choose whether to go to North Wales are another England Town. Chester England was the winner. The Jehovah's witness cult packed up and moved places when I started preaching. An older English lady thanked me for preaching because the youth were listening and asking hard questions. The Chester police showed up while I was preaching to the youth at my 2nd spot. I was given an

131

ASBO. What is an ASBO? We don't get these in America, so it was pretty funny. The red-haired cop had his tall English hat on and muscles popping out his shirt while writing me this ticket. ASBO means "Anti-Social Behavior Disorder." This must have gone on my record because my next trip to UK caused me trouble with immigration. I was accused of making a little girl and never saw any little children. Hey Chester, just another day in the office for me. It was just mostly youth the whole time flipping birds, singing about weed and wanting selfies. Chester police gave me the ASBO with a map of city. They banned me from their city for 4 hours and told me where I could be only during that time in city. Basically he wanted me to go back to Liverpool. Well, that was no small stir. Later, a Christian wrote about my ASBO in the British news. He defended me and shared a photo he took of me in Birmingham, UK.

My next preach in Liverpool got me covered with purple wine, nailed with strawberries to head and popcorn thrown at me by angry teen girl in circled crowd in city center. I asked her a hard question to break her pride to find out what the anger was all about. Soul doctors have to do hard work with hearts to help them see need for savior. I asked her as she threw popcorn at me if her father left her. The Word of Knowledge opened a wound in her heart. She begins crying on the nearest teen boy's shoulder. Fathers not at home hurts the family and children grow up wondering if God is there. As soon as she broke in tears, I extended mercy and compassion. Oil of the Holy Spirit to heal her wounds with words of love from Jesus for her. That I forgave her and no one will ever love her more than Jesus. Many of the teenagers in the crowd were well behaved, so I complimented them for character. Not during my time ministering to her of course. One group there wanted to sing with me and learn revival songs. I love Liverpool. If I had one city that I would suggest youth groups from America to visit to preach it would be this city and then go to Scotland. My heart breaks for these kids. Sheep having no shepherd. The song I taught them was "We will Ride." We sang it while I was in bible school in Pensacola. Great to hear the English singing this song in the town where Beatles were famous. Now, Jesus is more famous in Liverpool. Praise God! I love my job.

Scotland was a month, because I found a room to rent in Edinburgh for only $386 USA. My landlord was a wild woman pole dance instructor. This city is like a princess fairy tale video come to life. There was a good looking Scottish man I had been skyping since Spain that was from this city. My hopes got high that we would meet there and preach together in this incredibly romantic hometown of his. He even made plans to join me and us go to Glasgow together. It would have been like my first date as a Christian. Others on skype liked him as well. We had chemistry and would get lost into each other's eyes after talks about God and missions. He made a few videos of me on his YouTube channel talking about me and sharing my videos. Then he took them down for whatever reason. He was a mystery man. I loved his voice and how he said my name. The day he was to come he never showed up. I was dressed up for him, even had perfume on for this one encounter with my dream Scottish man.

He never said he was sorry or why he didn't come. He just ignored me. I cried. God encouraged me as only a Father could His daughter. God really did me a favor keeping Mr. Wrong away from my tender heart. He caught my attention and most men don't get me to do a double take.

Scotland outreaches had to continue even with a hope deferred at the train station one morning in my pretty new outfit under the Romantic views of Edinburgh castle, spring bright glorious flowers and bridge across troubled waters with bagpipers playing Amazing Grace. Jesus is still my hero. Waiting and trusting God is always wise. Father knows best. He sees what we can't see in the big picture of life. Missions is my Passion, next to Mr. Wonderful (Jesus).

Edinburgh youth would hang out in the main areas of city. I got to reach out to some of the same ones more than once. Great connection and one guy was a prodigal hungry to get answers. I preached in Glasgow and ate with friend from bible school. I preached in Inverness too. Visited the Isle of Skye on a bus and loved seeing snow in Scotland. Nice times of prayer and seeking God in His beauty. What a beautiful country. The youth in Glasgow seemed to struggle with their sexual identity badly. I prayed for a few of them and hugged them. Youth gone wild because of split families. A 68-year-old lady wrote me while I was in Scotland that she had been watching my videos for a year. She is now preaching on the streets. Praise the Lord!

God sent me to meet an older man and his family in a small community of Scotland where the first King James bible was printed. What a man of wisdom and enjoyed this fellowship. He street preaches at times and his whole family lives for God. His wife loves Israel. His daughter in her 20's asked why I was going back to America in October. I was shocked, because it was a great question. This wise father of many children answered and said "Because that is her birthday." Wow, he knew. However, I gave it some thought. Why would I go all the way back for one meal with my family to turn around craving to be on missions field again. Soon I was confronting myself with what is best for the Kingdom of God. Soldiers don't get to just go back anytime they want and God was calling me to return after Israel to more countries.

What a huge adventure ahead He was about to send me on. I changed that Sweden ticket to America in reverse to Bangkok, Thailand. Soon, God suggested for me to go to Australia from Thailand for my birthday. How cool is that? Yes, Lord lets go to Oz. Money in came in quickly from friends in Alabama to get my Australia plane ticket to Perth.

Bye Scotland! I enjoyed my month with you all. Meet some great Christians there and enjoyed preaching with them in Glasgow. Time for London, England to complete full circle UK gospel tour. I preached in 3 parks, Big Ben and London Eye area. When I planned London in 2014 for 420 day 2015 it was because of all the pot smokers that would be in Hyde Park that day. Some ladies showed up to join me from watching my YouTube channel. We had a good timing fishing together. Someone gave us a free ladder to keep. Vice London interviewed and said I had biggest crowd that day in Speakers corner.

We noticed huge crowds in another part of the park. Then, I remembered it was 420 day. I walked with the 2 ladies over there to crowds of thousands of pro marijuana people everywhere smoking it. I got on ladder and begin to confront them. I was surrounded quick with cameras going. Soon someone grabbed my orange bible and threw it way across Hyde Park. My heart sunk and grieving that someone hated God that much. I got down walking in that direction looking for my bible. I offered the crowd 50 euros for my bible back partly because the original picture of me with Steve Hill was in there from my first missions trip to Germany in year 2000. A young doper brought it to me. I thanked him. Then stuck it in my bag. A few minutes later he asked for the 50 euros. It was the smallest bill I had and UK doesn't use euros that is why I gave him so much.

He took my food money saved for Amsterdam. I told him eye to eye "Because you would take the money of a missionary. I am going to skip eating for 7 days. Fasting and praying for your soul to be saved is what I am going to do." I suffered too. It was really hard to not eat all week. I had many liquids, just no solids until I got out of Amsterdam on 7th day in airport. There I had a wonderful meal of just snacks of cheese, meats, crackers…Dutch foods waiting on flight to Sweden. Before going to Amsterdam I preached in York and Leeds England. Tiger Dan 925 did a short documentary on my life and ministry. Leeds wrote an article about my preaching there. Those youths threw books at me. Then, when I was done they followed me around like they loved me and wanted me to stay. There was a girl with cuts all over her arms in York that let me pray for her. 2 days later the same girl walked by me in Leeds right as I was about open air preaching. That had to be a sign to her of God's love. I love England! Really, the United Kingdom is what I love. My hope was in that 2 months to have meet my future husband, not just do outreaches. God knows who my future husband is and where He is in this huge world. Maybe my husband is not a UK man. I gave up wanting a Texas cowboy and started liking UK men. Now, I just don't even know anymore. Blonde hair and Blue eyes are still on the top of list though. I decided that at 5 years old. Where are you Romeo?

Amsterdam is my favorite city to preach the gospel. This year I got to see the world's largest garden in the world not too far from city. A bus takes you straight there from Amsterdam. Sweden was a city that I was going to end my gospel tour, but changed schedule 12 days after leaving USA in 2014. My ticket was now to Thailand. Matthew and I preached together in Sweden, then he took my clothes in a suitcase to Poland to hold for me until after Asia Gospel Tour. I was flying from Poland to Israel. Next time I will just give clothes away. It seemed like stewardship, but ended up too stressful. My fear was not having money for clothes in Fall. God always provides and should have just let it all go to a needy soul.

Welcome to Asia, wow this is my first time. I love it. Sweet Thailand! A country with 95% Buddhists and immigration says at boarder "welcome to Buddha land." My first hostel was $6 a night with roof top pool. So much nicer than Sweden's hotel for $50 a night and bathroom way down the hall. Bangkok's hostel had nice air conditioning and comfortable beds. I prayed that God would help me find a Cross to carry. Within 10 minutes of this prayer I saw construction on a new house in village with old boards to the side in a massive pile. I found the home owner and asked him for 2 pieces of old boards. He had his workers pull nails out. They cut the cross just right and nailed in place as I filmed the old rugged Cross. Everyone on his staff was looking at this cross being made for the smiling USA missionary. My cross had streaks of red paint on it and was so beautiful. I proudly carried it through village many times. One day I walked through the village without it and a Thai man lifted his arms. He was asking me where is the Cross? The

Holy Ghost is so powerful I trust He spoke to many through simple witness. I went over to preach where Katy Perry was doing her final tour concert and preached Jesus to the fans. Some knew what I was saying, not everyone spoke English. Taking a risk and it is worth it. I went around Bangkok singing and preaching with cross several times. Soon, it was time to go to Chang Mai, Thailand with luggage and Cross. My rent was $6 a day there as well, but had room to myself with Fox news.

Thailand is the home of $5 foot massages. Oh yes and it is the best. I enjoyed several while there. One day I woke up with serious tooth pain. I thought it was sugar problems. Another day went by and tooth still hurt. My friends on Facebook suggested I visit a dentist. What? Are you serious, I am in a 3rd world country. Many fears and my pain drove me to do something. Pain seems to cause action. I am in shock that there is a Dentist right across the street from hotel. I don't even have to get a taxi, bus or tuk tuk. I walked in and was extremely impressed with this office of professionals. This city is a training center for Dentists and they spoke good English. They cleaned my teeth, did x-ray and set up an appointment for me to get my wisdom tooth out in a few days. Several people sent offerings to make sure I had enough money. The bill was under $50 with dentist, surgery and medicine. I was able to walk home to rest after they drilled my wisdom tooth and popped it out. Great job! Now, I tell everybody to go to Thailand to get teeth done. They become my heroes.

My mother was in awe that God did this for me. It is a huge story of His provision. I sure do love Jesus. While I was in Thailand I carried my cross inside the Buddhists temple and sang about Jesus. The monks got upset with me, but not too mad. Thai people are sweet. Jesus still wants them to repent. I carried the cross in the mall in this city and instead of being kicked out. The security liked it and took my photo. A guy had a long talk with me outside the mall. It was a hot day and ran threw the mall sprinklers with the Cross. Then stood on the street corner holding Cross in air to all those driving by. Asia is truly a great missions field and looking forward to the whole summer there.

Hong Kong Revolution! I wanted to come to HK, China after seeing the protests on the news. I was not sure what they were upset about but I loved their passion. My bucket list was to meet the leader of the Hong Kong Revolution. God can make it happen. I packed my Cross to bring and upon arrival the airport had no issue with me carrying it through Hong Kong. Whoa, that was a rush. All for You, Jesus.

My first outreach in Hong Kong was by the beautiful riverfront where they have a lightshow free every night. I open air preached there and local man named Paul, was stirred by my witness. He was a Christian and God stirred him to consider going public with the gospel. God opened several doors for me in Hong Kong, with Kingdom connections. I simply added a girl to Face Book that has mutual friend and she invited me to her church. The second invite I decided to go. I connected well with the church member and her Pastor. Pastor asked me to preach at all three of her church services, when I returned in July after China. I accepted the invite and it was a great weekend in July. We all went out to eat at a Western restaurant along with the church leaders. The Philippine church made me a gingerbread house. I could see myself being there to train all 3 churches in evangelism. My nickname for these believers was "The Jesus girls." Many of those girls work so hard as maids in homes. They only get one day off a week and spent it in the house of God. Finally, a group of Christians asking to be trained. I wanted to drop everything for Hong Kong. God has a plan for all us and if He wants me there. Then, He will send me back for His Kingdom purpose. My heart is willing to train anywhere in the world.

While I was in Hong Kong, I meet Indonesian Christians in Victoria Park, while I was doing an outreach one Sunday afternoon. They were so kind and loved the Cross. Later, I went to their church and left the Thailand Cross there. I didn't feel at peace bringing it on the plane to China. That didn't mean I would not get a New Cross in China. God is in control, just need to get in first. Communist China is different from Hong Kong, Taiwan and Macau China.

Macau, is an island about one hour from Hong Kong. I also preached the gospel there with the wood Cross, I walked it through a casino without any problems the first walk through. I spent several hours walking with the Cross, through the crowded mall and chatting with people as the Lord brought them to me. This really was a fun day because of the few workers wanted to hold the Cross. There is a higher chance for someone to ask about Jesus while you carry a Cross. The mall looked like Venice, Italy with an indoor gondola ride on water. I sure was tired, hot and sweaty when I got back. Hostel life, also got divine appointments for the Gospel with an Israeli and others passing through. People chat in hostels, especially when you walk in with a wood Cross.

Time for China! The pastor in Hong Kong at an Indonesian church highly suggested for me to not wear Jesus t-shirts in China or carry the Cross. I rarely take peoples advice, even Pastors. People sometimes use Wisdom as an excuse to not take risks. I like taking risks and don't mind being killed for the gospel. Heaven will be awesome. God will protect me, if He wants me to stay on earth preaching the gospel.

Before I got to Beijing, China a young university student my son's age contacted me from China. He has access to Face Book and YouTube because of an app he bought to bypass the communist government. I bought this app for my computer also to make sure I could communicate with friends while there. China is a dangerous place. The university student wanted to know what city I was coming to in China. I only had 2 cities on schedule, one Beijing and the other was to go to a wedding of a guy's sister I meet only a few minutes' in Finland. Wild stuff, but I went to that wedding in China with my Jesus t-shirt on that day. Many Chinese wanted my photo in the city of Zhengzhou because it is not a normal tourist city. Pastor Ruben taught me the importance of Christian t-shirts and many that took that photo may have researched my t-shirt "Trust Jesus". Small seeds are better than no seeds. Go plant some seeds and let the Holy Ghost water them. Jesus is Worthy! I accidently got locked in the handicap bathroom also. So I thought it would be funny to record my escape from Chinese bathroom.

No persecution happened while I was in China, God gave me great favor with people everywhere. I wore my Jesus t-shirt and even found a pile of wood to make new Cross. A guy made it for me without him ever speaking English. I showed him what I wanted and carried the Cross, through Beijing China. Even past many police and security, not one problem. My brother in Christ just happened to live in Beijing, so we meet for the first time at the Great Wall of China. He was the University student that was writing me. The Great Wall of China is massive, but we had the connection spot made. Even without me carrying a phone God brought us together for the sake of the gospel. We ate a meal together before going on the long walk and gospel journey up the Wall.

I had two big bucket lists for Asia, well I take that back there were three on my bucket list. One was to sing, preach or do something Jesus related inside of a Buddhist temple. God allowed me to go inside three Buddhist temples in China and Thailand. China seemed like I might get in trouble for that one because the security are supposed to watch carefully who comes in there. However, I made buddies with security prior to bringing the wood Cross in, so they watched me just walk in with it.

My second bucket list was to meet the leader of the Hong Kong Revolutions, Joshua Wong, was only 17-year-old Christian when he rallied 300,00 followers to the streets to protest. He made Forbes 2015 for one of the most influential leaders. Joshua, also made Time Magazine. I like world changers. Even with a great mission's faith walk God had allowed me to live out, I still want to stay inspired by others. One Sunday afternoon after church in Hong Kong I heard a lot of noise in Victoria Park. I politely said good bye to the Indonesian Christians to go into the crowd to see if Joshua was speaking. God used a young pre-teen boy to point through hundreds of people to where Joshua Wong was standing quietly with his friends. I shook his hand and told him he inspired me. Then I could get a photo with this Hong Kong Legend.

My third bucket list was to go see the Great Wall of China. This is the whole reason I choose Beijing over going to Shanghai. I caught an allergy sinus mess in my nose and chest after walking down from the Great Wall. Arnold went with me, he is from Africa and speaks perfect English and perfect Mandarin. All over the steps of our walk up and down the Great Wall people wanted photos of him because he was black and of me because I was white. The color of people's skin doesn't matter to me in friendships. I look at people's hearts and get to know who they are as a person. Skin is not the problem in this world. Sin is the problem in this world.

One of the places I stayed was a divine appointment. The couple I rented from my first week in China shared a lot with me. The gospel was presently clearly and the man seemed to want to follow Christ. He told me with tears that God sent me there. I expect divine appointments; God didn't send me just to hike The Great Wall of China. God's plan was bigger than even my plan. I didn't know when I planned China that I would go to a wedding with Jesus t-shirt or that Arnold would contact me.

My last day in China I said goodbye to Arnold. He wanted my beat up free Cross. I was happy to give to him. He took me to his underground church one night too. The night he carried the Cross to his Beijing dorm, a Chinese Buddhist asked him about the Cross. He shared the gospel with him. The Buddhist gave his life to Jesus right there. Turned around made him a nice Blood Red wood Cross and sent me a photo of them both. Now he continues to carry that Cross in China. I love to preach the gospel, but watching new preachers rise up stirs me even more. Praise the Lord! That expensive Chinese Visa, was worth all the souls that were impacted by the Cross. The fastest growing church in the world is in China. 2015 Year of the Sheep. Behold the Lamb got to be used a few times in conversation with Chinese while I was staying in the dorms. Praise the Lord! Jesus loves China! Now, when I meet people from China I say to them in Mandarin "Jesus loves you." They always smile and are happy I know their language.

Singapore is a beautiful, small and expensive. I went to preach for their 50th anniversary of being a country. Most people speak English, but don not chew gum there. Chewing gum, is illegal there, they are clean freaks. Since Singapore was booked for three weeks, I decided to make one week a vacation week. Hong Kong Jesus Girls blessed me with a donation for speaking engagement. I went several fun places in Singapore. I went to the Night Safari, River Safari and Singapore Zoo. Yep that is it, besides, going to the water park. I saw elephant shows, giraffes from Israel, monkeys, pandas from China and Kangaroos. I screamed at Night Safari because of the small kangaroo running past me on sidewalk. I screamed "The Blood of Jesus!" That is pretty much what I automatically scream any time I get scared of something.

My first hostel had Jehovah's Witness family staying there and no doubt, they wanted to win me over to their cultish ways. One day a roommate from Hong Kong was crying. Someone on Face Book sent me a devotional in her language because she did not speak English. I just played them for her and peace came back to her supernaturally. A roommate from Mongolia gave me a key chain and invited me to come to her country. She was with her mother. Two Muslims, from Malaysia, stayed in my dorm room. I gave all my roommates my testimony tract. One Muslim stayed in touch with me. She knew I would soon be in her city and country. She still writes me even after I left Singapore and Malaysia.

Singapore has a beautiful waterfront and lightshow at night. It reminds me of Hong Kong a little. I choose to open air preach in Little India an area of Singapore when I moved to a new hostel closer to underground rail. A nice size crowd came, mostly men from India and they listened well. Since I was next to a vegetable and fruit stand the Holy Ghost put on my heart to talk about creation. Who do you thank for your food?

I was there for a good while and had a free Cross, made a few days before while going to Bugas post office. A Christian showed up named, Faith, and she sent me photos of me preaching to my email. However, after a couple hours the police showed up. Only two at first and then two hours later I was with six police and three well-dressed detectives. 9 cops for 1-woman preacher. They took photos of everything in my bag. They knew about my spy camera glasses and confiscated every testimony tract in my bag. After them keeping me so long in the humid outdoors, I was asking them, "to just arrest me, why don't you just arrest me? They let me go because they knew I was leaving for the Philippines in a few days. This works great with police. I am always telling cops my schedule and how they won't have to deal with me much longer. The Singapore police didn't know I was coming back for a few days thought in August to celebrate and preach at their 50th anniversary of becoming free from Malaysia. This was a huge bucket list and assignment. I knew it would be crowded that day on streets, the police let me go and the hostel got so stirred up after I returned. All my new buddies in the Singapore hostel from Indonesia, England and Scotland wanted to hear my survival story. They knew I was a Christian because of the Cross, my singing and always preaching to each of them.

Sunday was packed in Little India with thousands of men everywhere. I know the cops didn't want me preaching, but I couldn't ignore a thousand plus souls right by my hostel. I carried the Cross all over the streets until I knew everyone saw or heard me. Even Muslims were leaving their Mosque as I walked by with the Cross. No problems, yes of course I was by myself. No police came after me on this outreach and no Muslims threatened to kill me either. I felt like the only woman in the area that day. Yes, I talked to several people in English about Jesus that outreach. It was scary, exciting and dangerously wonderful.

Now, it's time to go to the Philippines, my schedule changed to add this country. Then, my schedule was changed again to add another airport and a two-hour bus ride to a faraway village with a church having a celebration. Manilla, was a lonely twenty-four hours and I was kind of glad. This has to be one of the worst airports and crowded cities to ride in a taxi I have ever been to before. Never, ever again it was just too stressful.

Bacolod was my next city. A twenty-four year old pastor's wife showed up to get me and ride the bus with me for two hours to her village. I spoke the next morning at an unforgettable church. No walls, no air conditioning, plastic chairs outside and people everywhere. I felt to just go and bring encouragement. The pastor and pastor's wife street preach and many of the church members do as well. We all went out to the streets and preached for a few days in another village. It began pouring down rain and the young men stood like warriors continuing to preach. I got great photos of them in the rain, while I stayed under tent. Children sat in rain to listen and people under the tents could hear the gospel. This had to be one of the most impressive group of young people that I have ever met. They go fish and sell door to door to survive. Life to them is very simple. Preaching the Gospel is what drives their lives. They mention coming to America and I shake my head, no please do not come to America. They may get sidetracked by the American dreams and quit the ministry. It takes a Cross from God, to keep someone dedicated to ministry in America with all the distractions from earthly pleasures. "Braveheart's", is the name I called these young men. We had a lot of fun together. They took me on a homemade boat to a small island. I could sit on the bottom of sand and hold a starfish. I could see straight through the blue water. I got very burnt and hurt for days. My hut I stayed in cost $25 a month and it was across from the church. The bathroom had concrete floor with a toilet without a seat lid. My shower was a large garbage plastic rubberwear bin full of water. I had to take scoops of water out with a soup handle and pour on myself. No worries though I used to do that while living in my car. I had many sink baths at coffee shops through America. A few times, I took bucket baths at the beach in California.

One thing I will not forget is the children in the neighborhood going through each other's hair. It was like a game to them finding lice in each other's hair. That was hard for me to watch, so I bought a few children lice remover for their hair. They didn't seem excited to get rid of it. I think if I had lice, then I would be washing those bugs out quick. It was no big deal to them. There were children hungry and begging in a few of the cities I saw in this country. One boy had no parents and thank God I had enough extra cash to buy him at least one meal that day. I had it so easy in the USA compared to some of these Asian countries that God sent me to.

A local school in the area asked me to speak on anti-drug message with the permission of the principle. I spoke my testimony to two classrooms, shared the Gospel and even hit the volleyball with them. They were so sweet and sincere. Even the children not in the class lined up outside the window in attempts to hear what I was speaking. Thank you, Jesus, I love my job!

Time to go to the next Philippine city, Puerto Princess Palawan is a place that Philippines' all want to go visit. It is a nice place. A street preacher family invited me to come and stay with them, what a blessing and nice visit. We preached a few places in town and I spoke a few minutes in the church. Mike showed me the 10 commandments concrete block in town. It was the Catholic 10 commandments, not the KJV Exodus 20 commandments of God. Catholic church changed the 10 commandments, just so they can keep worshipping their idols. Mike and some others were arrested earlier that year for preaching the gospel while the Pope was in town. Over 6 million people flocked to hear the false prophet, Pope Francis. Yet, the Christians with Real Gospel get stuck in jail. Repent Catholics! Read the Holy Bible and question everything about your church.

Singapore, was so packed on their 50th anniversary. I felt like I should take some photos that day to appear like a tourist. I went to a very crowded park. Planes were flying over us as the celebration begun. I began to open air preach. It lasted maybe thirty minutes before the police showed up. There were undercover officers blended in the crowd as well, listening to the speech. I was just about to preach on danger of Islam when they pulled their badges. At first I, did not think they were real police, yes oh yes, they were. I had fun explaining my Bible to one cop. He wanted to know why I had facts on Islam in my Holy Bible. I shared with him about the prophet Mohammed having sex with Aisha at nine years old. Islam says, blessed be his name (Prophet Mohammed), which is sick and twisted. Nobody deserves honor for raping a kid. They say it's their culture to marry children that young. No way was a nine-year-old developed in her little body to be having sex with a 54-year-old man. Poor Aisha. Jesus doesn't hurt people. He heals people and loves the broken hearted. Pope Francis says "Muslims and Christians serve the same God," No, I am a Christian and do not serve Allah Moon God head chopper. That is another lie of the Catholic church. Singapore wants all religions to get along and no one stir up anything. Had I known Joseph Prince had his church there, then I would have rebuked his Hyper Grace message on his church sidewalk. There was a Mega Church in news while I was there for stealing lots of money to make a singer in church famous. Singapore is a very wealthy country and yet needed the gospel very badly. I wasn't arrested on any of those Singapore outreaches, but I am not allowed to ever come back there anymore.

Kuala Lumpar, Malaysia spooked me out when I arrived on August 10, 2015, I almost booked another plane to leave immediately. My fears were heavy. I needed a place to pray. My cheap hostel upgraded me to my own room. I read this city was the #6 most dangerous cities in the world. It is a Muslim country and it just scared me. I had a large and small banner made by a Muslim with a picture of Jesus from Passion of the Christ movie with Him all bloody on cross. It said many attributes about Jesus from Isaiah chapter 9. Jesus: King of the Jews was main heading because I wanted to use it in Israel on my fishing trip one month away.

After prayer, God gave me new courage; I went to the streets to preach the gospel. One man stopped me to comment about my Jesus banner (small one was on my tripod), "what happened to this man and who is He". This is the power of the gospel, the Cross of Jesus Christ. He appeared to be from Morocco. I had great Joy sharing with him about the Son of God dying on the Cross. Then, gloriously was raised from the dead 3 days later by the power of God.

Here is a quote from part of my Face Book outreach journals, "My last talk was a Muslim that was shaking while he talked to me. We talked about 15 minutes and then security ran me off. The security walked me all the way to the end of the park to leave. This was after hours of evangelism and I was exhausted from heat and walking anyway. I told him I was leaving. They tried to get me to roll up my banner and I wouldn't. Never dealt with a real cop all day which is amazing. An Iran young man talked to me a while so many other I lost count. Huge lesson I learned about facing my fears. God rewarded me by allowing me to find $5. I need that $5 to use internet somewhere to Google how to get home since I was kicked out of park. That caused me to not know where I was in city. I don't use a cell phone to save on expenses. God is good!! Happy missionary gives Jesus His glory."

My roommate from room in Singapore was so nice and really wanted to see me. I was nervous because Muslims are taught in Koran to not make friends with unbelievers. *"O ye, who believe! Take not the Jews and the Christians for your friends. They are but friends to each other. And he amongst you that turns to them is of them. Verily Allah guideth not a people unjust."* Quran Surah 5:15

She seemed ok to allow to visit in my hotel lobby, so I agreed. When she arrived with her 2 sons we sat on sofas. She wanted photos with me and was so happy that I came to her country. I ended up wearing my Trust Jesus t-shirt and going to her favorite Arab restaurant in her car. Again, I trusted Jesus. We had a great time. She told me next time I come to Malaysia to come stay in her home. These are the kind of things that blow my mind. Christians rarely open their home for traveling ministries, but here is a Muslim opening her home to a Christian. Just because someone is a born again Christian doesn't mean they will give to world missions, fed the poor, clothe the naked, visit those in prison or even confront a local city council meeting over drag shows in the park. I have watched the church world my whole life. There will be people in heaven, because of faith in Jesus. You cannot get to heaven through works, it's all grace. However, those that did very little to help others will have no crowns to lay at Jesus feet. I don't think you have to be a Christian to have compassion. You do have to be a follower of Jesus Christ to make heaven for all eternity though. If being good saved people, I know a few that deserve heaven. However, it is God's plan of salvation that only the blood of Jesus can wash away sins. That is why I warn so many people, wherever I can find them. Come to Jesus! Repent and Believe the Gospel!

Back to Thailand, to finish my summer Asia gospel tour. I spend a lot of time in Thailand in 2015 and it has become one of my favorite countries. Maybe because they smile all the time, it's cheap, $5 foot massages and Pad Thai street food is awesome. When I preached in Pattaya Beach, Thailand the gospel stirred up a lot of demons, for weeks. All I did was simply walk on famous "walking streets" calling the English speaking men to repentance and showed banner of Jesus to girls trapped in prostitution. Two blogs were written about me in Pattaya, Thailand in English and one all the way in the Netherlands in English. I traced it on my website to see where all my YouTube hits may have come from. When someone blogs it helps for a video to go viral, over 10,000 views in a week, Praise God! Amazing how a video can reach more people sometimes than even the outreach. God uses the outreach to reach in person and the World Wide Web to reach the masses of people all over the world. Web is a good word for it also, some are caught in a web of sin and Jesus wants to deliver them from Black Widows of Hell.

Another interesting fact about "Walking Street" in Pattaya, Thailand is the song "God of this city" was written in a bar on this famous street. A Christian band got a burden from God and wrote that while worshipping Jesus there one night. Thai bar needed a band and the Christians offered to be that band. Incredible mission's song and many have used it for their promo videos. I did for a while on my website as well.

That night I meet a Chinese man name Enoch reaching all the Chinese tourists by the pier. Hundreds walked by constantly, so I joined him a few days to help his vision for China. He also had home lessons for local Thai children wanting to learn Mandarin Chinese. He had me come share the gospel to two of his classes. There were not over three kids in either class. Everyone needs Good News, even children. My last day there he gave me an offering and roses. Enoch was thankful for someone to join his crusade for a short season. God knows I do understand working alone. I really try to encourage other Christians everywhere I go around the world. This surely pleases Father God.

When I got off the bus in Bangkok with my bags, a UK muscle man with immodest bar working wife started an argument with me. They had heard me preaching on Pattaya walking street. They both defended the Thailand women's rights to be whores for income.

God didn't create any woman to have a career as a whore. Just like no one was created to bow to Buddha, Elephant or Mary either. Idolatry brings a curse to a land. Repentance will bring the peace of God. Girls are being rescued and turning to Jesus because of missionaries leaving their comfort zone and going to be a Christian Missionary. Christian missionaries are teaching these girls dignity and new ways to make money. Asia has a prostitution problem and God showed me first hand in 2015 what He sees every day. I hope to impart His heart for these countries in the next generation. Some will run in to the darkness with the light of the Gospel to bring the answer, Jesus is the answer, always. The gospel changes people. Jesus gives a New Start. New, New, New.

My room in Bangkok was perfect in every way including a pool for only $15 a day. I sat this season a side as a time to write and also fast for my Israel trip coming up soon. My fast was for sure ordained by the Lord because after days of the fast my mother sent me an email. My father was admitted to the hospital and was dying. That email made my world stop. I couldn't think about anything else, but his pain in the hospital. Here is the man that adopted me, raised me and rescued me with my baby at age 19 from an abusive situation. Now, my heart pounded inside with fear. I realized my Father may not live much longer. Every child deals with the loss of family at some point in their life. My pastor in California suggested I make my dad a video for him in the hospital. I tried to not break down in the video because I wanted him to know that I will be ok.

Imagine being the father of a daughter that makes the news for controversial issues, travels all over the world alone and lives in a small car in America. God has to prepare a father to have a warrior for a daughter. He prayed for me often, because he told me this fact. The last time I saw him he was praying over his breakfast in Chattanooga with his small orange juice on the Jerusalem coaster I bought him for his birthday. I heard the Holy Ghost quicken me to take the photo of my daddy in prayer. Thank you Jesus for this special photo. I poured out my heart in the video and others cried watching it as well. God has forgiven me so much and I have truly been blessed with a father that stood my me though all the news coverage about me. He never gave up on me. Daily, I waited to hear what was going on and after the 9th day of fasting I stopped the fast. It was hard to fast anymore. Sweet Daddy passed away Sept 3rd 2015 at 8:21pm. Mom is now a widow. I was so thankful for my son's strong arms to be there. My son is a caring young man that loves his family. I watched dad's funeral on YouTube the last week of Oct wearing Georgia Tech clothes to honor him while I was in Perth, Australia. When I got to Jerusalem, Israel, God gave me a vision of my father right after I preached on night of Yom Kippur. I was walking up the hill towards the Upper Room with the Chinese Christians to pray with them on the grass. All of a sudden, God dropped a vision in my heart like a movie. My father was in heaven and walked up to my spiritual father, Steve Hill. My daddy thanked Pastor Steve for teaching me about evangelism. I stopped and looked into the heavens with such thankfulness and joy. Now, my father is in the great cloud of witnesses no longer drinking orange juice on his coaster of Jerusalem. Dad just saw me preaching the gospel in Jerusalem with my favorite preacher. Amazing to have a God that cares daily for my heart and knows me so perfectly. Praise God!

"Wherefore seeing we also are compassed about with so great a cloud of witnesses, let us lay aside every weight and the sin which doth so easily beset us, and let us run with patience the race that is set before us." Hebrews 12:1

My father passed away and life goes on, souls still need to be saved and dad would expect me to stay the course. Therefore, I continue to follow Jesus as God's Word commands me to do. I am a soldier in the army of God.

Time for Poland, Matthew is coming to meet me with my winter clothes. We preached together some that week. However, it was not easy to be around anyone. His English wasn't so good and not sure he understood the impact of my father's death. I asked him, to please stay with his local Polish friends, so I could deal with my emotions. I allowed him to keep the suitcase and a few of the clothes for his kindness. Israel was next and had to make sure I was ready spiritually.

I passed out in the Wizz airlines office from stress in the Polish airport on my way to Israel. This was my first time to pass out from stress. It was very dramatic because a Polish Doctor came in to check me. I needed more vitamin C and iron. Sometimes I overdo it with my schedules. Now I make sure vitamins and health foods are shove them in me through smoothies. Long story short, they helped me and bumped me on early check in. I arrived in Israel on Rosh Hashanah in time for New Years.

Israel was stressful as usual, but had many divine appointments. My arrival into Tel Aviv, Israel was very easy this time with no questions. I purposely chose to fly out on Rosh Hashanah which is in God's calendar (New Year's Day.) I try to always do something prophetic on this day. I preached the very next day with a six foot Jesus banner by the beach front on the holiday. Had several good talks with locals and as usual some upset. One guy left France for good because of Muslim persecution there. That is a typical life for the Jews. God sent me 2 pugs my first morning there. I sat like a child and played with them for a minute thanks to the owner for stopping for a Pug fan.

My housing in Jerusalem was in 2 different hostels while there and met some Christians that were like minded. Then, this year I meet more annoying Christians than either trip. Of course, the ones that got on my nerves the most were Americans. There is a movement going on around the world called "Hebrew Roots Movement." Some people in this movement are cool and even support my passion to be in Israel with gospel. Then, there are those annoying ones that could care less about the Great Commission and are there to super spiritual during feasts. They attempt to tell me how I am can't preach there or that I am doing it all wrong. I am on a Missions trip, not an Israel tour.

Preaching the gospel in Jerusalem is already stressful. I have done it several times now and can feel the Spiritual Warfare. As usual I went to a place in Jewish quarters where they fed needy people for free. There I eat with the Jews. I do know how to do friendship evangelism and see its purpose is to share the gospel. Jesus ate with sinners. He wanted to share good news with them.

144

There are preachers in America filthy rich that brag about being alone in their planes, so they can protect their anointing. That is so un Christ like. Jesus was a homeless missionary with a donkey and sent his disciples out with very little.

One thing I know about the Jews is they love to hear a Christian talk about their loyalty to the land of Israel. Jews appreciate Christians supporting Israel. While I was there somebody that was a Christian went up to the Temple Mount with an Israel flag and got beat up. Not a good idea because the Muslims in this area passionately hate Israel. They believe it's their land and call it Palestine. I have not been up there yet. Tried a few times to go to the Temple Mount, but line too long or it was closed. Israel is a war zone. I knew this before booking ticket. It's one thing to go on a tour of Israel which still is risky. Going to Israel for preaching the gospel, sets a preacher up to be martyred. So far, no one has killed me. I look forward to my next trip in Fall 2016. I will share some outreaches stories with you in that chapter.

"Ye worship ye know not what; we know what we worship: for salvation is of the Jews." John 4:22

Jesus is Jewish. I love to preach about Him and what He did for the whole world. When in Israel I do say Jesus and Yeshua. Another thing I preach is "Yeshua is the Lamb of God" promised to Abraham. Christians have had our eyes opened, those of us that are born again and not just a church goer that Jesus is the Lamb. Yet Israelis still pray for their Messiah to come. The night of Yom Kippur Sept 22, 2015. Jews were circling live chickens over people's heads for Yom Kippur. I remember preaching about this last year in New York. You don't need a chicken because God gave you a Lamb. The atonement for sin already happened when Yeshua took sin on the cross. "it is finished." No more lambs, chickens, birds or anything has to be sacrificed. Jesus, Yeshua completed the finished work of God on the Cross for us to receive salvation. All hail the king of the Jews! God brought Christians from China to stand with me, South Korea, England and Africa. The police got on to me for banner this year and being loud. However, the only time I was permanently told to stop was when I preached at the Western Wall. That message lasted about three minutes. Police escorted me out and almost would not give my banner back to me. I wasn't banned from Israel either.

While I was in Jerusalem there was a huge white wedding dress hanging over David's Tower. So many of us are crying out for Jesus to come get us "the bride of Christ". It was incredible seeing it there. No note why, but possibly because a lot of brides get married during fall feasts. I have seen brides there now three times and they are always modest dresses. I also was there on the roof of the night of the 4th Blood Moon. My hostel had best view in Jerusalem (Petra hostel.) Since I was there for 1st Blood Moon of tetrad, I felt called to be there on 4th Blood Moon. Sept 2014 I was in a cabin in Maine resting from 20 country tour watching Pastor Larry speak on the 4th Blood Moon. He said it would be a super Blood Moon and Israel would see this one. I felt the fire of God to go be in Israel to be there for Super Blood Moon. Mainly, because the Jews would be outside looking at it. I am looking for a way to start conversations on the Super Bloody Lamb of God.

One year later I am at the Western Wall area where mixed people gather, not by prayer wall. There was the Pastor Larry that was talking on TV about the 4th Blood moon being seen in Israel. Whoa, that was cool. I went to shake his hand and thank him for the show. God used him to get me there for this Fall celebration to preach the gospel. The wild part about seeing Pastor Larry that day was because it was the night of the Super Moon. Double whoa! Whoa Whoa go Jesus.

Watching all the people outside at 3 am on roofs and in city was powerful. Many Jews walked to Western Wall to pray for their Messiah to come with something in their hand. There were people posting photos of the Super Blood Moon by the Western Wall. That is a photo shop. It was by a huge crane, very small and over the mall area. It was not even close to the Western Wall. Hey, everybody has a hobby. I personally enjoy bugging Jews reminding them Jesus is their King. It is fun.

Sept, 23 2015 "Divine appointment on Yom Kippur" Last night a man from Hong Kong invited several of us to meet a wealthy man this morning. He said "he will help us." I had no plans and knew nothing else. So, I showed up thinking we were going to meet with a Christian business owner. After a few hours, a taxi was sent for us all to come to the man's home. As soon as we started up the Mount of Olives that is when I knew we were in Palestine area. We were going to a Muslim's house. As soon as we walked in the house there was a greeting from this older wealthy man named "Abraham." We all sat down at the table. I begin to watch and pray. The word "peace" was all over the walls and photos of him. He has traveled for years as a speaker promoting peace and unity. This is when I noticed the One World Religion circle photo. It is the symbol of coexist logo. No one else noticed it. Several Christians were praising this man for PEACE. Hosea 4:6 "My people are destroyed for lack of knowledge…"

While I am sent by God to this Muslim man's Jerusalem home in America the President is meeting with the Pope of Rome on the same day. The timing felt historical. I had my "Jesus saves from Hell" t-shirt on and Holy Bible in my purse. I whispered to the older lady that Abraham was promoting false peace movement. The rich Muslim man kept commenting how "we all served same God." He stated that he may meet with Pope soon and come to USA to promote peace. You can't coexist with a religion that worships other gods or that wants to kill us. Where is the common sense in the Christians? Pope and Rick Warren are both leaders in the Ecumenical movement. Don't fall for this false peace movement flooding the world. (Matthew 24:24)

First, I rebuked the Christians. I said "look many of you are going on your emotions. You are not paying attention. You are not going on the Word of God." Then, I pet the arm (because he had petted my arm) of the rich Arab. I gave him a rebuke from Jesus in Matthew chapter 10. Jesus didn't come to bring peace, but a Sword. I begin to give him the Gospel and draw the line in the sand. I asked him twice "will you renounce all other gods and submit only to Jesus Christ?" He said "No." He continued to tell us how he believes he is helping bring peace, but refuses to follow Jesus Christ. I looked at him in the eye and gave it to him, as loving as possible.

"Jesus saith unto him, I am the way, the truth, and the life: no man cometh unto the Father, but my me." John 14:6 I told him that only Jesus will save him or he will burn in Hell.

Money will not buy me, No way! Jesus bought me with His blood. I am not for sale. I called him to repent and turn to Jesus Christ. He said "Do you want to go?" He called for us a taxi. One lady went with me and Japanese guy that wasn't even saved yet, both followed me out the false Peace house. He has a key of Memphis given to him from city. Interesting because Memphis sits right on the New Madrid fault line and if Israel is split, then Memphis may have an earthquake to split America. Today was a sovereign day. The Japanese man knew that Koran God and Holy Bible God were not ONE. This is why the Bible says "test the Spirits, be not deceived, watch and pray." So many people will fall for false Peace and take the Mark of the Beast. Be careful to not follow a blind guide because he will lead you into a ditch.

Israel airport was stressful leaving for me because I missed train and had to take taxi. I looked all over the airport for a working ATM. Time I found one the next train was arriving. I was so stressed that I thought taxi would solve my problem. I was in tears, but paid him. Got bags and got in the long line. I noticed the Japanese guy, but we didn't speak to far away to talk. Immigration asked me so many questions about my passport and wanted to know why I went to Malaysia. They realized I was going to miss my plane and helped me get through to get there on time. Amazing how much warfare comes after I preach in Israel. Crazy part was I tried to get there on time. The enemy just keeps putting road blocks in my path and it was hard to not cry. Israel airport stresses me to tears. I made it to Stockholm. They stamped me in and I ate a huge free meal. Since airline was late, we all got a free meal. Thank you, Jesus!

My next flight was to the London Gatwick airport in the United Kingdom. Sept 30, 2015 was the day that the UN raised the Palestine Flag. This was two days after the Super Blood Moon was seen in Jerusalem. I knew something was going to happen there and that is why I didn't stay much longer. I knew to get out of Israel soon. There is a Jewish Talmud Book of tradition. Jews believe according to this tradition "when the moon is in eclipse, it is a bad omen for Israel. If its face is as red as blood (it is a sign) that the sword is coming to the world" Therefore: Lunar Eclipse equal bad omen for the Jewish people and Israelis. Blood Moon means the sword is coming and a solar eclipse is a bad omen for the world. (Pray4zion.org) I do believe God uses signs to speak to Jews because it's in the Book of Joel and Acts. Many Jews were stabbed after I left, bad things started happening in Israel. However, I guess one could argue Israel is always under attack. Let's pray for the peace of Jerusalem, right now. (Psalm 122:6)

UK immigration man took my passport from my right hand. I was wearing an Israel flag sweatband. Only God knows if he hated Israel. I was pulled into interrogation room. They moved me to an upstairs room, took my bags and left me with nothing. It was cold in the room. Plus, airport security watched us through this glass room, as we attempted to sleep. We all had individual curved chairs or benches with light blankets. We had a bathroom. They did feed us small snacks, which I appreciate. They said it wasn't jail, but waking up to eat breakfast with an Iraqi looking at me that spoke no English was not planned. They finger printed me and told me late in the night they denied me entrance into UK. By morning me and a girl from Israel were walked to the plane before everyone else. When we arrived in Sweden, then we got our passports back.

UK told me I was denied because I had not been to USA in a while. I didn't have enough money. They called one lady that was hosting me my first night. She told them all about my ministry. I will never do a host home again for entering a country. All my other hotels and hostels were paid. I had $300 cash and ticket leaving from Scotland. I got some of the trip refunded. Huge disappointment and just should be thankful for my 2 months of gospel preaching there earlier in 2015. Maybe it was the ASBO in Chester, England that stopped me from coming in England. I still think it was my Israel sweatband.

 May 2016 London elected their first Muslim Mayor. God may never send me there again. It may become too dangerous for me to go alone. I will trust the Lord with His closed doors.

Where should I go, now that Sweden took me back? Sweden's hostels had recent reviews about Syrian refugees staying in hostels, so I felt to go to Riga, Latvia. Sweden had car fires the week I was gone from there and still having problems with Muslims.

Ferry ride to Riga was fun with a few divine appointments on the boat. I got sick from staying in cold UK immigration room all night. I bought a winter coat in Riga for $20 used because it was getting cold. After a few days I went to Lithuania. I saw a YouTube video that voted this country as #1 in suicides. So, it broke my heart. Latvia was #10 on list. Both countries I open air preached in city center. I preached two outreaches in Vilnius, Lithuania.

I didn't have much money because of my new plan to leave Sweden for safety. I walked for over 1.5 hour looking for this American rock band. Remember, I had a cold and was feeling horrible. When I rested in the warmth of the mall I almost quit looking for the concert from exhaustion, then the Lord gave me more strength to give the hunt another chance.

After getting to the concert "Kamelot." I pulled out big Jesus banner and began preaching to the rock n roll smokers outside. A sober beautiful tall man with long hair came out to meet me. His name was Oliver Palotai. He is the keyboardist of the band and wanted my photo. I got my photo with him too. Oliver was very nice and brought me a water. He listened to me with honor. This man was the very reason of my long journey on planes, ferry, bus and the last final walk to his concert. Praise the Lord! Oliver seemed frozen in deep thought when I asked him a quote from Jesus:

"For what shall it profit a man if he shall gain the whole world and loose his own soul?" Mark 8:36

Time to go all the way to Sweden, first by bus, then Ferry on Baltic sea and now to my favorite hotel made from a former plane "Jumbo Stay." I had breakfast with a man from Vietnam that needed prayer for his dying father and the gospel was given to him. Praise God! Time to go back to Thailand, so I can get closer to Australia. My bucket list for my 45th birthday was to get to Australia for the 1st time.

Can I refresh your memory? I left the USA in Dec. 2014 to go to Europe Christmas markets, UK, Amsterdam tulips and Sweden with plans to return to USA on May 9, 2015. However, only 10 days after I left my plans changed to go to Thailand. Why? Because of a video, I saw on YouTube of a few street preachers in Bangkok, Thailand saying "Come to Thailand. You can preach here." I had never been to Asia, but the video sparked me to believe God. I want to do an Asian gospel summer tour 2015. Now, check this out what happens when I arrive to Bangkok in the Fall of 2015. It's mind blowing.

I am now in Bangkok, Thailand for another visit and sitting with a Thai family. They are now my friends. Tony says to me that the video that caused me to book my Thailand ticket was a video he preaching on. I could not believe what an amazing divine connection. The man that made the video never preached again. However, Tony in the video continued with his ministry all those years. Praise God! Now, this Thai family is holding my winter clothes for me in a small bag, until I get back from all my next adventures with the One True God. Do you see the Sovereignty of God in all of this? Do you see why I am so inspired by the Great Commission? I don't sit with Pastors in some room trying to plan where I am going on the mission field. God leads my gospel tours in the most unusual ways. I love my job!

Australia gave me a year Visa, but I still was nervous if they would treat me like the UK did on Sept 30· 2015. New problems arose, when I left Thailand. I did not pay extra to go around the immigration in Singapore for my Perth flight. As soon as I got into Singapore they flagged me and put me in a room. The waiting room was 5 star and warm compared to UK. This gave me time to get on Facebook and ask for emergency prayers. I was only a few hours into my 45th birthday. Singapore knows exactly who I am, just like the UK. Guess I am marked as an Extreme Christian. Two workers in Singapore brought me to a comfortable sofa and asked questions, for over an hour it seemed. I showed them proof of my laptop email account that I was going to Perth. That was still not what they really wanted to hear. I finally just said that I am sleepy and going to just sleep. Then, get aboard the plane. I am not going into the city at all. They were concerned how I felt about all the religions in Singapore getting along so well. I had to convince them that I was not there to cause even a small stir. After that final plea with them they left to talk, came back to tell me I could go through. Praise God! Singapore trusted me, that all I wanted to do was take a nap before flight to Australia. When I walked through the airport door I watched some men hanging up a beautiful Christmas tree. Then, I went to find me a spot to take a nap.

Australia!!! Just simple machine with passport and hardly anyone talked to me. It was my birthday and paid for a taxi to go straight to my hotel. No time for a bus, today will be drama free in Perth.

All my outreaches in Perth were in the mall area of city center. Fellowship was sweet with a Hong Kong lady married to a local Oz man that I saw singing in the city center unashamed of the gospel. I saw kangaroos on a golf course by my first home. I took great photos of an entire Kangaroo family. There I ate cheesecake with a man renting a room down the hall from Singapore on my birthday and shared the gospel with him daily. My second home was by Indian Ocean, but I refused to go down there because of rattlesnake signs and hissing sounds. I have more Australian stories to share later in book of other cities. Perth was the calmest city and never dealt with police. The mall security seemed to want to help me, not shut me down. I meet several Christians sharing the gospel. Since leaving Perth the lady I rented from in the second home by Indian Ocean contacted me thanking for the inspiration. She taught on Acts chapter 1 verse 8 with her Sunday school class. An Australian from Perth contacted me about 9 months after I left she is now preaching the gospel. She found me on youtube and now is being disciple. Praise God! This is the fruit I am looking for in my travels worldwide.

Sex trafficking crimes in Cambodia bothered me while I was in prayer in Poland planning the year. When I got to Singapore in July that is when God called me to come to Cambodia, Vietnam and then go to Indonesia. I made a video with pictures of Cambodia and Vietnam and put on YouTube asking for $300 for plane tickets. Within 10 hours a complete stranger watching my channel named Mr. Wung sent the money for tickets. So, I took down video. Made a new video with proof of buying the tickets to thank him. God for sure called me to go. I looked at some rooms on Airbnb and found a brand-new home for $10 a day. I booked early because it was next to governor's home. My hope immediately was to talk to the governor of Cambodia about the problems with sex trafficking children in his country within an hour away. I got a quick reply of yes, you can rent. We then chatted online and I invited myself to his wedding. When I arrived in Cambodia he picked me up. He took me to his parents five story mansion. On a desk in my $10 huge room was a beautiful purple wedding invitation. It rained often that week, so I prayed and made smoothies. Health food became my new passion while in Perth. The wedding day was very long and over 800 were invited to the wedding party. I rode there with the family early, sat by strangers, tried new foods, filmed and people watched. The women all dressed beautifully and modest. No one danced dirty or started twerking like nasty whores. I appreciated that because western women with alcohol get nasty. Let me add many females in the western culture don't need alcohol to express their whorish behavior anymore. It seems to have become acceptable and celebrated by liberals. I sure didn't want to go to a wedding party to watch that mess. They thanked me for coming. This was my 2nd Asia wedding to invite myself to in 2015.

Next I moved to a hostel for $2 US a day. Hardly any tourists were in this hostel. My first divine appointment was while walking around Phnom Penh, Cambodia with a table of men. One man worked at American Embassy. He talked to me a long time about the One True God. His concern was that 90% of his country was Buddhist. He questioned how he could get out of this religion to become a Christian. He was humbly interested in what I had to say. Praise God!

I spent time watching more documentaries in my hostel room about Cambodia to break my heart for my mission field. I hired a driver of a Tuk Tuk for several hours at low price. He took me to many crowded areas so, I could preach the gospel carrying my six-foot Jesus banner. My hopes were even without someone helping me, that that the Holy Spirit of God would help me communicate the gospel. The picture of Jesus on the cross is the message that I wanted pierced in people's minds forever. I know it's not the REAL picture of Jesus, no one has the real one. Dramas work, pictures work, anything can work except apathy. Apathy is cruel and helps no one come to Jesus. This driver couldn't figure out what a brothel was or where. That meant I had to do my own research. Then I found it.

The worst place in the world that all these reporters in UK and USA had been reporting on was right here in a village outside of Phnom Penh, Cambodia called Svay Pak. Men come from Asia and western countries travel to have sex with teen girls. It is not just young girls. Little boys and little girls are victims in this wicked sex trade. I heard two little girls on a video talk about "yum yum" for oral sex and "bam bam" is for intercourse. Did you read that? These are children ages 5 saying what they have had to do with men. The governor is not stopping it quick enough. Sex tourism helps the economy of this poor country. Pure evil and the burden I had while there was heavy every single day for these Cambodian people.

I preached outside of a few brothels and called for the fire from heaven to fall in Jesus name. This makes God angry. This is my final story on Cambodia, then I will write about Vietnam and Indonesia. I pray that there will be some of you reading this that will quit your job and move to Cambodia to help these children. This night in Svay pak is one I hope to never forget. Tears come in my eyes as I write because they are so poor.

Nov. 12, 2015 A few girls wanted my testimony tract. I tried to do a drama about what I used to be like and how Jesus saved me. My tuk tuk driver held the Jesus banner. He was like a son to me. I helped him with advice on getting more business and beefing up his tuk tuk. He said he was taking my advice and added now, he likes Jesus also. Later I saw him again and helped him with tuk tuk , we needed each other. He suggested we go down into the village. Great idea and was blessed to have him with me. My heart was broken and then impacted by one small boy. The Holy Ghost showed up in a powerful way. This little boy got the Joy of the Lord seeing picture of Jesus from Passion of the Christ movie. He couldn't stop smiling and laughing. This caused me to start singing childrens songs. The village stopped playing sports and riding bikes to listen. Some clapped, one lady offered money. Of course I said no to her money. I am bringing the gospel to you freely, Cambodia. This is one of the poorest villages in the world, where parents sell their own kids out of desperation to pay debtors. I started to tear up. The village thanked me for coming. I prayed over them attempting to release Hope from Heaven to their village. Jesus was glorified. Yes, I meet some pimps. I sang them an improve song called "You don't have to be a pimp anymore. You can repent and serve the Lord."

Time to go to Vietnam by bus and leave Cambodia in God's hands. Our Bus stopped for a break at a store and 4 little children ran to the bus begging between 5 and 7 years old. One little boy had on a girl's shirt ripped and I can't remember any of the orphans having shoes. I went into the store to get me snacks. Then came out with little hands begging again. I gave them all my stuff and said share. I knew by looking at their desperation, they wouldn't share. I went back in store to buy them all something. They got mad at me for being a mom and getting them waters with snacks. They wanted sugar. I wanted them healthy though. Right as I was handing out the goodies another child runs to the pack. Oh no! The bus is about to leave and he doesn't have anything. So, I gave him the snack bought for me and he got the best. Now, I had no snacks. Believe me, I was not going to complain. Praise God, my son was not out begging with a ripped girl's t-shirt on with no shoes. God has been good to me and my son.

I share this story with you to let you know I have seen beggars in this the world. It is a real problem, just like the child sex trafficking. If you are married with children, consider teaching your children about the poor in this world. I see a lot of spoiled brats in western culture. People wonder why I don't miss America while I am overseas. It's because America has many Christians already and these poor Cambodians don't have clothes, food or even parents some of them. Jesus sees the whole world, not just your small world. Think about it. You can make a difference in the world. One life at a time. Do something.

Vietnam has always been somewhere I wanted to go because my uncle Dallas was a chaplain in the USA Army in Vietnam. When he built me a club house in our backyard, he put his Army chest in there for me. Very special and immediately bought me an Army hat with Vietnam on it. Then, got my son t-shirt for his 25th birthday. I knew Aunt Ellen would enjoy seeing Nick in that shirt. She is around 90 years old now and still working in her garden. God brought me a huge divine appointment in a coffee shop that day with a man for the UK. He confessed to me how he is so tempted by these twenty-four-inch waist girls here and they are the devil. He cheats on his wife with cheap hookers in Vietnam. His mother was a part of the Salvation Army, so he found talking to me interesting. We later saw each other another day right as he was leaving Ho Chi Minh. He bought me coffee and asked me to sit with him. He heard me preach that night on the wild street. He said he followed me, but didn't say he was there. He wanted me to know he wasn't bad that night and hadn't been with any hookers. Then he asked for another one of my testimony pamphlets. Praise God! Straight from Journal!

Nov. 17, 2015 Ho Chi Minh City, Vietnam I went to the street called "Crazy Street" that the England prodigal told me about where all the sinners hang out. This was the same street that a Philippine evangelist suggested I preach the gospel. I carried a camera tripod in right hand and Jesus banner in left hand. Hundreds of Westerns heard the gospel and many Vietnamese saw Jesus banner. Some of the locals wanted to hold the banner and read it. One man said I helped him because he needed to stop smoking and drinking. Not sure if he will truly surrender to Jesus, but I prayed he would. The outreach on crazy street drew tourists to gather around. The small crowd listening to me caused traffic to be blocked from flowing. Not one police showed up in this communist country to shut down the gospel. Glory to God! Lots of dirty old men and a few mouthed off at me. Vietnam is supposed to be one of the most dangerous mission fields and by God's grace I never even had one cop harass me.

A big breakfast buffet for $5 and preaching the gospel to a man from Texas. He lived in Houston and never heard the gospel until that day in Vietnam. Talked to waitress awhile and then a girl from Australia a long time. Everything seemed great until I woke up the morning of Nov. 19, 2015.

Jason kept telling me to get my tags renewed on my car, but because my father died, UK denied me entrance, Singapore stressed me out. I am 45 years old and learned a very hard lesson. No matter how many problems you have that you still have to renew your car tag anyway. This is called the real world. My car was towed and it was going to take a certified letter from USA Embassy to even get my home/car out of the tow jail. This became a huge drama for me and Jason. How would God get me out of this? It was my fault. Will God give me grace in my neglect? My car is all I have of value in USA besides family. Vietnam Embassy refused to see me because I didn't have an appointment. So I had to wait a few more days because it was a Friday. Monday, I am now in Bali, Indonesia and got an appointment. I was very sick because of fumes from bikes in Vietnam, cold airport in Singapore and smokers in Indonesia are everywhere. Some money came in from givers, Praise God! I got letter in mail and waited for it to arrive. In the meanwhile I am getting tag taken care of and my mother mailed that letter to Jason in Florida. More bad news! In my nervous condition to do paperwork, I wrote my name on blank space instead of Jason's name. Jason was so graciously helping me and they refused to release the car for my 2nd error. I was at Jason's mercy. Here I had to ask God again to rescue me from my mistake. Jason was the only one that could get Motel Honda out of towing jail. I was vulnerable. I went back to USA Embassy in Bali, Indonesia and the man treated me like his own daughter. I needed that because my dad was gone now and was mad at myself. He didn't charge me a fee at Embassy. When I got done with my pledge and vow over letter I concluded "In Jesus name." The USA Embassy older gray haired man smiled and said "In Jesus name." The letter arrived correctly in a few days from Indonesia. Motel Honda got out of jail with new tags. God provided Grace, Mercy and taught me about trusting others more. People have let me down often and now I failed myself with huge mistake. It was very hard testing and vulnerable time in my walk with God in Asia. Thanks Jason, bless you.

Happy Thanksgiving Day was spent in a doctor's office in Bali, Indonesia. My journal of the Dr. visit: Nov. 26, 2015 Happy Thanksgiving day from Bali, Indonesia. I went to the Dr. for $50 USA and got three prescribed meds. There is a name for my condition. Yes, it was caused by smokers, smog and air conditions. I have Laryngitis. Problem was more in throat. I gave all four men working in the clinic my testimony tract. Doctor was most interested and seemed to want to hear the gospel. He even implied that God sent me there. He is a Catholic. I explained to him how I connect to God, not just religion in a very kind manner. He thanked me and asked for a hug. Hug? Wow, it was a moment of being vulnerable again. It was my first time to ever need a doctor on mission field, so I hugged my doctor. Then, ate a meal in Bali in an American style diner. Sometimes, I do miss USA.

While I was carrying my wood cross around Hong Kong that I got in Thailand a lady named Yuliana meet me. She was from Indonesia and had me add her to Face Book. When I arrived in

Bali she flew over to visit as well. I went to her church and spoke a few minutes on evangelism. Her biggest connection for me to expand the Kingdom of God was with her friend, Ady. When I got to Bali Ady asked if I could fly to Sumba Island? I had an extra $100 come in and decided to try another new adventure. Mind blowing how God set me up for a major outreach and connect Ady to the Prince and Princess of Sumba Island.

Post from Dec. 5, 2015 "Red Light fruit stand killer gives Life to Jesus!!!"

The day has been filled with ministry on Sumba Island, Indonesia. There was only one Airbnb room for rent and I took it. Not knowing she was married to Prince of Sumba. She was not a Christian, but came to jail to be my translator for outreach. Sarah is from Melbourne, Australia. There were over 200 men in the jail for my sermon. Everyone else that didn't come I preached to them shouting from the door. I preached on Matthew 9 where Jesus told Matthew "Follow Me". It was a command. How Jesus came for sinners. I forgot I was in a jail, because every sinner is a prisoner. Jesus is only one that can set free. When I gave, the altar call the first man to stand up was on front row. Many men stood and came forward for repentance to follow Jesus. Praise God! The man that stood up first used to work the at a Red Light as a Fruit stand business owner. He was in jail for chopping up the man in pieces that had sex with his wife. This man wanted Jesus to forgive him, Amen. Jesus forgave Saul, the Christian killer and made him the Apostle Paul the missionary. After the jail, I went outside with the team waiting for the ride to next preaching assignment. I noticed many young children hanging out across the street. Let me go to them and try to have some fun. My weird chicken dance moves and jumping jacks drew a huge crowd close to 100 children. They were laughing and trying to dance like me. Behind me were for young women that were training in Bible school to be ministers. The crowd was stirred and awaiting a speech. Therefore, I wanted to draw a crowd, so someone would share the gospel. ANYONE!!! I begin to try to get any of them to come over to preach the gospel. Many of the children were Muslims, but the Bible ladies were too shy. They should have been ready to preach right then. It ticked me off because ministry is not a microphone. Ministry is servanthood. Hopefully, they will never pass up an opportunity like this again in future. No one can say being shy is a culture. Because when you are a Christian the bible says the righteous are bold as lions. Every Christian around the world needs to be prepared to share the gospel. This is part of our Christian duty. If you are shy, ask God for help to overcome. Just don't use it as excuse to not share your faith with lost souls.

Our ride came for us to go to the next village. It took over 1 hour and half to get there in rain. We walked through mud puddles about 30 minutes. My finger nails got full of dirt from falling in mud a few times going towards unreached people group. I told Ady that many of those men in jail would love to be out walking in this to share the gospel. It was a blessing to go through all that to reach a group that had never been to church before.

When we arrived there was this building with a tin roof, no windows, concrete block walls, rocks everywhere for the floor and wooden pews. The pastor was only around 28 years old and gathered them all to come hear an American woman speak about Jesus. My message was based on Isaiah 9:6 *"For unto us a child is born, unto us a son is given: and the government shall be upon his shoulder; and his name shall be called Wonderful, Counselor, The mighty God, The everlasting Father, The Prince of Peace."* Jesus is Mr. Wonderful. It was a compassionate message for such poor people without even a store to buy toothpaste. A man on the front row that used to worship and believe in rocks had never been to church. His teeth were solid brown from chewing wood chips. He came forward along with most of the church to repent and follow Jesus. Praise God! Great day, Jesus is happy. Heaven is rejoicing. Ady, really cares about the salvation of souls on his island. He had me on other adventures while there as well. Souls were saved and anytime I want to return the door is open for me.

Sumba Island felt like real missions. I gave my six foot Jesus banner to Ady. Also, gave him the key to my home to return to the Prince and Princess of Sumba Island. He had been praying for two years to connect with these Island leaders. My key helped bring the connections. What a mighty God, we serve!

Back to Bali, Indonesia for a few days to rest. Bali was one of my favorite cities in the world, until 6 months later. It is so beautiful and super cheap. I love the street chicken with peanut sauce and sticky rice. One day while I was in Bali I paid a man $25 to drive me 8 hours all over the island. He showed up with Jesus on his t-shirt and purposely drove me to a Hindu temple while it was packed. I walked in that place while people were on their knees worshipping idols and rebuked them all. Of course, they told me to leave, but they saw Jesus poster. 6 months after this outreach someone wrote a blog after my going into Hindu temple to rebuke those idolaters. The video got 13,000 hits after about 10 days and with it came more death threats then I ever had in entire ministry. Not safe for me to ever return Bali, Indonesia alone with the gospel. They were warned and didn't receive the word. Woe to Bali!

Well, just call me the Asian Wedding crasher of 2015. I invited myself to a wedding in China, Cambodia and now Indonesia. One day I was out looking for some lunch and looked over at a huge outdoor tent event close to my hotel. Being the bold woman of faith and power I decided to go see what was going on up in here. 2 young people just got married and there was a wedding party. I invited myself to come on in. I got my photo with the bride and groom. Then, got a free bottled sprite. Next thing I know I am at the back-meeting grandpa and the little kids. The groom showed me the amazing buffet and told me to get a plate. Glory to God, so I did and filled my plate full of good shrimp. Way too much fun and appreciate the kindness of all these Asians. So much hospitality, yet so lost without their Creator guiding their paths in life. Pray right now, for God to send more laborers to the nations. Don't tell me again, how America needs missionaries.

It is time for Australian tour part 2 starting in Adelaide with Brother David and ending in Jan. with Brad in Melbourne. There is no place like Australia. First, the country is massive and only place I physically felt far from USA. There is a park across my first hotel with a zip line. It was a lot of fun riding that after all the kids left. Weee!!! I love to enjoy free stuff.

Facebook post Dec. 11, 2015 "Australian outreach was wild and crazy!" We had a great team and several people jumped in to join us. Big crowds drew because I was preaching against Islam and their wicked religion. The gospel was being preached and over eight Adelaide police showed up. The team was amazed at how awesome the police were. They helped us all night. A woman, in her fifties got in my face saying how she wanted to cut my throat. Some of the crowd cheered her on to get her to kiss me. She attempted, but I quickly got her away from my face. The police helped and pulled her aside. Police openly rebuked her. Then a younger lesbian got in my face saying that I better watch my back. The police then pulled her aside to deal with her preacher bullying. Later that night the young lesbian threw a bucket of water on the street trying to get it on me. By the end of the night, she lost full control and threw a glass of vodka on me. Vodka got in my hair, tongue, ear and splashed on other Christians. Persecution only made everyone on the team more joyful. We had great fellowship after the outreach.

Tonight people asked good questions as well. What must I do to be saved? Who is God? What is the final exam? There were too many good questions versus the haters. Many stayed for long periods of the night with interest. The police never corrected me. David said tonight was a blessing and beautiful!

Adelaide, Australia was very hot in December. It was their summer time. Before I booked my ticket to Adelaide, I asked David how he felt about Santa Claus. Some people will tell children about Santa without the fact that he is dead. This is one of my top 10 pet peeves when people don't tell the truth about Santa. David agreed it was a lie. We connected well in the Harvest field.

How did I find David and Brad? Well, social media has been a huge help to me. I get supporters from YouTube and Face Book. People suggest me to add people in other countries and then many times go meet them for the sake of the gospel. First, before meeting new people I get to know them. I want to see videos and read posts. Not every street preacher needs to meet me or work with me. I try to choose wisely based on personal convictions.

The glory of God makes someone more attractive. December 2015 I got a marriage proposal from someone I never met and then another man wanted to get to know me for possible courtship. Both men I was not interested in for romance. I am very picky and both did not have good jobs. Why would I be attracted to a broke man, when Jesus sends me all over the world? There was only one man in 2015 that I was interested in over in the UK. Oh, the blue eyed Scottish man. Deep sigh…. I bought perfume for our preaching date that he didn't show up for in Edinburgh. God closed that door. It's probably a good thing because I might have grabbed him and kissed him while the bagpipes played Amazing Grace by the smooth river. We had serious chemistry and was ready to start courting him for marriage.

I recently had a man from Africa write me to tell me I was his missing rib. NO, I AM NOT YOUR RIB! I am not even his Cole slaw or Baked Beans and Corn Bread.

If you are a single woman preacher then, guard your heart, ministry and anointing. Do not throw away your calling for some muscles or a man wanting to rescue you. If you are called to get married and serve your husband, then do it for the glory of God. Singles can be free to work full time for God. Praise the Lord! Don't settle and be miserable because you think you need a prayer covering either. Jesus is praying for you. Don't get all lonely and needy. Blow Jesus kisses while you preach, it works for me.

My time in Adelaide was just a few weeks. I preached with David at an Elton John concert and then city one more time. I preached with a man named Peter and Mark also. We had great outreaches and many teenagers sat to listen to the gospel for the first time. Glory to God! It was very hot in this city.

Vickie became a new friend from this city. We went to preach on the streets by ourselves and it was spiritual warfare. The lesbian that attacked us with vodka on the weekend came and pushed me over 5 times in chest across the outdoor mall area. She said "I am willing to go to jail." Jail is ok, but Hell is forever, these people need to understand the consequences of sin and rejecting Jesus. Vickie took me to the airport to fly to Sydney. This is a city that I had wanted to go to pretty much my whole adult life. There is so much to do there, if you have the money to spend. I don't have the extra cheap thrills money so, I go preach the gospel by those crowded tourists spots. Taking photos and walking is always free. My first outreach in Sydney was going to be Christmas day on George Street. However, it changed the morning I woke up in Sydney looking for a church to visit.

Dec. 20, 2015 Hillsong Sydney Christmas rebuke. Taxi, two trains and a bus finally almost two hours later I arrived while Sun was still out. Prayed over the campus and looked for the best sidewalk entrance to reach this church. Security knew my "Jesus saves from Hell" t-shirt was way different from Hillsongs "You are loved" banner. Security banned me from the church property. The security also warned me that the police were coming. Well, he lied because police never showed up. Church lied also. I saw the Santa throne on church property. With my camera on I asked Hillsong workers "Did you tell the children the truth about Santa?" Hillsong volunteer said "No they will find out later, he wasn't there to judge". I said "I am here to judge." Later as he drove off with Santa throne I said "Liar, Liar, pants on fire."

On the bus the Holy Ghost gave me a pearl from the Word of God in John chapter 2. Jesus rebuked the ones in temple for selling doves. Scriptures says Jesus saw sheep, oxen and doves sold. However, Jesus rebuked those selling doves. That is what Hillsong does by charging for their Christmas program. Two services today were sold out, they seat 30,000 and they charged $5 a person. That is $300,000 in one day big money. There is a possibly, I have gotten my numbers wrong in this thread. However, I did see the price that they were charging, saw they were sold out and found out the number of seats. If I am wrong, please forgive me. I am trying to make a point in this post about churches getting making money off Christmas program and being dishonest about Santa Claus. If someone wanted $5 back, they can ask. Not sure how many asked for a refund. The Dove represents the Holy Spirit. It is possible to prostitute the anointing for profit. This is the same as selling doves. I stood outside rebuking Hillsong for over an hour. Repent! For idolatry and lying were my main points besides the money loving issues. I told them they are just as bad as Mormon's adding Santa to the Christmas story. Luke 2 does not involve Santa coming on a sled to Bethlehem to bring baby Jesus presents. Many churches deserve side walk prophets. Hillsong, London just put out a very immodest Christmas show that was going viral called "Silent Night." A New York Street Preacher Woman was confirmation to me to go when she wrote me five minutes after I decided to go. Coming back to my home that night took hours and many divine appointments on the way. Obeying God is not always convenient. Read the book of Jonah.

Sydney has several nice places to preach the gospel. I preached close to Opera House and near the water where the ferries roll in daily. It was a great spot for folks to sit and listen. After an outreach one night in Sydney I was coming up the escalator to get on the train, still feeling bold as a lion and completed 100% yielded to Jesus. A Muslim woman smiled at me. I noticed her daughter on a rug praying in those long Islam clothes. Her husband was praying on another rug. Without even thinking what I should do; my mouth opened praising Jesus really loud. I praised Jesus for being the Son of God. Praised Jesus for being the Way! Praise Jesus for being awesome! I praised and preached until they stopped bowing to Allah. Everyone was looking at me and then I stopped to wait on the train. That's how you stop Muslims from publicly praying in a Sydney train station. I wasn't embarrassed. My goal was to embarrass those demons operating and lift Jesus higher for all to see His worth, His fame and His glory. Worthy is the Lamb!

New Year's Eve in Sydney is one of the most popular places in the world to be for the fireworks on Harbor Bridge. I went that night alone to preach the gospel. Never saw any Christians preaching, passing tracts out or with any banners. Dec. 31, 2015 Happy New Years from Sydney, Australia! It is now midnight and just got in the house fifteen minutes ago. Nice peace and quiet again. I preached to many lost souls tonight as they walked by George Street on the way towards the Harbor Bridge that a few years ago lite up the word "Eternity." The police accused me of disturbing the peace because a few complaining about what I was saying. Police woman, said "What if someone reading a Quran out loud?" My response to the police was "Muslims don't evangelize with reading Quran. They evangelize with bombs on their back, sharp knives and explosives." Anyway they moved me 75 meters west. I still reached the same people going in that direction to fireworks. Another male policeman showed up and asked me to not speak against Islam. I said "ok I will only preach Jesus then." He didn't think he could handle that either and asked how long I would be there. We agreed on 10 PM which was a long time. I had a few one on one talks, but mostly people walked by to Harbor Bridge. Police put their fingers in their ears a few times over my loud voice. At the end of the outreach I was talking to believers from Indonesia and my heart also begin to burn for India. New Year's Eve was then spent alone in a rented room off Airbnb. I really liked my roommates there. One from Spain and the other from Indonesia. I enjoy staying in hostels and homes to get to know people. God always opens the door for the gospel. As I reflect on my three homes in Sydney, I can say there was a deposit of the Kingdom of God placed in all homes. Thank you to the "Most awesome youth group ever" in upper state New York for doing a fundraiser for my ministry and paying my rent while in Sydney. It was cool to visit this church in person after returning to USA to thank them in person. God bless you, MAYGE.

Victoria, Australia is for sure the state that I will always remember the most. What a wild place to preach the gospel. I went over there because of Brad. By the end of my trip I had linked up with many more preachers in Melbourne. Many of them had seen me on YouTube already. They just didn't realize when I was coming there. Maybe I need to make YouTube subscribers more aware of my schedule. Hard decision because I get death threats from Muslims, Hindus and angry hecklers around the world now. I have documented past three years very well of world missions.

Jan. 2, 2016 Melbourne, Victoria Australia "No small stir Melbourne, Australia outreach. World Vision day was a borderline Riot. It got immediately. As soon as I began preaching from Isaiah 40, a wild man came up next to me to begin publicly reading from Stephen King book. Wild man helped to grow the crowd. People began coming forward to sit and watch. Several cursed me and one man brought a microphone for the heckler to continue Stephen King tribute. I changed my location to get inside the crowd on the grass of hill by library. The heckler got bored and stopped reading.

Side Note: Hey, it's my meeting and there is an art to holding a crowd. Use hecklers to gather crowd, but never let them take over the crowd. I learned this from selling cars. My boss taught me how to walk in authority. Years ago I sold cars for a season in Pensacola because all the car salesman got fired. I was the cleaning lady and my boss was desperate. My boss was not a Christian, but saw me open air preach before. He said "If I can get you to use that same passion that you put into preaching, then you will sell a lot of cars," He taught me to always walk ahead of the customer and never let them lead me. I learned valuable lessons working for this mean boss. Now, years later I am in Australia preaching alone on World Vision Day and refuse to let a Stephen King fan take over my meeting. This is my Holy Ghost church service, not the church of Satan!

My new focus was to walk on the grass to the people face to face with my eternal questions. Soon a divine appointment came on hill with a sincere homosexual asking questions about God. The Holy Ghost gave me a word of knowledge in my spirit the name "Kevin" I said "Kevin is that your name?" He said "yes." I said " How would I know that?" Kevin answered, "God told you." He then allowed me to lay my hand on his shoulder to pray for him. He said that he felt the Fire in my hand. I almost cried because of God's love for him. Praise God! I don't lay hands on everyone for prayer or shake everyone's hands. There are times I know God wants to touch a person to show His Power. Follow peace, amen. Later that day the crowd got wild, again. Three people surrounded me reading books out loud. Then someone threw water on me. Yet, several people sat quiet watching and listening. One was a girl from China. She asked for my testimony tract along with a few others at the end of outreach. A policeman showed up and threatened me with a ticket if they were called to come back there. The police warned me not to offend anyone.

This is not even possible for a true ambassador of Christ. The Word of God is offensive, it's a sword that cuts the rebellious heart. When the police left those serious to learn more about God's Kingdom stayed. The ending was peaceful and rejoiced to be somewhere the gospel was really needed. Victoria, Australia allows nine-month abortions with two doctors signing a yes. This is evil!

My first home I rented from really enjoyed my two night stay so much that they gave me a free ride to Ballaret, Australia, this is a city that my Face Book friend lives with family. When I first planned the trip I didn't understand that Victoria was a state and that he wasn't even near Melbourne. Because I travel so much everything seems close on a map. Brad is close to my son's age. We had a nice first meal with his friend across the street from a Catholic church. Anyone that knows me knows: I have no respect for the Catholic church because of all the compromises and Mary worship. I also have no respect for these USA televangelists going to eat with Pope of Rome. This church had strings all over it and I wanted to find out why. Those colorful strings on this Ballaret Catholic church were for the victims of child sexual abuse. Ballaret has a dark history of priests molesting children. I read a lot of new coverage about this city after seeing all those strings on St. Patrick Church. According to the news, Australia's worst pedophiles were in the city and possibly molested a thousand children. This priest is up for parole in 2019. Cardinal George Pell is hiding at the Vatican refusing to come testify in Australia. This is the same thing that happens in Los Angeles, Ca. with, Cardinal Roger Mahoney refusing to speak. He hides out at the Vatican. The Catholic church covers up so much sin, while many victims killed themselves for mental relief.

2016 Academy Awards in USA Best Motion Picture of the Year and Best Writing went to "Spotlight." A true story about the Catholic Church in Boston covering up child molesters in the local Catholic Archdiocese. I was preaching in Hollywood in 2016 the day they announced this win. Praise God! I normally don't rejoice over a win in Hollywood. However, thank you Hollywood for another winning movie to expose this church. HBO movie prepared me in 2013 to rebuke the Vatican.

Preaching in Ballarat got the locals all stirred up. After being there a few hours the police told me I can never preach there ever again until the head captain retires. Maybe this Cop was a Catholic or Catholic sympathizer. Let me share about the outreach. Jan. 4th, 2016 Only five cops showed up for Brad and I, after two hours of evangelism. We were told we can never practice free speech or hold banners in this city ever again. Brad got it all on film. One of the police was heard to have said they got around forty calls at the police station about my preaching on their emergency phone line. Not five calls, but forty calls on which 000, which is like 911 in USA. Why so offended locals? Are you Australians not offended with the priests that raped your own children in your town? God sent us to confront and shine a big LIGHT.

People listened and sat down awhile. People lined the walls of the mall. The whole two hours we were there the mall security tried to get us to leave. I told Brad on the way there that I hoped for a low key, non-extreme day partly because it was just Monday. My tripod wasn't even packed because I thought it would be an easy outreach. Well, it wasn't a calm day. A teenager girl spit in my hair walking by me.

God used Brad with his awesome large banner. The gospel is one side and a strong rebuke, fear God warning to sinners on the other side. He is great to work alongside on the front lines. After we left Michael was working crowd, sharing the gospel. He had several good conversations because of the open air-preaching explosion. This city needed a good Bible spanking awakening. 1 Corinthians 15:34 *"Awake to righteousness, and sin not! For some have not the knowledge of God: I speak this to your shame."*

Melbourne, Australia has several great places to preach the gospel. Federation Square was a place set up like a church. I loved this spot because people lined up row by row to sit. It was like a church service and a man even hit me. I asked the cops why they didn't arrest him? They said I had to press charges. Wow, that was shocking. USA the cops would have arrested the man without me asking because he broke the law. We preached there and other places in the city. People pushed me, ripped up my Bible, poured drink on my head and persecuted other preachers, as well. These people are like wild animals, especially around the train station. My last day there preaching, ended up with fifteen police showing up. They were glad to know I was leaving soon, just another day in the office for me. Many Australians watch my channel and a few new people from this city now that I left. I have free housing and invites to return there anytime. Praise God! Maybe I will in 2017. Australia was over a month of my life and love the wild bunch. They need missionaries. I would love to go around the entire country by car, even if it means being in desert hours.

A fun day with Brad and his little sister, was spent at a Ballarat wild life park. I enjoyed feeding kangaroos with my hand. Koalas were cute in selfie photos. Tasmanian devil was an interesting little critter with loud mouth. I had so much fellowship in Australia, that I dreaded being alone again over in New Zealand. Yet, I got to keep on the gospel road. I can never get too comfortable.

New Zealand is where I flew after Australia. When I arrived it was cold and rainy weather. After a few days of rest I felt God calling me to lay down the ministry and fast for a season. Fasting with water only 7 days made me better in tune with the Lord, but also very moody. I traveled to Dundin for a week on fast. God put a girl from Tonga island on bus there and back to Christchurch. She was a Christian and wanted to hear all my stories. When I look at New Zealand I remember how thankful I am for her friendship. Later in 2016 she surprised me with $100 offering. It was fun seeing her at the Chicago Cubs game this year on Facebook when they won world series. This is where her mom lives in USA. I remember her stories she told me, as well. Someday, I may go to Tonga to preach the gospel.

One day I felt the house shake in Christchurch and discovered it was a 4.7 earthquake. I had never felt an earthquake before. Soon God released me to preach again. I preached on earthquakes because they have had so many in Christchurch. This is Ray Comforts home town and where he started his open air preaching ministry. It wasn't a good place to draw crowds though. I went to the famous area with big church and hardly anyone was around. New Zealand was not as thrilling as I had hoped it would be. It was hard because of the water fast. If you have money and a car for sightseeing, it's a different story. God sent me to fast, rest, preach and write. New Zealand is where God spoke to me to call my book "Inspired by the Great Commission" instead of "Motel Honda." My story was bigger than a Honda.

Super thankful to finally leave this city and go to Auckland. This city has great places to open-air preach. The crowds listened and took photos at my last preaching spot. Great day to preach there because it was "Auckland day." God put that on my schedule. Perfecto!

As I was leaving, I began to talk on the sidewalk in Auckland to a tall college student from France about noticing him listening to my message. He just had arrived from France the day before to go to the University of Auckland. I told him I had just arrived that day as well from another island. He had never seen a street preacher or heard the gospel before. I told him that I preached in his city Nice, France in 2014. Shared with him how to pray and seek God for truth. Praise God for this divine appointment. New Zealand was country #40 for me since beginning world missions in 2016. Glory to God! Update on his hometown Nice, France later in July 2016 there was a huge terrorist attack on their big holiday. 84 people were killed as a truck purposely drove through the crowds mowing people down like grass. We never know when we will die. The Holy Bible tells us are days are numbered. I will never know if he was in that crowd that day 84 were killed. I reached a guy in Scotland from Nice, France and even gave him a French bible. Now, I reached a young man from Nice, France in Auckland, New Zealand. It is important to preach to the crowds and, talk to the ones that were listening while you preached when possible. God wants to save lost souls. What an honor to be someone's FIRST Christian street preacher.

Here is where the long journey begins back to America. My two choices were to go from New Zealand to Hawaii to LA then on to Fort Lauderdale, or go to Thailand to Finland to Fort Lauderdale. I choose to go to Finland on the way back to spend Valentine's Day in snow with Jesus.

Bangkok, Thailand was awesome, as always. I feel asleep getting my cheap foot massage because of jet lag. I enjoyed Pad Thai and other Thai cheap meals. Preached with local team there and expressed joy of one day coming back to stay longer. Thanked them for watching my small bag of winter clothes and had a showdown with UK man on the streets of Bangkok. Some African black man followed me alone down a dark road while I was going to get my Pad Thai. He wanted me to help him get into USA. He even sat with me while I ate, which I did not invite him to do. By God's grace I got away from the African stalker and jogged back to hotel. He didn't follow me because he had a phone call. I am amazed how God watches over me all over the world. People have no idea the spiritual warfare that comes with this kind of international ministry. I make a crazy schedule sometimes, without thinking about how my body will react to that plan. Great deals, sometimes have strange hours on the plane. Oh well, better than not going at all, amen.

I traveled from Bangkok to Oslo, Norway for a day. Oh wow, I was so blessed by the place I rented in the city. The owner was in Copenhagen, Denmark and left the high-rise apartment for me to enjoy. The sunset was gorgeous and sun rise. Thank you, Jesus, for allowing me to see Norway in the winter even for just one day. Happy thoughts of this day because I almost slept in the airport to save money. Then, provision came in so I could go into the city for a night and morning. May sound simple, but it was long journey back to USA after 14 months on the mission field. God was allowing me to slowly enjoy my way back home. Yet, where is home? I don't have one. I must be talking about my family. Maybe "Home" is all 50 states of the USA. I don't know where home is anymore. One thing I do know, I am happy traveling overseas nonstop. It makes me feel alive. Meeting strangers for the purpose of the gospel is awesome.

Finland is one of my favorite countries because of its forest snow winter beauty with reindeers. I saw a beautiful picture of Helsinki in the snow in 2014 and decided to go there. The trip was so incredible that I asked God to please let me go there on my way back to America. I had free housing. She used my laptop in a Jerusalem hostel to Skype her family in Finland. We became friends. However, she warned me of a sickness in her home with fever. My plans changed, quickly. Now, I had to budget in housing. Finland was not cheap. 30 countries in 14 months, would God fail me now? No way, He had an adventure to Russia for me again. Surprise!!! Seriously? Oh yes, I drug my body to 6 countries in a week. Australia was an airport stop over city making it 6 countries in a week. Why not? Russia, here I come.

Why not go to Russia on the ferry again? It was only $93 for the boat, housing and bus ride inside St. Petersburg. God provided extra for my last few weeks there. I bought a $10 bag in Helsinki mall for my stuff since I had broken my wheel on my bag. When I walked outside in the snow I noticed street preachers. What!!!! I didn't know anyone in Finland was street preaching. I was smiling eagerly wanting to cross to meet this team. The man said "Angela Cummings!!!" Ed knew my name because of YouTube. He had become a preacher over the past year. He enjoyed my videos and others on YouTube street preachers as well, influenced him to step out into street ministry. I got to preach as the big snowflakes came down and rejoiced with new family in favorite country, they gave me Russian Bibles to take on my mission to Russia and gospel tracts. What a great divine appointment.

Russia showdown with the Harry Krishna Cult members, as they all danced and chanted to demon gods. I cried out to them how they were breaking God's heart. One of the men pushed me and another one came to talk to me because it began to rain on their demon party. They were forced to stop because of rain. He was very confused, but glad he was angry enough to talk to me. Apathy is horrible. Anger is a good sign of conviction in many cases. I gave the Bibles out and tracts very easily. This trip had snow all over St Pete. I enjoyed some Russian soup and bought my mom a Russian magnet for her fridge. I shared gospel all over the city. Then went back to my cabin room on the boat to Finland. Hey, Russia almost didn't let me in the country, thanks to UK stamping a denial on my passport. This hurt me at the boarders in a few countries after that. Not cool at all UK. I sought advice from a seasoned missionary on my passport problems. He suggested I just get a whole new passport and start over.

Simple Russian gospel adventure on St. Pete's line. Update on Russia, Putin just passed a law in summer of 2016 that it will now be illegal to preach the gospel in Russia on the streets. That is horrible news. I am glad to have gotten another chance to reach them before this law was established in Russia.

When I returned to Finland I reconnected with the same street preachers for ministry outside in the cold and inside in the metro. My last day in Finland was spent alone on Valentine's Day in an amazing apartment for under $40 USA by the airport. This was my choice. I soaked up all the views and just walked around my large apartment in awe. Pretty sure this was the most comfortable bed of all 30 countries. Great last day memory on the mission field. Happy Valentine's Day Jesus! You are my heartbeat. I used to hate Valentine's day as a single, but now my life is too exciting to share with someone else besides God. Paris in 2014, Spain in 2015, Finland in 2016 and South Korea is on my schedule for Valentine's Day for 2017. Makes you wonder just how jealous is Jesus for me to stay single? Not sure a husband can compete with how Jesus has treated me all these years. He would have to be pretty special for me to slow down and take notice. I love World Missions!

When I came back to America Jason and his wife picked me up at airport. He told me eye to eye that my car was in the worst part of town during the time it was towed. This made me more thankful for him and then I hugged my car. My home was saved from Towing Jail. Thank you again those that helped save my home and car.

Motel Honda is ready for a road trip to Tampa to see friends. I preached in Alabama in church. Drove to Texas to get flight to see my home church: Bible believers fellowship. Some Facebook friends opened their home to me and it was fantastic. I preached three days at Catholic Convention, Academy Awards and at Cal State in Fullerton. Every day was filled with Christian fellowship and I enjoyed all of it. Very edifying to be around people with same goals and heart Kingdom work. Watching Ruben Israel smash a Mary Idol at Catholic convention is epic. The Catholics all started freaking out and praying the rosary on their knees. You can get away with a lot more in America than you can other countries, yet so many Americans still get scared to share their faith. Never fear, the Holy Ghost is here.

After California, I flew back to Dallas. I spent a few days with my best friend, Gail on the road. We went to Steve Hill's grave together and laid pink roses. I will always love that preacher like a spiritual father. Even his grave fired me up for the gospel. The grave had awesome quotes on it. We found out that we were first to see it since they put it up. Praise God! Told my buddy bye and went to Little Rock, Ark. to see Oliva and get my hair done.

Olivia was like my nurse in a hair hospital. My hair was ruined in Philippines by a man clueless on doing blonde highlights. I attempted to fix it myself in Asia and Israel. Then I got a bad cut in Australia by a man with shaky alcoholic hands. My hair looked like it had a mullet. People don't realize what all I go through in traveling around the world. She spent four hours fixing my hair back to health and reshaping it into a proper cut. Going to 30 countries is not the same as driving

30 states. Some of these countries have bad water. Now, I am on a cleanse to purge my body from any possible problems.

After Little Rock, Ark. I drove to Jackson, Tn. where my son was born. I preached two services there and enjoyed some good fellowship. Finally, I made it to my hometown to see my mother and son. I loved hugging my mother and sat in my daddy's chair missing him. Mom gave me one of dad's bibles. I bought my father yellow, red and orange roses for his grave. Mom and I went to his grave together the next day and I left some roses. I was able to see my son's girlfriend and Nicholas briefly. I got a hug and photo with him. Got Motel Honda ready for the next trip and out the door I went for Jonah Tour in USA. What is a Jonah Tour? When God asks you to preach somewhere you don't want to and you only do it because of the Fear of God.

March 17, 2016 Well, it has been five years today since moving into my car to live. I hope you have enjoyed all my stories and having stirring in your heart to know God if you know Him yet. My parents adopted me at three weeks old and walked us to church in the snow one year. I will always respect my family for the value they taught me at a young age for sacrificing for Jesus.

With that being said, I dedicate this book of my 5-year journal to the man that chose me, adopted me and gave me his name. Harold B. Cummings III. I miss you, Daddy.

God told me to take this picture. It is my last memory of my daddy.

Chapter 14

Jonah USA tour chapter

My goal was to finish the book at the 5-year marker with dedication to my father, but so much more happened in 2016. I was not too excited to be back in America after going around the world several times. Now, what am I supposed to do in the states? Topeka, Kansas was having a Holy Ghost conference with major Mega Church pastors speaking and asked me to come teach on Evangelism during conference. I even went to eat with the church leaders and one of the Mega Pastors from Dallas sat across from me. I told him why Dallas, Texas was the most annoying city in USA to me. There are churches everywhere. 4 years I lived in DFW and rarely saw anyone out on the streets sharing the gospel. One time I preached alone at Justin Bieber in Dallas. Why? Justin is the #1 youth star possibly in the world and no one thought to send their youth group out to share the gospel with the Beliebers? Then, I find out while sitting at this table that Justin Bieber was in Kansas City that night. I wanted to skip the Holy Ghost conference that one night. It was not my night to speak. I could go preach the gospel. The leaders felt I should stay in town and go to church. They were an awesome church. Normally, I would have put evangelism before a conference. When Saturday came for me to speak over 80 people showed up for my evangelism training. The Pastor told the group of people out of all the speakers that I inspired him the most. He likes my YouTube channel and is an open-air preacher too. This church became special to me and reminded me of the book of Acts church. They were a community that prayed together, meet in homes, did evangelism and had meaningful church services that welcomed the Holy Ghost.

After leaving Topeka, I went to Chicago to street preach at a huge concert because people on my YouTube invited me often. I made new street preaching friends that weekend in Chicago and even stayed with them a night. Detroit has a Jew living there that has watched my channel over 2 years. God made a way for me to meet David in Detroit. He asked me to preach there, but I wanted to preach in Dearborn, Michigan. Dearborn is the home of the most Muslims in USA. I went over there and preached in the city on street corners by myself. Nothing bad happened to me, praise God! Jesus be praised the One True Son of God. Jesus is not a prophet of Islam. He is the Word of God made flesh. Read the Gospel of John.

> 1 John 4:15 KJV "Whoever confesses that Jesus is the son of God, God dwelleth in him, and he in God."

I was told by a seasoned missionary to get rid of my passport with all those stamps. He suggested I get a new one, so no one at the immigration would see the UK denial stamp anymore. I invested $140 in new one and mailed old one to the state. My passport came back so quick along with old one to keep as souvenir. A lady that has known me awhile had just given me $1000 cash while I visited her in Louisiana. That was my ticket out of USA. I decided to go to Costa Rica and see about the land. Someday, I may want to live in another country. I wanted to check this country out for their lifestyle. Valentine's Day in Helsinki, Finland I watched a YouTube video about why Costa Rica was better than Thailand. The cheapest ticket to Costa Rica was from Albany, NY. I was scheduled to speak in 3 NY churches in middle of May until June. This worked out perfect. I drove from Topeka to upper NY reaching several cities with the gospel on the way.

Matthew 10:7 KJV "And as ye go, preach, saying, The kingdom of heaven is at hand."

Jesus talked to His disciples about as you are going, preach the gospel. This is why I try to preach my way across the world, instead of spending thousands on one ticket to only reach one city. I told one of my supporters on the phone 2 weeks ago that with the travel knowledge I have now, that I would have done 2013 Europe trip different. I could have stayed 2 months on the mission field, instead of only 3 weeks. This is all self-taught and now a passion for me. When I see someone raising funds for a mission trip, immediately I look at the price they are asking. Talk about a holy frustration because most of the ones I see are overpriced. If I know someone pretty well, I go to them to try to help get budget down. This is just a side note. My biggest blessing has been skyscanner.com. I try to find the cheapest way to go and flexible with days. I got the cheapest ticket to Costa Rica from NY. Parked my car at a YouTube subscribers home for 3 weeks and he took me to airport for my escape plan. I wanted a place to relax from all this travel. USA is not a place to relax for me and hasn't been in years. Costa Rica was a great get away. It was nice, but don't see myself ever living there. I plan on looking at other Central America countries in the future. USA citizens have been leaving for other countries in seek of a new life. I don't need a home, because I travel nonstop doing missions work. My lifestyle seems to work best as when I need a break, that I just find a place to rent in someone's home on Airbnb. This is one of my biggest blessings for cheap housing in my mission's budget. The places I stayed in Costa Rica had divine appointments. One guy was all the way from Australia with his wife from Switzerland. I was fasting for future ministry trips. This caused the atmosphere in the condo to clash. Darkness in him versus Light of the gospel in me and I volunteered to leave the condo, if the owners would give me full refund. This happens at times where I stay. John 3 writes that people hate the light. The glory of God was resting on me and he didn't like it. No worries, God brought me to a new place to have alone to finish my time in Jaco. I stayed all over Costa Rica and shared gospel as I went. Praise God! One of my landlords asked me to preach at the Sunday markets and it was a quiet ride back. There were so many new age idols in the home, that I was glad to preach the gospel.

When I got back to the USA the street preachers were stirred up over Target stores allowing men to now use the women's bathrooms. The only requirement was for the man to self-identify as a woman. Oh goodie, welcome back to the USA. Let the war games begin, right? Well, the church I was scheduled to speak at in Upper New York decided not to allow me to speak to the youth. I was in shock, because I drove 3 days to get there. My friend that scheduled me wasn't the head leader. We just had to say ok to whatever they decided. This was the youth group that raised $300 for my ministry and covered most of my rent in Sydney, Australia. I still got to tell the youth thank you for that. The senior pastor even asked me to speak that Sunday morning to the whole church for a few minutes. After church we meet in back of church for anyone that wanted to hear more about my world mission's trips. Only a few were interested. That night Danny and I went to a Target. So many preachers had already gone into Target to rebuke them for their bathroom policies. I promised the street preachers that started this movement that when I got back that I would go rebuke a Target too. Eddie was the one with the idea. It was his birthday. Danny held the camera and I went into a Target rebuking them for their bathroom policies. Many people laughed because store was fairly empty, but the video got over 100,000 hits. It caused a huge stir in Upper New York.

 Next thing I know my boredom kicked in and I drove about 25 to a city in Vermont looking for a High school with good sidewalk. Universities were closed by now because it was the middle of May. Just a simple preach that day exploded my YouTube to over 14,000 hits. I started getting emails to come to other schools in Vermont. The best letter I got was from a grown lady older than me. She wanted to get right with God and told me all about the mess in Vermont with drugs.

God sent me to the next church in NY. They moved the meetings to the outdoors, so I could preach to anyone fishing in this small community while having church. I spoke 2 services and enjoyed getting to know the Pastor. He was a fire ball for God and always sharing the gospel with someone. Pastor Fred didn't care what his denomination thought about having a speaker like me in the pulpit. He wanted to meet me. We are Facebook friends for a long time. I didn't mind driving there because he was such an encouragement, even if only 15 people showed up for church. After I left there I went to preach in 3 more Targets trying to cover some states that don't have as many street preachers. I preached in another NY one and that got removed from YouTube for some reason. Massachusetts and Connecticut are the 2 other states that I rebuked the Targets for their bathroom policies allowing men in women's bathrooms. My favorite was Holyyoke, Mass. because it was over 4 minutes. I asked girls in store if they wanted men in their bathroom? They said "No." I said "There you have it, America has spoken." Pervert revolution!

I found another High School in NY to visit now. It had a great sidewalk and was very small town. Whoa! I was not expecting such a huge response. The students gathered across the street and were listening. The Vice Principle came out and was so mad at me. He grabbed my tripod, but I held it tight. I got it back and continued to preach, warn and say thought provoking end time topics. The police came and were not going by the law. They clearly wanted me to just go. I left and the video got over 100,000 within in weeks. So many news reports started popping up on the internet. Either about my preaching at Target or at this school. I turned down interviews. Why? Because it was a Jonah tour. I didn't even really want to be in USA, but was making my rounds anyway to the open doors. See the power of fasting? I was fasting for Europe 2016. Yet, NY had an explosion when I got back. Praise God! A friend from bible school suggested for me to stay at her mom's house. The next morning her son that she adopted from Africa came in kitchen. He said he saw me on the news the night before. So, I decided to just go. I didn't want to cause my TN tags to cause problems with their neighbors and have to defend me. I drove to Albany to take one interview with ABC and stay in a hotel. I wasn't in the mood to sleep in my car. Only a few times I stayed in my car when I returned to states to do Jonah tour. Once was in Rhode Island at Walmart and then I was startled awake up at 4 am by loud employee playing heavy metal in his jeep. Pretty sure he did it on purpose to wake up all the campers in parking lot. I walked in that Walmart that morning to give them a rebuke for hiring jerks. I changed my mind when I saw all the senior citizens.

Now, back to the ABC Albany, NY story. When I arrived at the news station I asked for permission to film the interview on my camera. The lady doing interview said it should be ok, but they changed the interview to another news reporter. When he walked into the room my camera was rolling. He clearly refused to do the interview with my camera rolling, so I blew him away by cancelling the interview. He said "you don't want to be on TV?" Nah, not that important. It was epic moment to cancel and get on film. Many New Yorkers were watching my channel at the time and countless numbers of young people wrote me. I got so many comments, emails and inboxes that I had to turn all comments off on my YouTube.

Even during this season Bali, Indonesia was going viral 7 months after I left. They were over there threatening to stone me to death. Many Bali and Bali tourists wrote me angry. I would say the most death threats of my ministry came from there that week in Indonesia.

Some young man in Ireland begin stalking me and telling me to kill myself. He looked miserable in his photo and asked my friends to pray for him. He was stalking me on Facebook and YouTube. His mother found one letter and wrote me. She was from Bethlehem and moved with family to Ireland. She was embarrassed for her son and apologized to me. She then said this happened for a reason because she used to be a follower of Jesus Christ. She was backslidden. God was using this to invade this whole family. Thank you, God, that you can turn this whole family around and help this young man and his mom. You must realize I deal with these kinds of things daily. You can't be on the frontlines of battle and expect none to hate you. If a day goes by and there is no hate mail, it seems strange. Persecution is part of my life because of my bold stance for Christ. Jesus is worth it, because He is the perfect Lamb of God sacrifice. I love Jesus! He is my redeemer and friend.

John 15:14 KJV "Ye are my friends, if ye do whatsoever I command you." Jesus

My point is the nations are contacting me, even it is to say how they want to kill me. I would rather get a death threat, then be ignored. Angry is a sign someone is awake. My goal is to wake up people, including the sleeping saints. Some saints are even sipping saints. Gail told me that a lot of people in DFW region are beginning to drink alcohol in the church now. Including leaders thinking its ok to drink alcohol. What changed? Why would a Christian need alcohol? John Maxwell says "You teach what you know. But you reproduce who you are." Do leaders really want to reproduce a church sipping the booze while reading the pure Word of God? I miss Steve Hill. He preached holiness with fire in his eyes. Good role model for me and many people had high standards that sat under his ministry.

One person even made an info page on line about me. I accidently found while googling for photos. The photo I used for the cover of my book was found on google. Everipedia.com/angelacummings91 Some of the articles written about me have the craziest titles. It is easy to find videos of me on YouTube too. All I must do is type in "Crazy woman preacher." Some of the videos that come up are Sister Cindy and some are of my preaching. We are friends and love preaching together. It is awesome to have been written about by Friendly Atheist several times and Huffington Post over 4 times. Making Christian news isn't as fun, as the secular news. Light belongs in darkness. I have a feeling that if I were still in a normal church setting or in a bible school that all this press would get me in trouble with church leadership. Years ago, my evangelism mentors at BRSM said "God told us that you are not just a revivalist. You are a revolutionary." Bible Believers Fellowship house church in Los Angeles area rejoices with me when I make the news, even if it calls me a "Transgender phobic." I don't get to go to my home church much anymore because of my travels, so I stay in touch with my pastor by internet. A few times I have called on skype or on a phone in USA when in the country for advice. My pastor was in NY for a TV interview on Samantha Bee show while I was in the area. This worked perfectly for my schedule to ask him to pray over me before I flew back to Europe and Israel. Street preachers don't always get a friendly welcome in the local churches. Yet, we still need the Body of Christ. I find churches in my travels to visit and worship with them the King of Glory. Yahweh created a perfect custom plan for me to be who He created me to be as an Ambassador of Christ to the nations. All through this book is a testimony of God using me to reach the lost and encourage young preachers. Glory to God! No one could stop me, except myself. Therefore, the enemy of my soul attempts to attack my joy. The joy of the Lord is my strength. This is not prideful. My confidence is in the Lord's perfect plan and provision. All my hope is in Him. I could have never done 3 world tours without His help. #happymissionary

Proverbs 18:16 KJV "A man's gift maketh room for him And brings him before great men."

When I got to the Bronx, NY the last weekend in May a lady from the church was getting her hair done. She left the beauty parlor with hair dye in her hair to come meet me. We begin sharing the gospel and later I ended up in her home. What a great place with air conditioning in my room and soft comfortable bed. Sophia made me feel welcome in her home. Sunday was a busy day for me. Harvest Army booked me for 3 different churches. I love this church because they encourage everyone to be a preacher. They travel the world and share the gospel. They found me on YouTube preaching outside NY Fire Department about being a firefighter for God. Now, they call me "Fire woman" and "Most traveled evangelist in the world." This is another church in the states that is street preacher friendly. They even got me scheduled in their Atlanta church for the next week, when I returned home to mom's house in Chattanooga. I preached on Jeremiah at one church, Blessings of Persecution at main headquarters and last church spoke on the Nations. I spoke from my heart mostly with the scriptures God gave me. World Vision Day is 4 times a year. This church birthed WVD. They encourage everyone around the world to go preach at noon on the same day on those 4 days selected in the year. I have only missed one World Vision Day in the past 2 years because I was really sick. This is why it's good to raise up an Army of Harvesters. Go Harvest Army! I love this church. One time I said to someone in their church how I was surprised a church likes me so much. He said "We don't just like you. We love you!" I never forgot that. Thanks for allowing me to speak and do life with you all.

Transition time is at hand now that all the NY churches were finished. I have to get to Chattanooga, TN to prepare for a huge mission's trip to Europe. One of big supporters in 2014 was now a house mommy with bright blue eyed boy. I made it a point to stop by and see baby Bobby. She cooked Indian food by my request. Years ago, she was a missionary to India all by herself. Her story inspires me. I enjoy her friendship. There I stayed just a night and hugged that sweet baby boy. Mama took our photo. I had one more Target scheduled to preach with someone in TN. So, I swung over to this city to be the camera holder for a lady that said she wanted to preach in local Target. When she arrived in the city everything changed and she no longer felt God wanted her to do this rebuke. The next day I woke up thinking about how I told people that I was going to do one more Target. This was not something I was too happy about because this detour caused me to miss 2 extra days with my family. Finally, I just called my Pastor in California to ask what he would do in this situation? He said "You need to go preach at a Target by yourself and it will speak volumes of your character." Alright then, this what I did. I rebuked a Target in Knoxville, TN on my way to Chattanooga. The video got over 28,533 hits as of time of this writing. When I got to Chattanooga my mother asked "What was it you had to do?" I explained that I made a vow to preach in a Target and was close to Chattanooga. To avoid making any stirs in Chattanooga I choose to drive all the way back to the Knoxville store to preach. She appreciated me not stirring up Chattanooga. Amen, I didn't want any hometown drama either. It was just another day in the office for me. I would not even have told my mom what I did, but she asked. It's nice to have peace with my family and hometown now. God is good.

Time to stare at all my stuff on my childhood bed and decide what was most important to come with me to the nations in a small bag. All my plane tickets were paid until Jan. 2017. I did not pay for check in bag fees and wanted to try to go without paying this expense. I enjoy being a good steward of finances. It's great to laugh about getting a $21 plane ticket. Paying $20 to $40 for a check in bag sort of kills the moment of laughing of cheap tickets. However, a friend of mine that does my hair said "God will provide those check in bags." She was right about the Thailand Dentist, so I listened, thoughtfully.

I told my son goodbye. He was now in charge of Motel Honda while I was gone. My mother wanted it this way. I told Nicholas that I may never come back after this trip because the Muslims may kill me this time. There was a Muslim in Amsterdam, Netherlands that said if I ever came back there that he would kill me. Nicholas told me to have fun and be careful. Mom took me to the small Chattanooga airport to drop me off for NY. I flew to NY. Stayed in an Airbnb home a few days. Joined the NY street preachers for Beyoncé outreach and Korean fun, food and fellowship after we preached the gospel over 3 hours. Bulldozer from Harvest Army picked me up from my Airbnb home and took me to eat, then airport. I then flew on Norwegian for around $200, maybe $225.

Chapter 15

4 police cars in 4 countries in 4 months

Yeah!!! I am in Bergen, Norway with my first European stamp on new passport. My Airbnb host picked me up free and brought me to house. She cooked for me an amazing breakfast and other meals while I was there. I had jetlag and purposely rested for those 2 days. I only booked Bergen because it was cheapest way out of USA. At 1 am in the morning the sun was still not fully down and by 3 am it was still not fully dark. Winter brings dark winters that cause the Northern Lights to be seen. Summer is the reverse and has a phenomenon called "Land of the Midnight Sun." I love the free beauties God provides along the world missions journey. The back of her home had a nice hiking trail and got some exercise there. I never spent any money the whole time in Bergen, except what I prepaid to rent her downstairs room. She gave me a free ride to airport. Praise the Lord! My next stop was Paris for only $24.00 plane ride. I purposely wanted to preach the gospel in Paris because of the terrorist's attacks that killed so many people. Righteous anger caused me to buy that plane ticket and go deal with the cruel effects of Islam. Jesus is not their prophet and the Koran is not the Word of God. I serve a Loving God, not a god that beheads people.

1 John 4:10 KJV "Herein is love, not that we loved God, but that he loved us, and sent his Son to be the propitiation for our sins."

Paris, France was going to be a 10 day trip, until I meet some street preachers in Finland in Feb. Sitting with 2 young new women converts in Finland desiring to be used by God was refreshing. Jemppu invited me to come back to stay in her small apartment. I looked over my schedule several times. Everything was already set up already. So, while I was in Costa Rica I figured out a way to return to Finland to encourage this group of street evangelists. It was about $300 extra for me to work this into my schedule. God provided for the new tickets. Praise the Lord! I preached in Paris a few days. Euro Cup 2016 was surrounded by men coming to party hard in Paris for football/soccer game. I reached many people with gospel. It was an unforgettable night because someone saw my USA bandanna on my head. A tall man from Ireland grabbed the USA flag off my head with a small clump of my hair. OUCH!!! That hurt my head so bad. He then stomped on the USA flag and strutted off like he did something heroic. I just kept preaching the gospel, after saying ouch a few times to myself and God. The next day I meet an older lady from Congo in a Paris suburb. She saw my Trust Jesus patch. She had prayed for God to use her in her morning prayers. Then joined my mission to preach the gospel at the Eiffel tower. Her weight was hard on her feet, but she pushed herself to come be with me to glorify the Lamb of God. Just the day before the famous tower was in rainbow colors to honor the shootings at Sodomite bar in Orlando. She stood with me, even when the police showed up. We reached people from different nations. My first time preaching here a couple told me that I was more exciting than the Eiffel Tower. Christians should be more exciting than a building, amen. We are Lighthouses carrying the Glory of God. Shine, Church, Shine!

Paris has 3 airports. One Paris airport has cheap flights, but costs $15 for the bus ride to that cheap airport. It is also 90 minutes to get there, because it is not in the city of Paris. Watch out with this when buying cheap flights in Europe. I had to go to the toilet so bad that it was hard to sit still in my bus seat. I prayed with tears and stomach pain. Finally, I got up off my bus seat in humiliation to ask the bus driver to pull the bus over just for me. How embarrassing having to walk up in the woods of France to relieve my bladder. It made me laugh while up in the woods. I could see the bus while I was squatting in relief and laughing because my prayers were answered. No more tears or tummy pain. Just a bus load of people to stare at me when I got back on the bus pain free. There's the lady that couldn't hold her bladder a few more minutes. Yep, God knows how to keep me humble. Once again, Motel Honda trained me for not being overly embarrassed for this completely natural action.

It got harder after getting to airport. My Airbnb host picked me up and took me to his house. He seemed to not know English and I was scared in his home. My question was where is your wife? Because he had a woman in profile and thought I rented from a couple. He put hands together and showed me they had been fighting. He didn't speak good English and no lock on my door. He offered his bedroom for me. Oh no! I went quickly to his bathroom. Then, grabbed my bag and walked 1 hour back to airport. It took a long time to get there. Finally, a lady picked me up hitchhiking to carry me to airport. My goal was to contact Airbnb and try to get another place. They didn't take care of me quick enough. I don't use my phone because it costs money. The airport kicked us all outside. I was forced to sleep with my bags outside this airport. This is something I have never done before. What a rough night and when Airbnb found out they gave me a refund. They are such a good company. Next Airbnb surprised me with giving me June fees back and $200 future coupon because I slept outside. It was nice to see new friends in Finland after all that France drama. We preached together, ate together and laughed together. Finland is pretty year around. I really love those Christians over there. It is a country that I could be happy living there. I day dream sometimes of being a Finland tour guide for the Northern Lights, instead of being a controversial preacher. There are Christians that would love for me to get a real job and stop traveling the world. Even, if they never help pay for any of my expenses. What matters in the End at the Judgment Seat of God is hearing God say "Well Done!" No one else's comments and thoughts will matter except Almighty God. Live for Eternity and one day you will have Crown to lay at the feet of Jesus. This is my best advice, besides preaching the Cross.

Back to Paris a few days to catch my flight to Venice, Italy for a week. Venice was such a small place. My favorite divine appointment was with a young man on a bridge as the sun was going down. A Missionary to Turkey from USA attempted to correct me telling me how I am doing evangelism all wrong. Then, the nice young man stops her to tell her he is listening. I felt like God sent me there for him. His name was Nicholas, same as my son. He was brokenhearted over losing his grandmother and lost faith in God. The Holy Ghost was drawing him back. I spent time with him in the scriptures and then prayed for Nicholas of Venice, Italy. Praise the Lord!

Malta was next on my mission's schedule. It was World Vision Day weekend. What a beautiful place and by now in my journey I am using a real bag. One day I sat down and added check in bags to all my tickets. That way, I could actually enjoy the trip more. God did provide, just like Olivia said before I left USA. Malta was full of young people talking to me. Some were locals and some were from Sweden on vacation with their school. I always go to the most crowded tourist's spots looking for souls. No police bothered me in Malta and the lady I rented from gave me great review about my zeal for God. July has arrived and huge schedule ahead, How exciting! I love making my own gospel tour schedules. Praise God!

Naples, Italy is known for Pizza! I stayed there a few days and even found an African church to visit twice while in the area. God sent me on a mission to Sorrento and ended up by a beautiful Italian wedding. I made a video with music and the couple. It has become one of my favorite Europe videos. God healed my broken heart this week over some past hurts. The Italian coast is breathtaking and have wanted to go for a while now. Italy is the home of the Mother Catholic church. This country needs the gospel, just as much as Thailand Buddha worshippers. Catholics are more loyal to Mary, then to Jesus Christ the One true son God. Here is what happened to me when I preached the gospel in Amalfi Coast, Italy:

"July 8, 2016 Almost arrested in Amalfi Coast, Italy. The police are so nervous right now that I am going to preach again. They gave me a ride in police car to my hotel. Lately, I have been talking about how religious people have NO JOY and appear to be sucking lemons. When they had me in the police department over an hour, they could not understand why I was so happy. I am wearing my JESUS superman t shirt. I told them it was Jesus and the Holy Bible. The chief police came in the room and called for the paramedics to check me out. They could not understand my singing and reading the bible in jail. One cop enjoyed my police station visit. He took my photo and videoed my Moses drama. Moses Drama is where I raise my camera Tripod in the air and say "Let my people GO!!!" He was the officer that dropped me off at my hotel with the Captain riding with me in the back of police car." The 3 paramedics asked me if I was normal? I said "Yes, I am a normal Christian." The Chief police didn't like me preaching in the city center outside their Mega Catholic church. They took me to hotel and put me on house arrest. I told them that I could still preach out my window and it made them all nervous. It was so much fun and what a great view for house arrest. Later, a girl told me it's a good thing I didn't swim in that sea there because she was stung by jelly fishes. Next day, I went to Capri island on the way to Naples again. I didn't want to ride the bus again round those narrow steep roads.

Naples, Italy to Switzerland for 2 weeks in July was my next huge mission. I preached in 4 cities in Switzerland. Basel, Zurich, Lucerne and Geneva Switzerland and had a hard time with police demanding me to turn camera off every city. Several police even grabbed my camera and it caused bottom screws to mess up on tripod. Switzerland is special to me personally because of a powerful prayer meeting I had alone back in bible school days in Swiss. I believe in was 2003 on my second visit to Switzerland with BRSM. Everyone on trip went to Alps and I choose not to go, again. Kurt gave me the money back, which was nice. Then, I stayed in my room playing Rita Springers song "You said." I read Psalm 2 and cried asking God for the nations that day.

Little did I know, that 13 years later I would be writing a book about going to 45 countries. Wow, I am in awe of His grace.

A month before I got to Switzerland a young man named Simon added me to Facebook from Switzerland. I shared with him that I may go to Beyoncé concert in Zurich to preach. We both decided this outreach needed to be done. He rode his bicycle over 3 hours there in the rain with 2 rotten apples in pocket. We preached some. I went to my room. He went and preached again by himself and rode 3 hours' home in rain. This young man impressed me. It takes a lot to impress me. That weekend I got to share in my friend's church in Basel from BRSM. We all had great fellowship and even went to a zoo type place in another city. The food is so expensive, but they wanted to bless me anyway. Andy paid for me a meal $30 USA for Pad Thai by the lake with gorgeous Switzerland Alps in backdrop. It had been over 10 years since I have seen my Swiss Christian family. This was so good for my soul. Praise the Lord!

Geneva is the home of United Nations and CERN. I preached outside of both places. Several local Muslims chatted with me at the UN. I allowed them to borrow my tripod for photos and then shared gospel with them. It was the big divine appointment God set up for me there. Praise the Lord! Here is the outreach update from CERN:

"July 26, 2016 Turn or Burn CERN Outreach update: Well, I went to CERN today and was fired up to preach the gospel. When you walk in this place it says on the wall "Where did we come from?" Hello, perhaps they need a preacher to help them out with some answers. 1 Corinthians chapter one qualified me to go do this today. I was at a good street corner between 2 CERN buildings and catching people going in and out. CERN's logo looks like 666. It has a Facebook page. I got about 30 to 45 minutes of preaching in today before the police came to take me away to the police station. It was sad seeing little kids going in there with adult leaders. When one of the leaders saw me he said "Jesus" in a way that demeaning to His holy name. I preached to that man very hard. People teach kids science and laugh at God's Word. Not today CERN!" God gave me many awesome scriptures to declare over the area. Soon a few workers from CERN came out asking about my bible and if it was a good book? Maybe he was stalling me for the police. It was still fun showing them Genesis 1:1.

Geneva Police took me in the police car to the station. All the way there I read the Word to them in backseat, sang to them and prayed for Switzerland. Everyone knew a Christian was in the police station when they brought me inside the building. I walked in the police station singing and praising the Lord with a loud voice. Praise the Lord! Then, they demanded I get partially strip searched by a female cop with gloves. They did not erase my film, thank you Jesus. They allowed me to go and warned me. If they catch me singing loudly in Geneva again, that they will lock me up in a hospital. When is the Joy of the Lord a crime Switzerland? One cop asked as I was leaving if I am going on the TV show "the Voice?" Guess, they didn't realize I was preaching more than singing. Whatever…Just another day in the office for me. That was a lot of fun. Later I googled my name on the web and CERN. I found a blog. This is classic moment. There is a guy called "Friendly atheist" that blogs. He wrote about me twice while in USA and many shared his blogs. Then, after I preached at CERN he did a blog. What he doesn't understand is my highest goal with the CERN outreach was the film all CERN. I knew I wouldn't draw big crowds there. I have preached over 15 years and knew this already. My goal was to make a video outside CERN to reach silly atheists online. The fact that he blogged was a great sign that my fishing online works. He took the bait. Praise the Lord! 1.79 k shares. Thank you for free press and many atheists may have watched the video with my bible truth on Genesis 1:1. He calls me "Scream preacher." Call me whatever you want friendly atheist blogger, but I am a Friend of God. God is laughing with me, atheists. See Psalm 2:4 for details.

My first night on the Greek island was a hoot. The local restaurant was having a weekly party and people were throwing plates for entertainment on the dance floor. Then, they set the floor on fire as people danced to the music. I did not throw a plate. Just got some Gyros for my room and enjoying the palm trees. This was a brief rest for me to work some on the book again. My evangelism outreach drew people to take notice and listen sitting down. Yet, not everyone was happy to see a street preacher. The Police were upset with me demanding I move locations. No worries, so I moved to preach somewhere else. A few people thanked me for preaching the gospel. This is my second time in Santorini, Greece. It's one of my top favorite rest spots in the world. Here I celebrated alone with God 22 years Crack cocaine free to the glory of God. July 31st, 1994 was my last time ever smoking that poison from Hell.

Sicily, Italy was my next missions stop on the European summer gospel tour. This time a couple of California missionaries joined me. The first thing I paid for in 2016 with Christmas money from a friend was $21.80 plane ticket from Greece to Sicily, Italy. My second goal was the hotel in Sicily that had a huge waterslide that goes into the blue seas with Italian views all around. It was under $100 for hotel and the one fun thing on my schedule all year. Then, the 2 brothers show up and got to enjoy it with me. One brother was feeling very sick by 2nd day. Nate and I went to preach in city center. Then, Nate got sick. We were now staying in a low-cost place in Sicily, as a team. We did a few outreaches around Sicily. Then they went to Africa. My original plan was to go to Ireland for 2 weeks. I had a cheap ticket from Sicily. God changed everything when a brother in USA posted a picture of a young street preacher in Germany. He said that he was preaching the gospel faithfully to his city all by himself in Germany. God had me add him to Facebook. Then my plan changed to go to Germany to encourage this street preacher and cheer him on to keep going strong for the Kingdom of God.

First, I went to Rome, Italy. I was sick a few days and even saw a huge fire outside my hotel room while recovering from cold. Fire department got the blaze put out before it got to my room. Teenagers were cheering for the fire truck and hope they were not the cause of the fire.

I went out to preach in Rome. Crowds booed me at Roman Coliseum and 9 days later there was a huge earthquake in Central Italy. They have had many earthquakes since I preached all over Italy this summer. God is clear in His Word about Judgment starting in the house of God, FIRST. I warned this Catholic country that claims to be Christian about their abominations and idolatry before God. Repent Italy! Sad, they boooed me, after reading this verse. Was God avenging the blood of the saints?

Revelation 6:10 "And they cried out with a loud voice: "Lord, the One who is holy and true, how long until You judge and avenge our blood from those who live on the earth?"

My next stop was Eindhoven, Netherlands. I wanted to preach in another Netherlands city, because I had reached out to Amsterdam a lot in past 4 years. I got punched in the nose by a drunk girl in Eindhoven and needed to defend myself. It could have turned into a riot, but the restaurant owner allowed me to escape out the back door of his place for safety. I should have not gone out there that late, but did because I was running behind from arriving from Rome. The city had to be reached because I was heading to Amsterdam the next day. A few local street preachers discovered I was in Eindhoven from my YouTube channel. They wanted me to stay to preach the next morning with them before going on train to Amsterdam hotel. I suggested we sit down and talk first. They didn't show up on time or at place I said to meet me. I went looking for them. Great, they had already started and stirred up an area. I still wanted to fellowship before the outreaches begin. Why? Because I don't want to hang out with every street preacher that asks me. Some of the street preachers I have seen are trouble makers, more than history makers. Not every street preacher is a good role model, either. I look at the old street preachers like Charles Spurgeon, John Wesley, George Whitefield, Aimee Simple McPherson and William Booth as good role models. Aimee used to be a single mom of 2 children and drove across USA putting up her own gospel tent. God called me to be a street preacher after reading her story in God's Generals a month after the fire of God came on me at the Brownsville Revival on 2/27/1999 with my original call to preach. A Street Preacher is a scary calling, compared to a church Evangelist. Huge difference and anybody can be a street preacher that is willing to take the persecution. It's my Christian duty to use discernment who I work with on the frontlines. Character does matter to me, as wild as I am for Jesus. I do care about character and integrity. God only knows the motives of why every minister does what they do in the first place.

1 Thessalonians 5:12 "And we beseech you, brethren, to know them which labor among you…"

The 2 Holland street preachers seemed to want me to just simply trust them. I broke my own rule and started preaching with them. I regret doing this outreach, but God used it to speak to me about several things while I was in jail. See, I preached all over this small city with them. Then, was taken to jail for "insulting Islam followers." I was arrested for stirring up the city with gospel, but the police used what I said to him as a reason to jail me. He was looking for a reason to get us off the streets. 31 hours later, I was finally released. If I had of gotten to know these guys more and learned that they were arrested often, maybe I would have not been arrested. Allow me to share with you more details of this day and what it is like sleeping in jail in Holland.

All the way to the police car I preached exposing the Netherlands police. When they got me in station I preached for a few hours in my cell that was next to their main office. They moved me after 6 hours to another cell upstairs. They purposely sent me a Muslim police officer to take me as a test of what I would say. I stayed silent. My jail cell had a bed, personal toilet, Dutch magazines, clean water and radio on wall if, I wanted music. It was clean and bigger than the tiny house that I almost built in USA. My free attorney came and saw me several times. I meet with him in another room. He is an attractive man with nice eyes, dark hair, well-groomed beard and nice strong build. The only man I said WOW over in 2016, besides a cowboy on a video blog in Texas. He had never had a case like this, but he sure helped me. When I gave my statements to be recorded they mistranslated me several times. His English was great and truly helped clear up some misunderstandings of my statements. This upset my attorney that the police department had a horrible translator. My court date is Dec. 21st, 2016. I am facing a small fine for a hate crime, but hopefully I won't get banned from EU. I have bought a plane ticket to go to court, even if I don't have to be there. He wrote me today giving me instructions of when he will have me speak in court. I am going to be there early to go over this case with him. I do not think they have evidence of me yelling insults about Islam. The Police must prove it and he has no proof. He arrested me based on what I said only to him about Islam. Beware: you don't have free speech in Netherlands to insult Islam. I am not the only one under attack in this country for insulting Islam. I came to Netherlands to call them to repent and turn to Jesus. They are making a bigger issue out of it, so I want to make a bigger issue out of it too. Put the News cameras on me and let me reach all of Netherlands on Dec. 21st. Because I will tell you who is Lord! It's not Islam or the courts of Holland. Jesus is Lord!

Trial of Geert Wilders, a member of the House of Representatives of the Netherlands, has been in news since 2010. This man has stood for what he believes, even if it has nothing to do with the gospel. Not everyone wants Islam to take over their country and bring in Sharia Law. Can you sing like the Germans did to the refuges "You are welcome, here?" I am about to share my German stories with you next. Europe is not the same place that I visited in 2000 on my first mission trip. Islam has invaded and wants to take over.

When I got out of jail in Holland the biggest fear I had was that no one would even notice that I was missing. 2 people wrote me in concern that I wasn't online. They prayed. Thank God or my heart would have been crushed. I depend on prayer warriors and the night before my nose was punched. I made a blog for YouTube and quickly got videos up online. 4 am I was attempting to rest 2 hours in Amsterdam before getting up in morning for breakfast and train to Germany. The police were tricked by me in jail. I carry 2 cameras. When they stuck my stuff in a box, that is when I covered up my yellow camera with USA scarf. The chief police on my case walks in my cell with orange camera hoping evidence was on it. I wanted to laugh because he had the wrong camera. Preacher woman outsmarted the paid police working there for years. This is only reason I got film updated and soon the news media wrote about my arrest. My YouTube exploded with views from Netherlands. Praise God! The gospel got out even more after the arrests. I told the Foreign Police working on my case "You only helped my cause." She was a different department from local police and gave me 30 days to leave Holland in writing. She asked me to please not preach in Amsterdam when I arrived though. No preaching, just rest and go to Germany. 31 hours in jail was a long time, because I had never sleep in a jail. Holland was my first and the police upstairs treated me like I was famous. Simply, because I was from the USA.

God spoke to me on my walk breaks in the sunshine while in jail. They give walk breaks where the smokers take smoke breaks. The sun felt so good on my face. God said "Go back to America after Israel trip in October". I was not happy about this and felt like Jonah in the whale. God then spoke to me again "I will bless you if, you do not complain." Still not truly embracing this because I had a great schedule. Israel to Poland to Denmark to Thailand to Hong Kong to Taiwan to Japan to South Korea and all these plane tickets were paid for already. Talk about a major let down, but God is in control. I begin to make new plans after I got out of jail. The end of book has good news and can hardly wait to share with you how God blessed me for obedience.

Train ride to Germany was amazing because I saw over 10 castles on the way. I met up with Christoph. He was the street preacher in photo that someone posted. I cancelled Ireland to come this route. Soon God had me cancel Spain tomato fight as well. I just went to Romania early. Christoph and I ate at Pizza Hut my first day in Germany. Then he invited his girlfriend and her sister to preach with us. She knew Arabic and got to witness to several Muslims in their language. Germany is full of refuges. We preached in Darmstadt and Dortmund. We saw protests while there and almost a few fights with the Turks. It was not the Germans causing problems. It's those that moved there from other countries. He is a faithful young man and recently got a fine in Germany for preaching the gospel. He plans on rejoining me in Koln, Germany at Christmas markets before I go to court in Holland.

Then, I went to a super small wealthy country called Luxembourg. Oh how I wish I had a week there. When I preached in the city center the youth showed up all around me asking questions. One guy was from Los Angeles and was a subscriber to my channel. Another guy said "did you preach in NY by fire department?" Someone stole my video and it got almost 400,000 hits. OK with me because the gospel is getting out. I enjoyed talking with those young people. I took off on buses and trains for Brussels, Belgium. There I preached in city center in same area that I did 2 years ago. Many Muslim teens gathered around me and at times I sang because they looked like they may snap on me. Peace! Singing changing atmosphere and I do that to shift everything quick in spirit realm. It is spiritual warfare. Imagine being a woman only 5 foot 2 feet and doing this alone without even mace to spray for protection. God protects me and no one can hurt me without God's permission.

Bucharest, Romania is not in the Schengen zone of EU. This is what I wanted was to get stamped out, to save me the extra days in zone for returning to USA in October. When I arrived a in Romania a well-traveled older man suggests me to meet some Americans that were living there doing missions work. At first I complained thinking they will only tell me how I am doing it all wrong and ruin my day before I go to Israel. Super glad I ignored my first thoughts about these people I had not even meet. They loved street preaching. Immediately they got a team together and we went to preach. I love these people! We all got along so well and reached this city as a team. Praise the Lord! An invite for me to teach on evangelism came on Sept. 3rd, 2016 at their church. What a day to teach and brokenness was in my heart. My daddy died a year ago this day. This was a sweet gift for me to be used by God to encourage and teach on kingdom advancement by fulfilling the Great Commission.

Almost time for Israel trip and I was quietly preparing for the trip in my room. God asked me "How would you like to go back home?" I said "Iceland!" Send me to Iceland Abba God! RT.com has an article on Iceland being 100% atheist ages 25 and under. How can a group of teenagers that experience the Northern Lights be so blinded to not believe the lights shows were from their Creator? I wanted to go over there and find as many as possible to confront this foolishness. Simon from Switzerland got interest in going to Iceland with me after reading that article too. Quickly after a 3-day fast God brought in the money to get me back to USA. I changed my Copenhagen to Thailand ticket to Iceland to Boston. I then bought a Boston to Chattanooga flight. Plus, Israel to Switzerland ticket and Switzerland to Iceland ticket to complete my obedience to God to return to USA from Israel in October. Everything I did was on a great budget, praise the Lord! Wait till you hear at the end of book what God rewarded me with for going when He said Go.

Israel, the apple of God's eye, here I am again. Yes, you do need to let me in this country lady at Immigration booth. She got mad at me for saying I was a missionary. When she got off the phone she stuck my entrance paper in my passport with a mean look handed me my passport. I said "I can come in?" She said "Yes, but I got my eye on you." That was Jezebel working the booth that day and trying to tell the preacher to be quiet. No, I cannot be quiet. This is a mission's trip, not an Israel tour.

My first outreach report from Sept. 15th, 2016 "Jerusalem The Shuk Outreach report: Spit, Spit, Spit! You ever had an old Jewish lady spit at you and on you before in Israel? Lots of these Jews spit tonight and hundreds were given the gospel. God made me brave. I will have to say this was the most in your face people of 2016. That is heartbreaking because of JESUS. Sometimes tonight I did not even record because they surrounded me like wolves. They grabbed their own private parts, slapped their own butts and called Yeshua names. These were Jews dressed in Orthodox clothes. My biggest hater was a Jew from New York…" I ended up doing 10 outreaches while in Israel, praise God! I feel such a victory from this trip because I tried so many new places in Jerusalem besides just Jaffa Gate. Thanks to a few brothers on YouTube posting their videos of new fishing holes. They inspired me to try new area.

My first week I rented a room in a college students apartment on Airbnb for $15 a day. Praise God! He and the other girl were my son's age in their 20's. Here is his response to my staying there a week in the apartment:

"Merry is very clean, respectful and quiet. I learned a lot about Christianity do to her daily work on the Bible." D.B went away for the weekend to stay with his parents on Mt. Carmel. When he got back I told him about what happened at "The Shuk" because he suggested I go preach there if I wanted to reach many people. This opened the door for him to watch videos and share how this is what I am used to as a preacher of righteousness.

Airbnb gave me a $200 coupon because of my night sleeping outside that France airport. I used it for a room with a Russian Jewish family a few minutes outside Jerusalem. The city where

Solomon received wisdom and Joshua told sun to stop. A 19-year-old young lady new convert from Finland came over to stay and do outreaches with me. We enjoyed eating 3 meals of Shabbat with this family. We watched how these Jews do life on weekends. I was not in a mood to sight see at all this trip. All I wanted was more time to myself whenever I could get it. I had not shared a room with same person in over 25 YEARS for that many days. I did several outreaches by myself before she got to Israel. World Vision Day I did alone because she doesn't believe in preaching the gospel on the Sabbath. Jessica was very helpful with holding camera and it was extremely exciting the day that she stood up to preach the gospel in Jerusalem. Bravo Jessica!!! She did great and spoke from her heart. One day was unforgettable for both of us. The crowds were getting really rowdy and then cops came. I sent her away with the camera and tripod. Then, clicked on my 2nd camera to point towards the police with machine guns running my passport. After they were done cops left me standing there with a crowd of Jewish children. They hated me and spit on my arm, skirt, hair, backpack and just covered me with their saliva. Even my friend, Kara, was spit on just for being there loving Yeshua. Jessica showed back up and had been watching quietly. We were all heartbroken over the 5-year-old flipping me a bird and sticking out his tongue. Their behavior had to been taught to them by school, family or even Rabbi.

Jesus said "Blessed are the peacemakers, for they shall be called children of God." Matthew 5:9

We obeyed Jesus and did not fight anyone back. We just kept shining for the Lord. That night I saw a brand new 12 stone Jewish priest ring for sale for $50. After praying about it, yes I bought it. That ring will always remind me of the night in Jerusalem where I was covered in spit for simply sharing Yeshua with the Jewish people in HaDavidic Square. God helped me gather so much footage with police saying that I have free speech to preach there. Hopefully more preachers will go over there. This trip I reached more Jews than before and had the biggest crowds. It was good that I tried all the new preaching areas. It was a well-documented missions trip. One day there will be The Two Witnesses on the scene preaching every day for 1,260 days. (Revelation 11:1-14) Happy New from Jerusalem! Apples and honey to you a sweet new year. It's now Rosh Hashanah in the year of Jubilee 5777. I had a great exit from Israel airport with no problems or even hard questions this time. Praise God!

Matthew 23:37 KJV "O Jerusalem, Jerusalem, thou that killest the prophets, and stonest them which are sent unto thee, how often would I have gathered they children together, even as a hen, gathereth her chickens under her wings, and yet would not!"

Geneva, Switzerland was a great route home because it's airport is close to city and my hostel gives free travel passes to city. I stayed in hostel 2 days and meet a street evangelist. He followed me to hostel and begin preaching to everyone on their smoke break. The next day I went to church with him and really loved the message on faith from pulpit. I needed a message on faith, because I didn't want to go to America. God was making me go back and wasn't sure why. Now, I understand it was to publish this book. I had worked on this book over 3 years.

While I sat in the Geneva, Switzerland airport about ready to get in line for the Iceland trip a surprise showed up. Simon from Switzerland had his father drive him over. He had checked in a huge backpack was not just visiting Iceland. Simon had plans of moving to Iceland and trust God for everything. When we got on the plane I was on the front row and airline lady allowed him to come up to sit by me. This made a man so upset, that he moved to 2nd row. Hey whatever, man. Simon and I had so many divine appointments on the plane, that people would come back to get in line for toilet to ask more questions. Praise the Lord! God was already moving by His Spirit before Team Jesus of Iceland touched the ground.

A whole group of students waved bye to us as they went into airport terminal. They talked to us while we waited to get our bags. I made a personal vow after Israel trip to never pay for anyone's rent again that joins me. Even if I have a coupon. It wasn't easy to walk into the freezing rain of Iceland and leaving Simon for my warm room in a hostel. However, just like I lived in my car for the gospel. He has to trust God for his housing that night. I can't rescue these young people and then go broke myself. Everyone needs to flex their own faith muscle. Praise God, Simon was ok. He slept in bus terminal and the next night on a playground inside of a clubhouse to stay warm.

We met up to go preach the gospel in the afternoon. We did not have a plan in Capital city, so we just begin talking to people. Soon, 3 teenagers mentioned a local college up the road with pot smokers. We walked to this school and waited for them to dismiss classes for the day. In America it would be called a High School, not college. Here come the teenagers and my big mouth begin to preach. I asked if it was true that 100% of them were atheists? Within 10 minutes a nice size crowd was drawn at the top of campus and 2 groups of students gathered behind Simon across the street. I wanted Simon to address the crowd. He walked up and begin preaching to them. 25 minutes these students stood there to listen, not all across the street stayed though. A motorcycle police officer middle aged showed up to confront us and ask us to leave. Good news is Iceland does have free speech. We walked to the Mall for tea to ease my throat. Over 3 students came with us to talk some more and get to know us. They wanted to know more about what we believed and why. They had to leave for a school competition, so we just begin to walk back towards city center. We saw a nice size crowd. I asked Simon to go follow them to preach. I would catch up with him. Someone on the sidewalk wanted to do an interview with me and it was already stirring up the city. News spreads fast because of social media. The Holy Bible predicated technology being advanced in the last days.

Simon was surrounded and a few students pushed him. They were angry that we didn't accept homosexual lifestyle as normal. God told us in His Word what He thinks about it, so why would we as disciples of Christ condone abominations? We want to Fear and Obey God. The crowd walked into a field of hundreds of youth. Maybe 300 to 400 teens were out there in this field. We took over the school debate with the gospel. Students blew smoke in my face and I just let them. They pushed me and yelled at me. I got a clear gospel presentation to the crowd after I could get on the hill to throw my voice to all the listeners. Same attacks happened to Simon in the crowd. Many students were like animals and pushed us out of crowd straight to the Police car. We were taken away in the police car, but not arrested.

We saw beautiful rainbows several times that day and rejoiced together on his 23rd birthday. The police tried to make us feel like we were stalking children. These "children" are allowed to have abortions at 16 without a parent even knowing. They are not children, if they are having sex and abortions. Apparently, Iceland has many drug problems and #1 in fatherless homes according CNN. God was only trying to extend His loving grace to them and a few wrote us they believe in God now.

Soon, we were famous in Iceland. News agencies started writing me and asking for interviews. Some news already went up online and we made appointments with 3 reporters to give our stories. One in the hostel lobby at night and the next morning at the donut shop in city center with another reporter. Both stayed awhile and really enjoyed talking with us about our hope for Iceland revival and truths from the Word of God. A student meet us at Donut shop during the interview because he seemed harmless. He wanted a photo with us both and told me he was inspired. The day I left Simon did radio interview alone and the reporter asked him to pray for Iceland. That was so cool. We did a few more outreaches and stories could be shared on them as well. Simon is in a challenging country and continues to reach out to them. I still get have hate mail coming in from students, even 40 days after I have left. One student sent me porn pictures to upset me. It was pure filth and God will deal with him personally. I assure you that. Simon wrote me one day that he has dealt with police over 17 times and they all seem to know him. A detective told him to contact me and tell me to contact her. No way lady! I left. Get over it! She most likely wants to WARN me to not come back. It's in the EU and can easily go back with a simple plane ride. Once I am in the EU, then I can run around freely country to country preaching the gospel. Good news is now the Finland street preachers are heading there in December 2016 to bring the Word. Praise the Lord! Great ending to 45 countries by 45 years old…All hail the King of the Jews. I am one Happy Missionary.

Now, for the good news, God is allowing me to leave America again for the mission field. Yipppppppeeeee!!!! Not much happened when I got back in the states and my car only got worse. I believe God brought me back for just a few people, family and to publish this book. I leave in a week to begin my next world mission's gospel tour.

My schedule is Denmark, Sweden, Germany, Netherlands, Croatia, Slovenia, Austria, Switzerland, Israel, Japan and South Korea. All the tickets are paid in full. Thank you, Jesus, and partners of this ministry. I wanted you to know this because it was hard letting go of my schedule to return to USA. My biggest fear was God using me in some big revival in USA and me giving up world missions. There are so many Christians in USA. Street preachers are everywhere and don't know many that desire to go to the nations. TigerDan925 in the UK made a movie on me and thanked USA for sending me to his country. Americans should not be upset that I don't want to be there. Rejoice that you are sending an Ambassador to the nations and that the gospel is being preached around the world. Glory to God! I have been Inspired by the Great Commission!
Angela Cummings

Chapter 16

The Grand Finale:

You know this is not my first book. The first book I wrote ended up in the trash can. Someone said "Your life is just now getting started…" Johnathan was right. He told me this in 2011 after I finished the first book. 2013 I rented an office for $100 and begin writing my story about living in my car. My original plan for this book was to call it "Motel Honda." I was so excited to write about going to a few countries and being arrested at the Vatican. My story felt like it should end in 2013, until I had a huge stir in my hometown. Then, God sent me to 21 countries in 2014, 25 countries in 2015 and already 22 countries with 29 states in 2016. Now, this is the Grand Finale. When, I got to Country #45, Iceland, with Simon it was a height of my journey in so many ways. Turn the page to the next chapter and I can see my future filled with Jessica's from Finland and Simon's from Switzerland wanting to be World Changers. God is going to give me more sons and daughters to train for the end time Harvest. There are many young people out there that don't want a Bible School diploma in a classroom. They want a real life Evangelistic experience with the lost souls. They want it now! This generation has burning hearts and wants to share what they know about Jesus. They want to stand up and speak to the masses. They want to be that trumpet and a voice crying in the wilderness. Prepare ye the way of the Lord! When young people find people like me on YouTube, then they expect me to encourage them to do the same.

Some churches seem to be us in the pews and the Professionals on the stage were the anointed ones. I felt like I was trained to be a professional clapper for those on the stage. That is why my destiny was hindered from growing, because some churches don't want you to have personal dreams. They want you to only think about their dreams and their church vision. Not many churches know how to mentor Evangelists. The Church should be trying to get under these young people and lift them up to their destiny. I don't think we need to be raising up Evangelists in million dollar buildings, either. Jesus raised up His disciples on the streets and didn't allow them to bring much on their journey. The journey with Jesus was about having burning hearts from walking with the Master. He is the King of Glory!

If you feel like you are a professional clapper sitting in a church and no one is encouraging your dreams. God sees you. I see you, too. Oh, let me tell you how I have longed to encourage you and my hands were tied from getting to you. See I watched the church operate my whole life, except the years I was a prodigal on the run. A few churches I have visited would encourage everyone in the entire congregation to be a preacher, be a voice and be the hands and feet of Jesus. See the church is not a building. If you are a Christian, then you are the church. That is why I can say "I see you." I see you desperately wanting to rise to do something for God. You may never get to be in a leadership role at your church. I used to clean my church for free and be a prayer warrior at church. It was not like I was teaching evangelism. Don't feel stuck and stare at that road block. Go around it in Jesus name! Rise and go outside the church building. Now, look at your mission field. Do you see the homeless, single moms or dads, crippled, veterans, elderly, teenagers, alcoholics, drug addicts, gamblers, sick, afflicted, religious or your neighbor? You can make a difference in others' lives, one person at a time. You can meet a need, pray,

184

give out tracts and share the gospel with these lost souls. I have rarely heard a Pastor share his personal experiences with a lost soul he has meet during the week. You can't wait for your Pastor to encourage you to share the gospel. This book is hopefully sparked you to realize you can be a World Changer.

I pray for you to rise and just go do something, now. Don't wait any longer. Just get started helping someone and sharing the gospel with a lost and dying world. Maybe you will inspire your Pastor and Church to start sharing the gospel, just like you. The only person stopping you is you. I hope this encourages you to Go.

Do know Jesus as your Lord and Savior today: What are you waiting on? Get right with God. Repent of your sins and Believe the Gospel.

1. Jesus died. 2. He was buried. 3. God raised Him from the dead. 4. This is per the Scriptures. 5. Jesus was seen by over 500 people.

    I am not going to pray a sinner's prayer with you. If you want to follow Jesus, then you will without me praying a prayer with you to surrender. This is your call. I can't make you marry Jesus. It's a covenant vow. You don't date Jesus or try Jesus. You leave all other gods and follow ONLY Jesus. He is the Way.
    John 14:6 for details and biblehub.com if you need a bible to get started on your journey for free.

My hope is that you have seen in this story just how much worth and value the gospel is to God. No one loves lost souls around the world more than the ONE TRUE GOD. He allowed His Own Son to be slain, nailed, whipped and hung naked publicly shamed on a Cross for the proud Americans and all the other Nations of this world.

All glory and honor go to my Hero, Jesus Christ, for this story of His faithfulness, protection, provision, guidance and most of all, His Love. I love Cowboy Jesus! One day He will return on a White Horse. I long for that day, my Love.

WORTHY IS THE LAMB!

59133104R00104

Made in the USA
Lexington, KY
24 December 2016